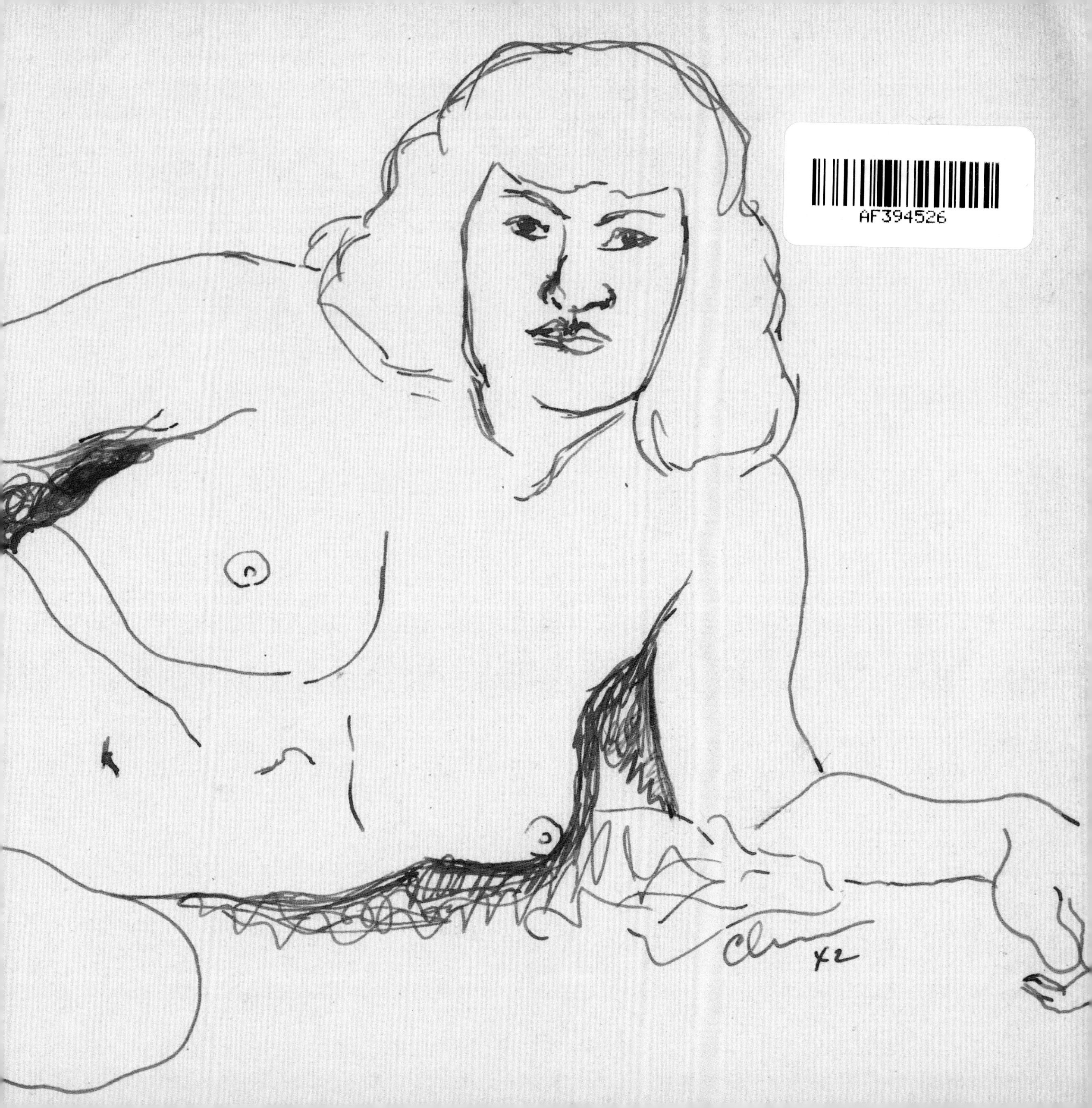

JOHN CLEMMER

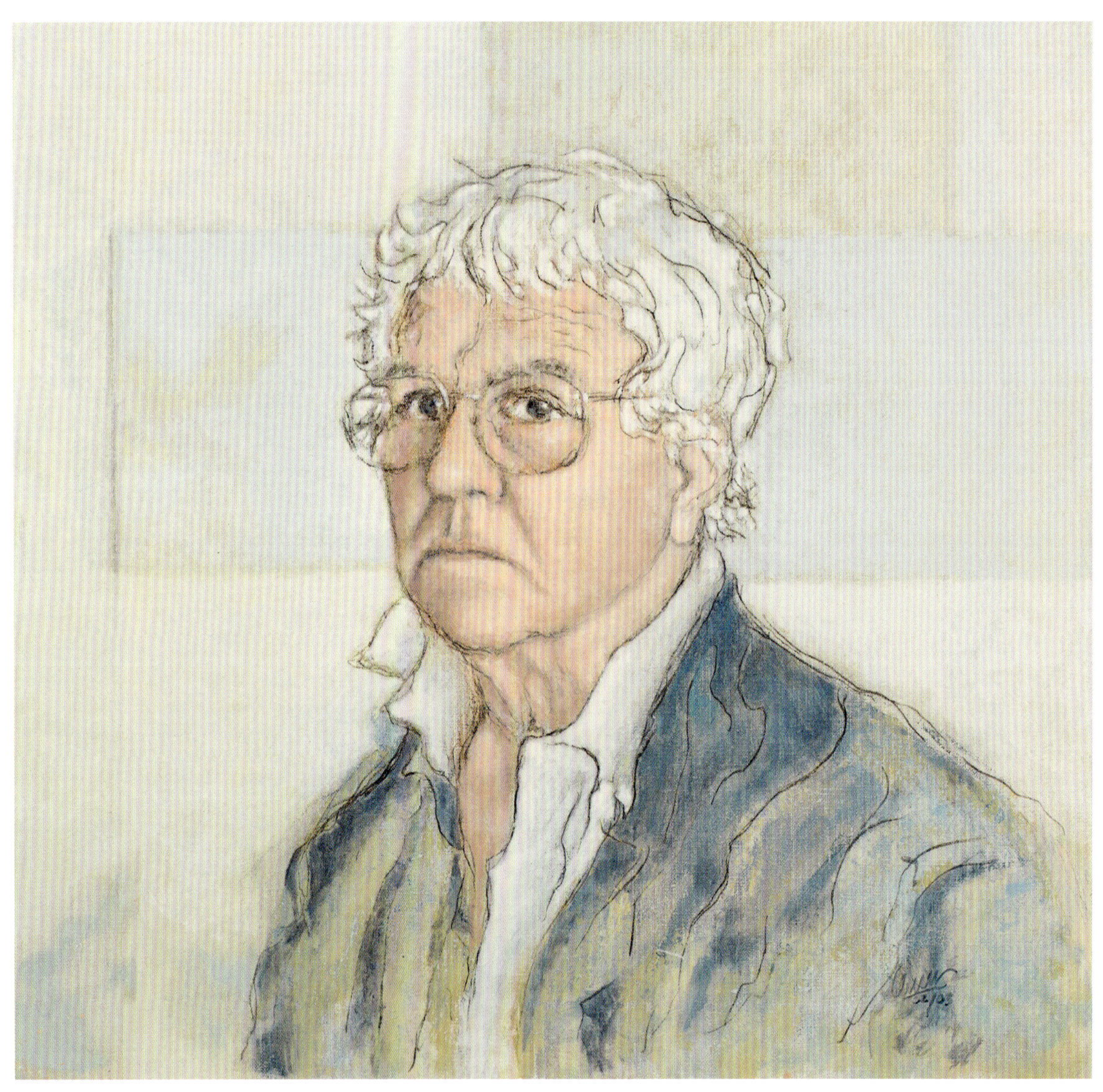

Self-Portrait, 2003, oil on canvas, by John Clemmer, 19 ¾ x 19 ¾ in.,
courtesy of 3618 Studio, LLC, New Orleans, LA

JOHN CLEMMER

A Legacy in Art

with essays by

Judith H. Bonner

John Ed Bradley

David Clemmer

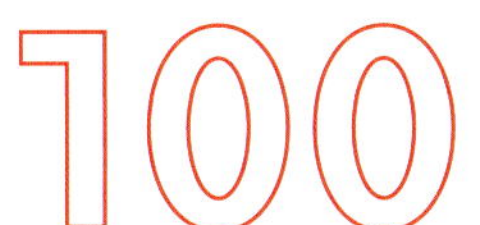

Published by The Historic New Orleans Collection in conjunction with the exhibition *John Clemmer: A Legacy in Art* (July 21–October 31, 2021), presented on the centennial of the artist's birth

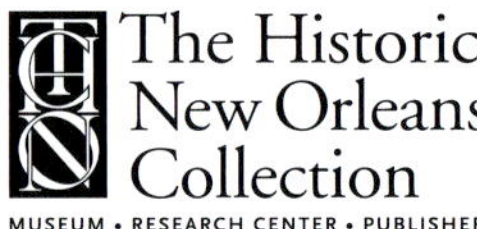
The Historic
New Orleans
Collection
MUSEUM · RESEARCH CENTER · PUBLISHER

The Historic New Orleans Collection is a museum, research center, and publisher dedicated to the study and preservation of the history and culture of New Orleans, the lower Mississippi valley, and the Gulf South region. The Collection is operated by the Kemper and Leila Williams Foundation, a Louisiana nonprofit corporation.

Project editors: Dorothy Ball and Siobhán McKiernan
Director of publications: Jessica Dorman
President and CEO: Daniel Hammer
Design: Alison Cody Design

Typeset in Scala and Scala Sans
Printed in Florence, Italy, by Conti Tipocolor
Distributed by the University of Virginia Press

© 2021 The Historic New Orleans Collection
533 Royal Street
New Orleans, Louisiana 70130
www.hnoc.org

25 24 23 22 21   1 2 3 4 5

ISBN: 978-0-917860-86-7

Library of Congress Cataloging-in-Publication data
Names: Bonner, Judith H. Clemmer's circle. | Bradley, John Ed. Artist remembers. | Clemmer, David. Works. Selections. | Historic New Orleans Collection, organizer, host institution.
Title: John Clemmer : a legacy in art / with essays by Judith Bonner, John Ed Bradley, David Clemmer.
Description: New Orleans, Louisiana : The Historic New Orleans Collection, [2021] | "Published on the occasion of the exhibition John Clemmer: A Legacy in Art at The Historic New Orleans Collection, July 21–October 31, 2021." | Includes bibliographical references. | Summary: "Created to accompany a 2021 exhibition commemorating the centennial of John Clemmer's birth, this catalog includes three essays that offer insight into Clemmer's life and art, as well as full-color plates of numerous works and an exhibition checklist"-- Provided by publisher.
Identifiers: LCCN 2021003213 | ISBN 9780917860867 (hardcover)
Subjects: LCSH: Clemmer, John, 1921---Exhibitions.
Classification: LCC ND237.C5725 A4 2021 | DDC 759.13--dc23
LC record available at https://lccn.loc.gov/2021003213

[COVER]

To the Beach, 1997, oil on board, by John Clemmer, 15 × 15 in., *The Historic New Orleans Collection, 2014.0464.11*

[ENDPAPERS]

Reclining Nude, 1942, ink on paper, by John Clemmer, 8 ¼ × 11 ½ in., *The Historic New Orleans Collection, gift of Dorothy, Jonathan, and David Clemmer/3618 Studio, LLC, in memory of John Clemmer, 2016.0041.29*

Untitled (Legs), 1940s, ink on paper, by John Clemmer, 6 × 9 in., *The Historic New Orleans Collection, gift of Dorothy, Jonathan, and David Clemmer/3618 Studio, LLC, in memory of John Clemmer, 2016.0041.26*

[OPPOSITE]

Nude with Still Life, 1951, oil on canvas, by John Clemmer, 36 × 48 in., *courtesy of Don Fuson*

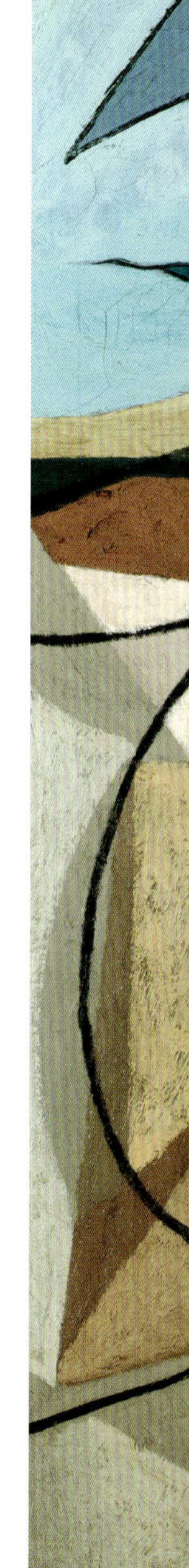

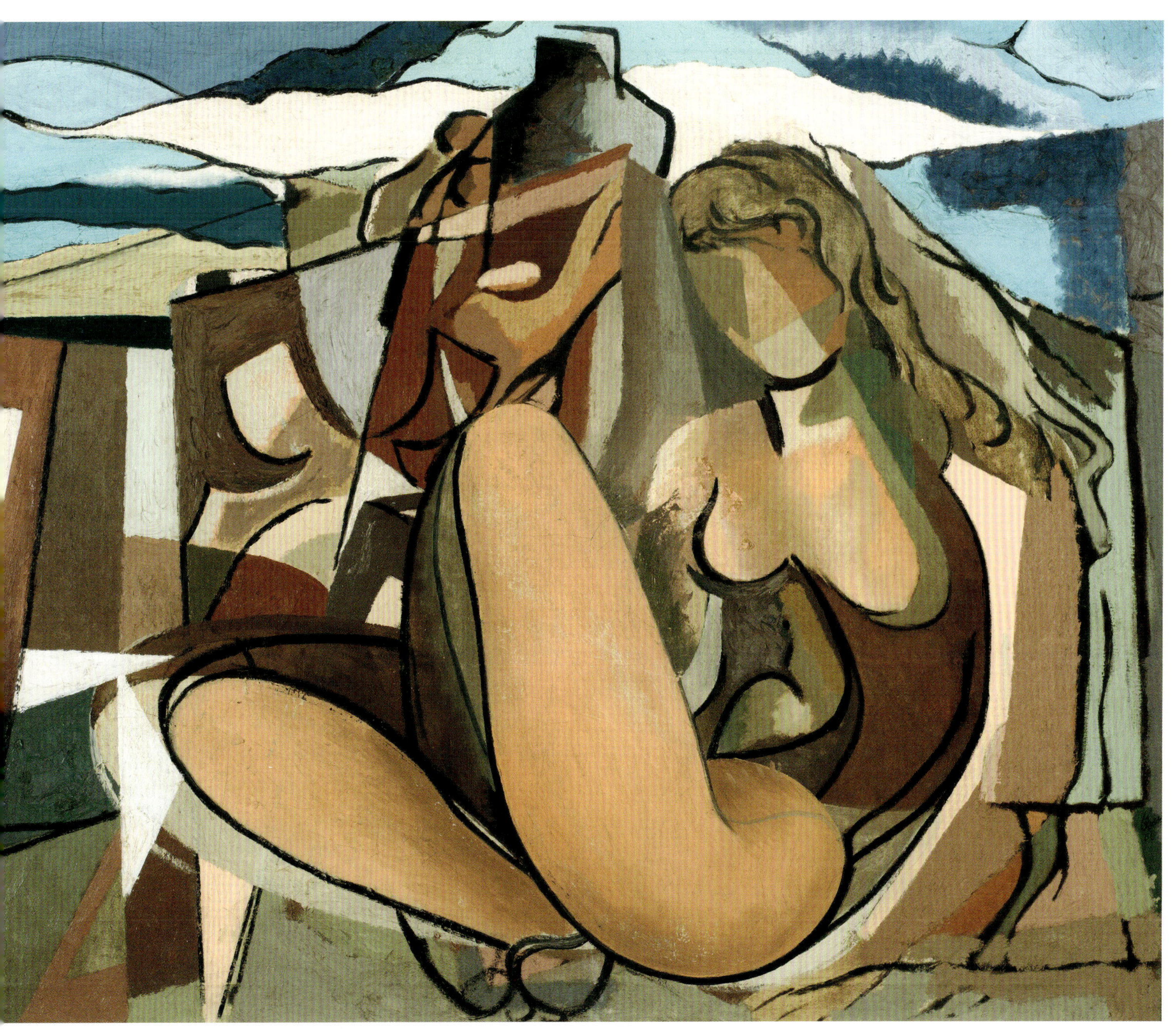

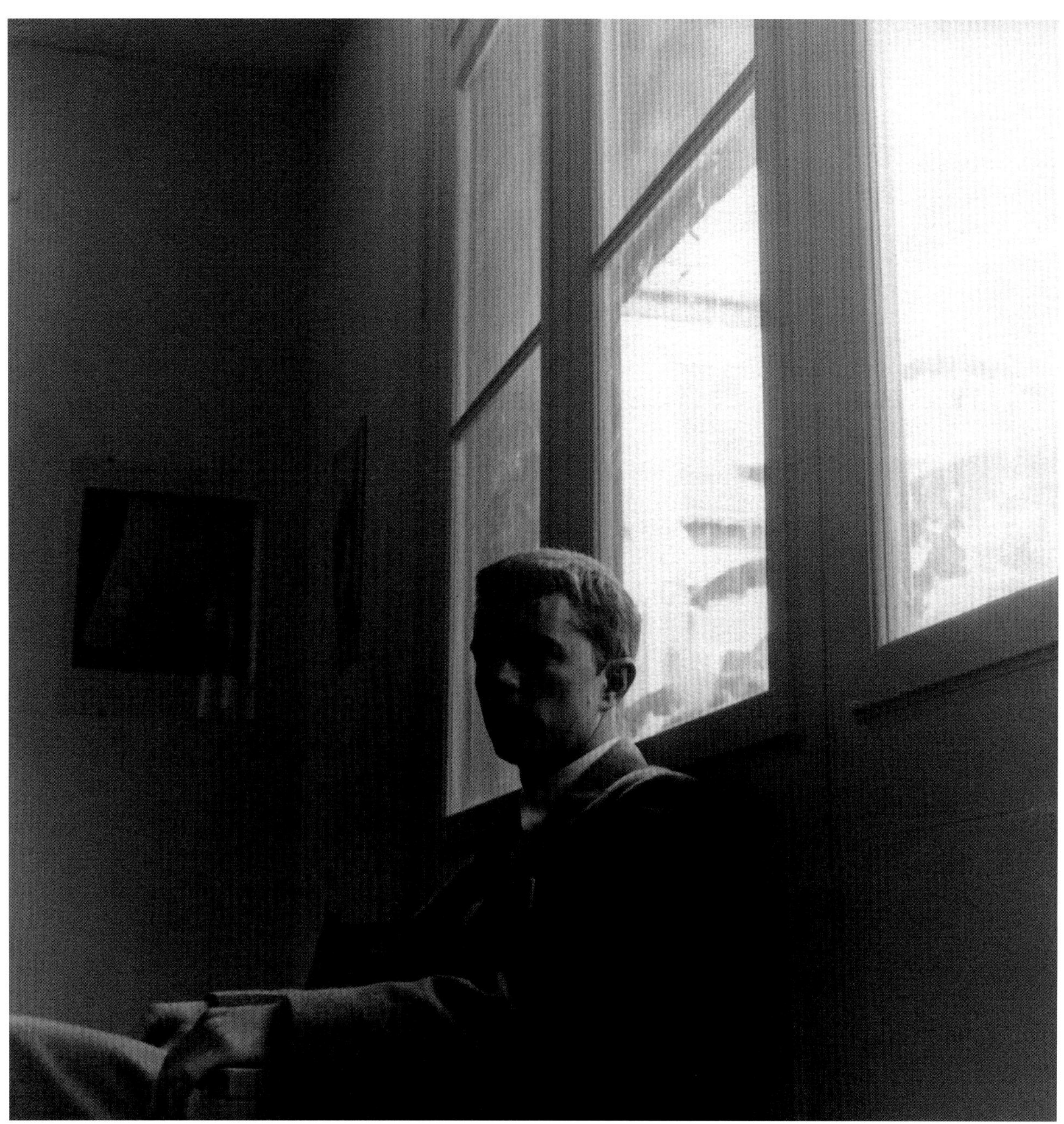

CONTENTS

1

A Painter's Progress:
Reflections on the Work

by David Clemmer

2

Clemmer's Circle:
Modernism in New Orleans

by Judith H. Bonner

3

The Artist Remembers:
Sharing a Life

by John Ed Bradley

PLATES

[OPPOSITE]
John Clemmer in the French Quarter, 1948, photograph
by Elliott Erwitt, *John Clemmer archive, courtesy of
Elliott Erwitt / Magnum Photos*

LENDERS

The Historic New Orleans Collection gratefully acknowledges the following lenders for their contributions to the centennial exhibition:

3618 Studio, LLC, New Orleans, LA
Mathile and Steven Abramson
Martha and Rick Barnett
Jacqueline Bishop and Herbert Halpern
Florence Macdonald Boogaerts
Kimberly and John Ed Bradley
Virval Bradley
Brooks Emery Braselman
Andrés Calandria and Antoinette Calandria
David Clemmer, Santa Fe, NM
Jonathan Clemmer and Michael Barnes, Royal Oak, MI
Don Fuson
Priscilla and John H. Lawrence
Edwin and Donna Lupberger
Mr. and Mrs. Matthew J. Martinez
Newcomb Art Museum of Tulane University
New Orleans Museum of Art
Ogden Museum of Southern Art
Ashton Phelps Jr.
Private Collector
Dr. Joseph J. Roniger and Mary Sue Roniger
Michael Wilkinson

This exhibition catalog is supported by the John F. Clemmer Fund of the School of Architecture of Tulane University. The John F. Clemmer Fund was established by Newcomb College alumna Martha Walters Barnett (1969) and Tulane University alumnus Richard R. Barnett Sr. (1968).

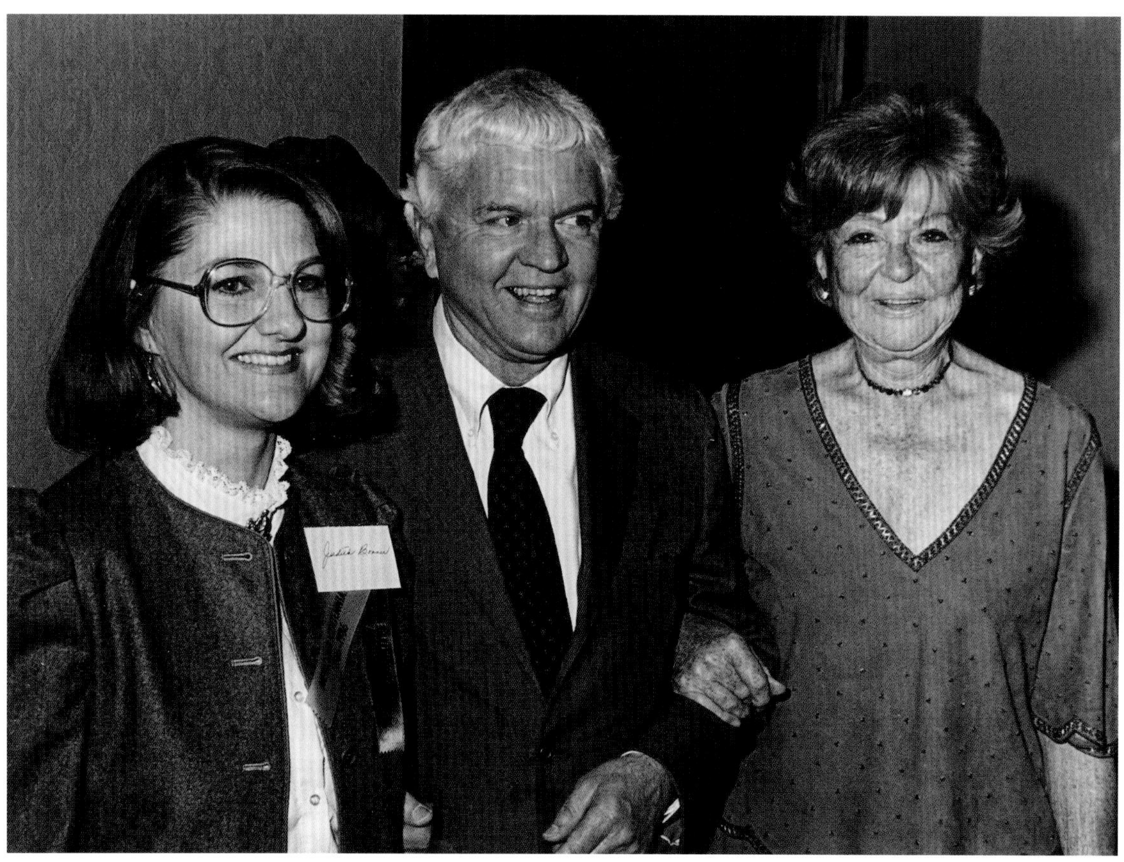

Judith H. Bonner (left), John Clemmer, and Ida Kohlmeyer (right), at New Orleans Museum of Art, 1987, photograph by the *Times-Picayune, courtesy Capital City Press / Georges Media Group, Baton Rouge, LA*

ACKNOWLEDGMENTS

The Historic New Orleans Collection has mounted a major exhibition in celebration of the life and career of New Orleans artist John Clemmer (1921–2014). Opening on July 22, 2021, the centennial of his birth, *John Clemmer: His Legacy in Art* focuses on his art and career from his student days to his years as a teacher to his later years as an independent artist.

A second section of the exhibition presents a selection of works by Clemmer's art circle: his teachers, his students, his mentees, and his colleagues. These include his teachers and students at the New Orleans School of Art and his fellow artists at the Orleans Gallery, the city's first artists' cooperative gallery. This complex exhibition includes 76 artists who worked in a variety of artistic styles and media—many of them experimenting with combined media. A number of these works were donated to The Historic New Orleans Collection or the New Orleans Museum of Art by Clemmer, who collected his colleagues' work through the years.

An unassuming and generously spirited man, Clemmer introduced others to decisive opportunities throughout his life. During his time at the Arts and Crafts Club and its subsequent Arts and Crafts Gallery, his tenure on the faculty of the Tulane School of Architecture, and his chairmanship of the Newcomb Department of Art, he arranged exhibitions in the galleries to showcase the work of students, faculty, and both emerging and established artists. Clemmer was the impetus for the Smithsonian's 1985–1987 traveling exhibition of Newcomb pottery, *An Enterprise for Southern Women, 1895–1940*, as well as for the *Newcomb Centennial 1886–1986* exhibition held at the New Orleans Museum of Art in 1987.

As with any major endeavor, developing the John Clemmer centennial exhibition and the catalog was challenging and could not have been accomplished without the assistance of many people. Martha Barnett, Rick Barnett, John Ed Bradley, and David Clemmer were present during the initial planning of the exhibition, as was John H. Lawrence, emeritus director of museum programs for The Historic New Orleans Collection. The project received the blessing of Priscilla Lawrence, former president and chief executive officer, and continued under Daniel Hammer, president and chief executive officer. Jason Wiese, chief curator, also lent his support.

David Clemmer, who proposed the exhibition to celebrate the centennial of his father's birth on July 22, 1921, has given invaluable support throughout the preparation for the show and the publication of this catalog. He spent many hours working with the Clemmer inventory and showing me his father's artworks in his collection and the collection of the 3618 Studio, LLC. We also appreciate the support of Dorothy Iker Clemmer and Jonathan Clemmer with their gifts of a number of drawings from the 3618 Studio to The Historic New Orleans Collection.

This project was initiated when Kenneth Schwartz was Tulane University's dean of architecture. It was brought to fruition under his successor, Dean Iñaki Alday, Richard Koch Chair and Dean of the School of Architecture. Thanks, too, go to Chelsea Borries, development officer for the Tulane University School of Architecture Office of Advancement, and Lauren Michel, director of gift planning for Tulane's Office of Advancement, as well as to Jack Pruitt, director of development and community relations at The Historic New Orleans Collection.

As news of the impending exhibition spread, many private collectors enthusiastically and generously offered to lend artworks. We are most grateful to these lenders, including the 3618 Studio, LLC; Mathile and Steven Abramson; Martha and Rick Barnett; Andrés Calandria and Antoinette Calandria; Jacqueline Bishop and Herbert Halpern; Florence Macdonald Boogaerts; Kimberly and John Ed Bradley; Virval Bradley; David Clemmer; Jonathan Clemmer and Michael Barnes; the late Lin Emery; Don Fuson; Priscilla and John H. Lawrence; Edwin and Donna Lupberger; Mr. and Mrs. Matthew J. Martinez; Ashton Phelps Jr.; Dr. Joseph J. Roniger and Mary Sue Roniger; Michael Wilkinson; and a private collector. We also wish to thank Lisa Rotondo-McCord and Mel Buchanan of the New Orleans Museum of Art, Sierra Polisar of the Newcomb Art Department of Tulane University, and Bradley Sumrall of the Ogden Museum of Southern Art for their gracious loans. Others have donated Clemmer's artworks to THNOC in advance of the exhibition, including Valerie Charles Beaudette, Lois Charles, Susan Brill, and Michael S. Hershfield. It has been an honor and a privilege to work with these lenders and learn of their experiences with John Clemmer. We especially thank Dean Iñaki Alday of the Tulane School of Architecture for his generosity in supporting the exhibition catalog via the John F. Clemmer Fund.

Finally, I thank the many colleagues at The Historic New Orleans Collection who have helped to bring the exhibition and catalog to fruition.

Museum Programs: Jason Wiese, chief curator; Matt Farah, associate curator, exhibition coordinator; Maclyn Le Bourgeois Hickey, coordinator of curatorial conservation; Amanda McFillen, programming manager; Elizabeth Ogden Janke, special projects and programming coordinator

Collections: Jennifer Ghabrial, head registrar; Monika M. Cantin, associate registrar; Rachel Ford, associate registrar; Susan Eberle, associate registrar

Photography: Keely Merritt, head of photography; Melissa Carrier, photographer; Tere Kirkland, associate photographer

Preparation: Joseph Shores, head preparator; Robert R. Gates III, associate preparator; Christopher L. Deris, preparator; Lindsay Rowinski, associate preparator; Peter Hoffman, assistant preparator

Publications: Jessica Dorman, director of publications; Dorothy Ball, senior editor; Siobhán McKiernan, associate editor; Matthew J. McKnight, freelance editor

Technology: Carol O. Bartels, director of technology; Lisa Griffin, network administrator; Kacell Hmaidan, computer client services technician; Candy Ellison, interface/interactive designer; Andy Forester, developer/programmer

Reading Room and Williams Research Center: Alfred E. Lemmon. director of Williams Research Center; Rebecca Smith, head of reader services and technical processing; Heather N. Green, reference associate; Brian Lavigne, records manager; Heather M. Szafran, reference associate; Robert Ticknor, reference associate; Kristin Hébert Veit, curatorial cataloger. —JUDITH H. BONNER

John Clemmer (third from left) teaching a class on the balcony of the Arts and Crafts Club (wife Litza at far left), 1949, photograph by the *Times-Picayune, courtesy Capital City Press / Georges Media Group, Baton Rouge, LA*

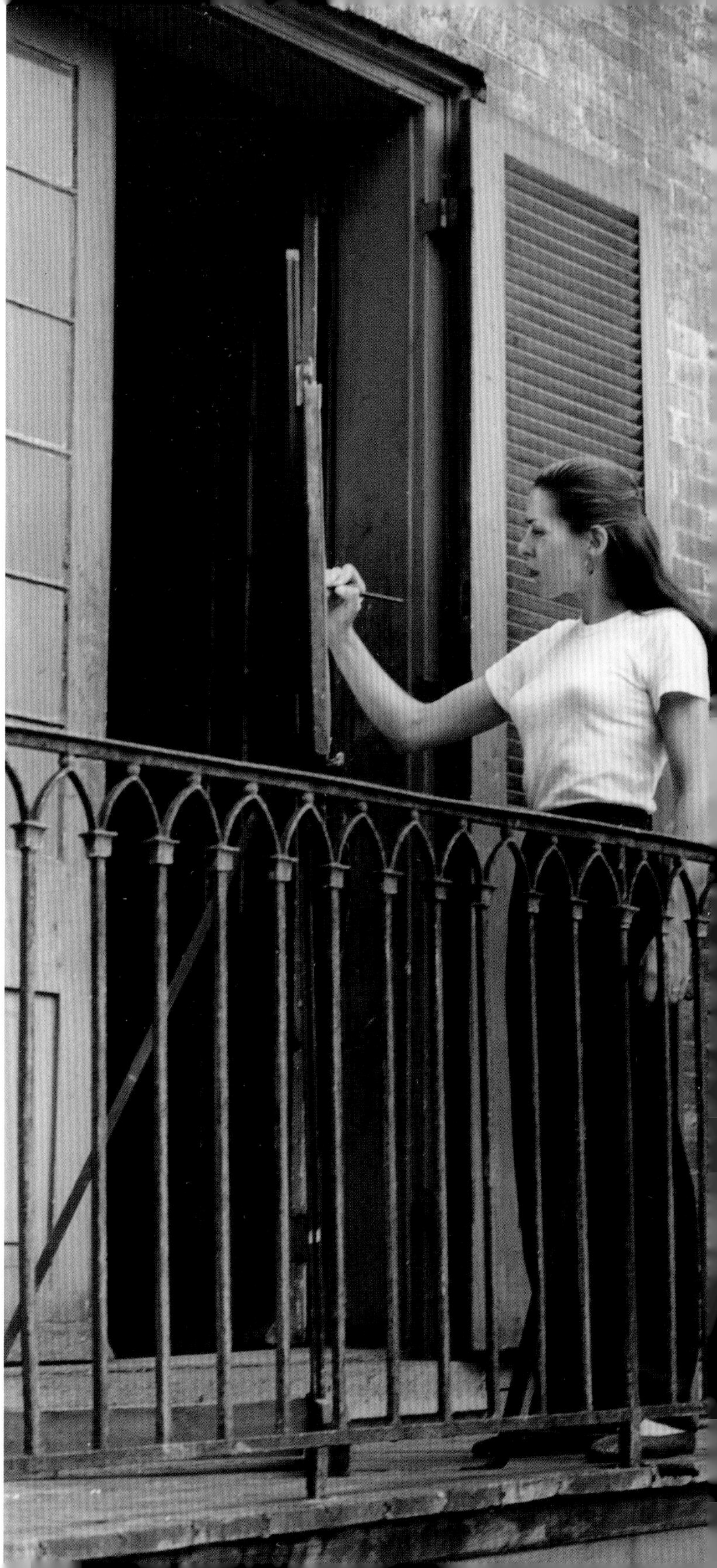

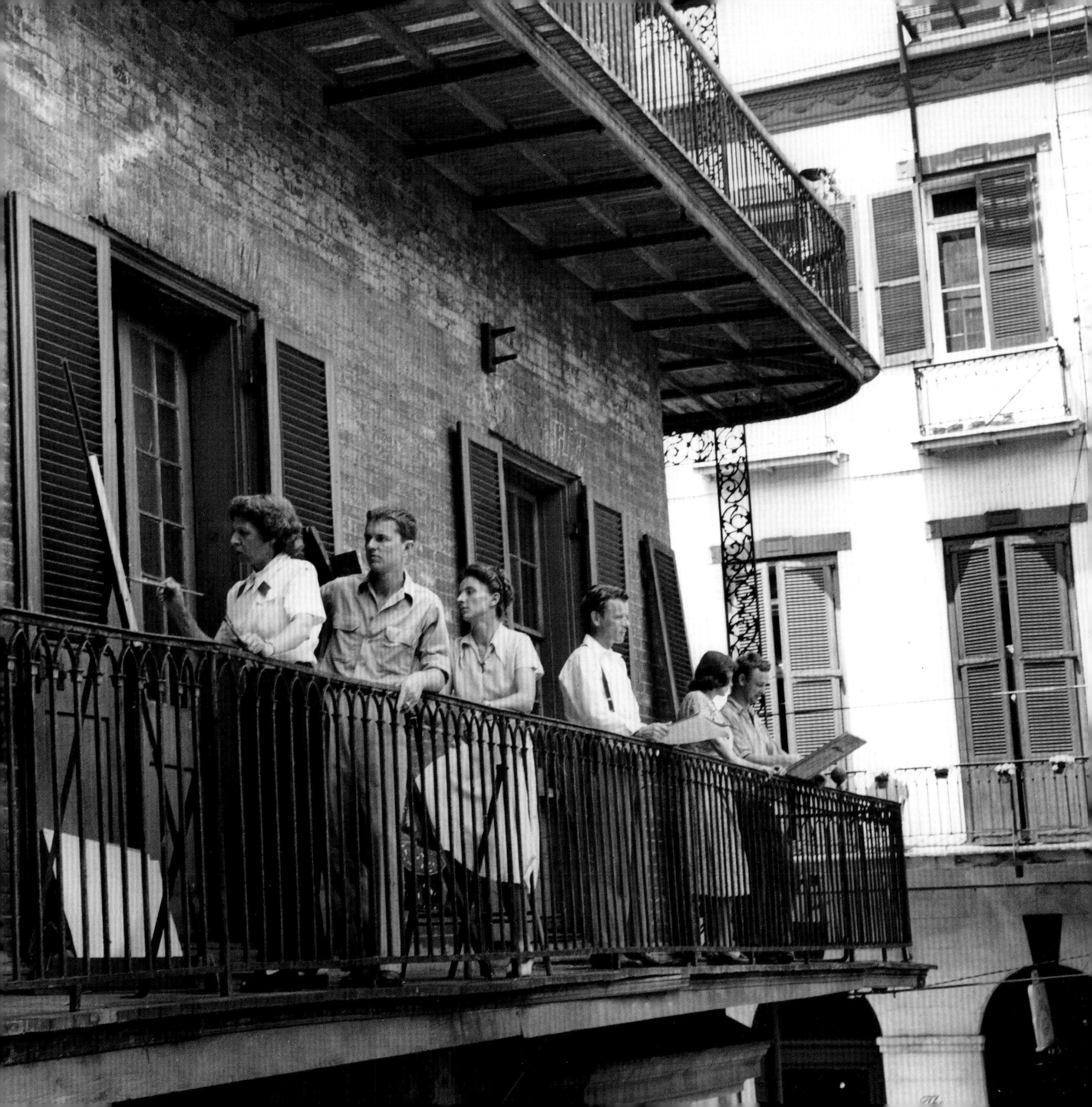

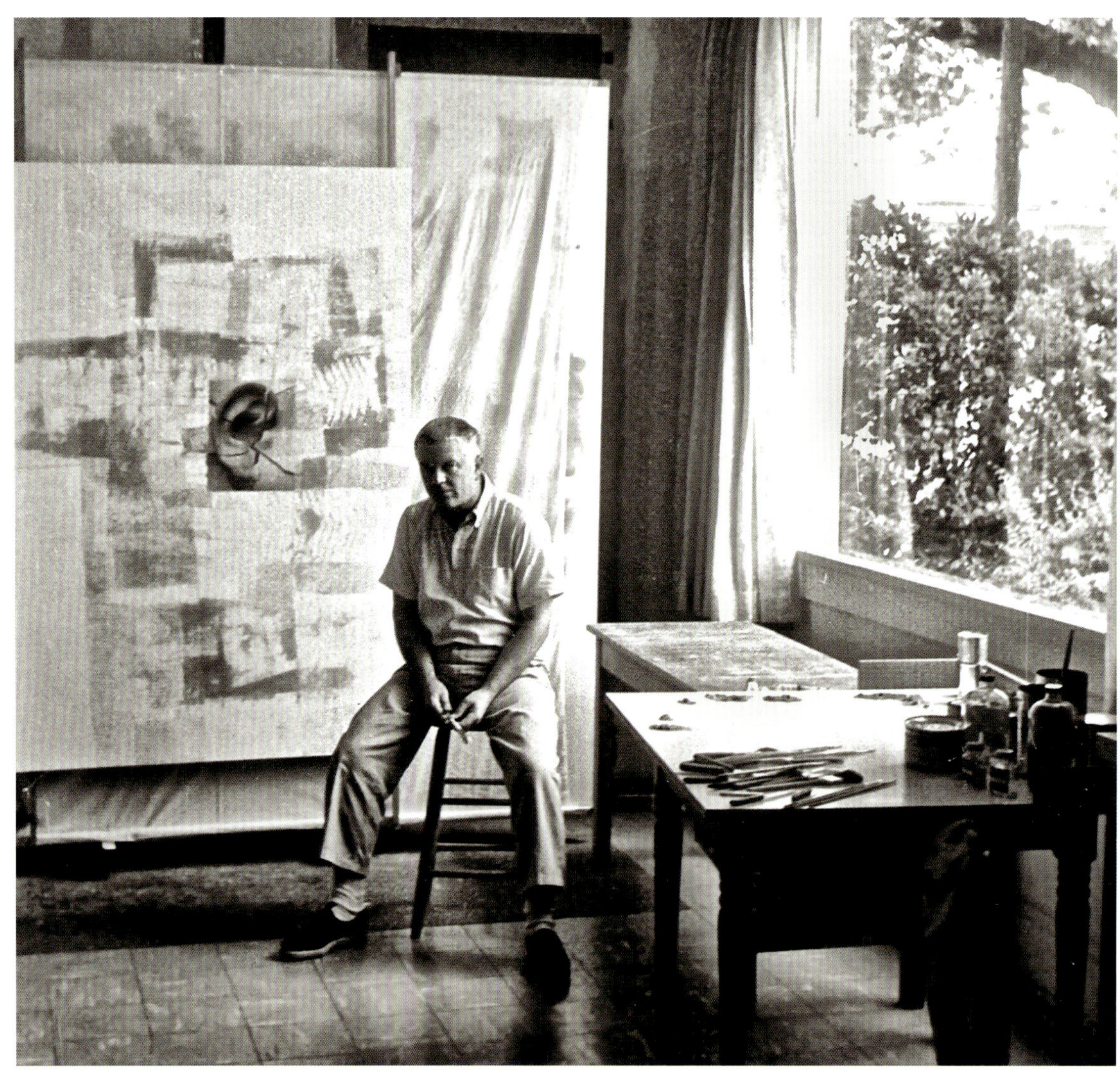

John Clemmer with *Almedia* in his Foucher Street studio,
New Orleans, ca. 1965, photograph by Milton Scheuermann Jr.,
John Clemmer archive

A Painter's Progress: Reflections on the Work

by David Clemmer

FOR MOST OF MY LIFE, I have been asked "What kind of artist is your father?" It has long been my default response to describe him as an abstract painter. It's an admittedly simplistic answer to a complex question. But I do believe that the majority of people well acquainted with my father, John Franklin Clemmer, and his oeuvre would tend to characterize him the same way. Abstraction, with influences from cubism and other early to mid-twentieth-century non-objective movements, was at the core of his artistic practice. And yet, an overview of his eight-decade career reveals an exceptional diversity of styles, motifs, materials, and subject matter.

In addition to abstraction my father worked in portraiture, landscape, and still life. He used oil, acrylic, mixed media, watercolor, ink, graphite, collage, sandcasting, and assorted graphic media. He also worked in a variety of sculptural modes. In the early 1960s, he began to produce three-dimensional wall pieces utilizing the technique of sandcasting—a process he explored in great depth over the following two decades. He became exceptionally fluent with oxyacetylene torch and brazed metal techniques and utilized them extensively for sculptures he made throughout the 1970s, '80s, and '90s. He often used photographs—his own and those taken by family members—as source material for his work. He routinely culled pages from magazines and newspapers, keeping files stuffed with images that caught his eye and spurred his imagination.

Considering the completeness of his oeuvre, John Clemmer is admittedly a hard man to pin down. He had faith in his muse and followed it where it led him, daily manifesting his friend Mark Rothko's dictum that "the most important tool the artist fashions through constant practice is faith in his ability to produce miracles when they are needed."[1] Clemmer adamantly resisted reductive labels, that of the "southern" artist in particular. "I'm not a *southern* artist," he would often say. "I'm an artist who works in the South." To wit, he worked extensively in the North (the upper Midwest, to be precise) as well, but was never labeled as such.

Regardless of where my father hung his hat (invariably, a black wool beret purchased on one of my parents' many trips abroad), his surroundings frequently inspired and infused themselves into his work, whether literally or through purely abstract ambience. An illustrative case is my father's large abstraction *Almedia* (1962) [FIGURE 1.1]. The mixed-media painting is titled after a hamlet upriver from New Orleans in St. Charles Parish; my father recounted that he noticed the name on a street sign while driving on Airline Highway one day. Completely devoid of any literal representation of the former plantation turned subdivision, the composition of cloudy red-brown forms and chevrons on a cream white ground incorporates a large photographic image of a shattered sculptural ear, torn from a copy of *Life* magazine and gessoed onto its surface. The word *Almedia* suggests "all-media" and the piece has always evoked for me dusty white shell driveways, tidal movement, and the hue of old growth cypress. The collaged ear perhaps reflects my father's love of classical music, or perhaps just the sense of sound. The combination of elements is enigmatic yet highly evocative.

For the generations of artists who came of age in the first half of the twentieth century the influence of cubism—of Picasso in particular—was

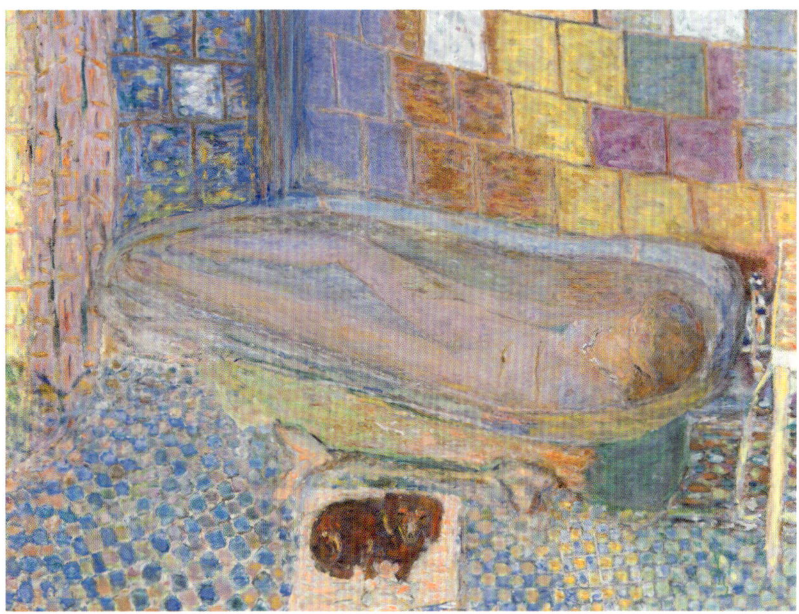

inescapable. Cubist-informed fracture of the figure and object can be seen in my father's early work. By the mid-1950s the abstract expressionist school of New York–based artists was ascendant in the art world, and his work from this period reflects the move toward elimination of the distinction between figure and ground, toward an "all over" compositional sense. In the next decade, his work showed an even greater ability to synthesize his disparate influences. His interests in Paleolithic cave painting and the art and architecture of ancient Greece, Rome, Byzantium, the Middle East, and the Italian Renaissance found expression in his work from the 1960s onward.

Later in life, my father came to regard Pierre Bonnard as the greatest artist of the twentieth century, finding endless fascination in the artist's uniquely poetic balance of the pure materiality of paint with scenes of intimate domesticity [FIGURE 1.2]. I recall a visit to the Metropolitan Museum of Art in New York and my father standing in front of Bonnard's *The Terrace at Vernonnet*, transfixed by the rich tapestry of color, pattern, and form, murmuring half to himself, "How does he *do* that?"

My father was an avid fan and scholar of classical music, and references to various compositions and composers began to appear in his work from the mid-'80s onward. He invariably listened to classical music while he worked, and in the late 1990s he executed a series of more than thirty intricate ink drawings depicting scenes and characters from his favorite operas.

Though my father's formal education extended no further than his high school diploma, his knowledge of art history and the modernist enterprise was extensive. He was possessed of a keen and relentlessly inquiring intellect and was a voracious reader. He was well aware of how his modest background and lack of a college degree might color him in the eyes of others as he progressed through his four-decade career in academe, but he was not afflicted by self-doubt or anxiety regarding his abilities. Rather, he had the confidence born of knowing that his accomplishments were honestly earned and not conferred upon him by dint of pedigree or privilege.

Like any artist of substance and originality, my father was much more than the sum total of his influences. Central to his genius was the ability to acknowledge and absorb the myriad influences that informed his personal aesthetic preferences while remaining very much his own man at the easel. Once he began to come into his own, his work less and less resembled that of anyone else. Biased though I may be, I feel that his work possesses an undeniable gravitas. This trait was equally manifest in the man himself: a quality of solidity and intellectual integrity that continues to speak eloquently across the decades.

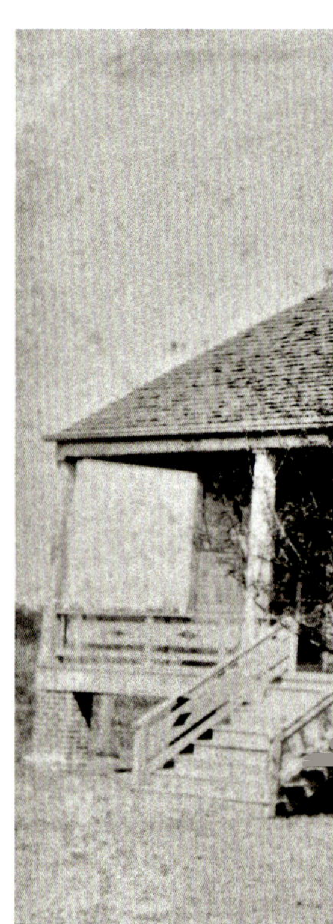

THE PHRASE "HUMBLE BEGINNINGS" is scarcely sufficient to describe my father's early life in Ascension Parish [FIGURES 1.3 AND 1.4]. His forebears were impoverished country folk living in the Bayou Goula and Donaldsonville areas—his father a transplant from Monroe, Wisconsin, and his mother a descendant of French colonials who arrived in Louisiana in the late eighteenth century. Just before the onset of the Great Depression, my

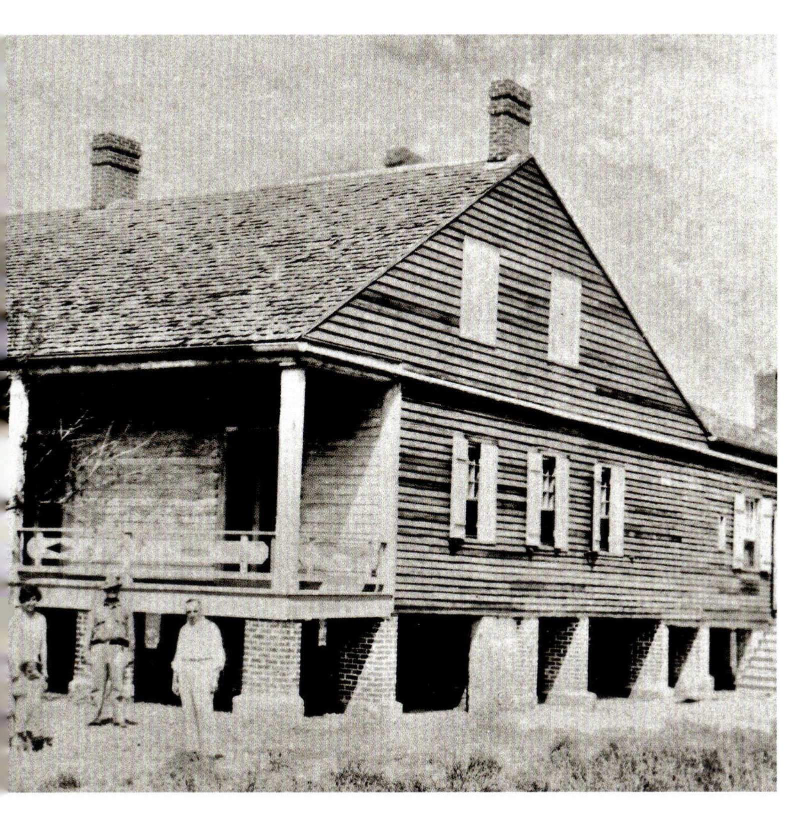

[FIGURE 1.3]
The Clemmer family home, Ascension Parish, Louisiana, ca. 1922,
Clemmer Family archive

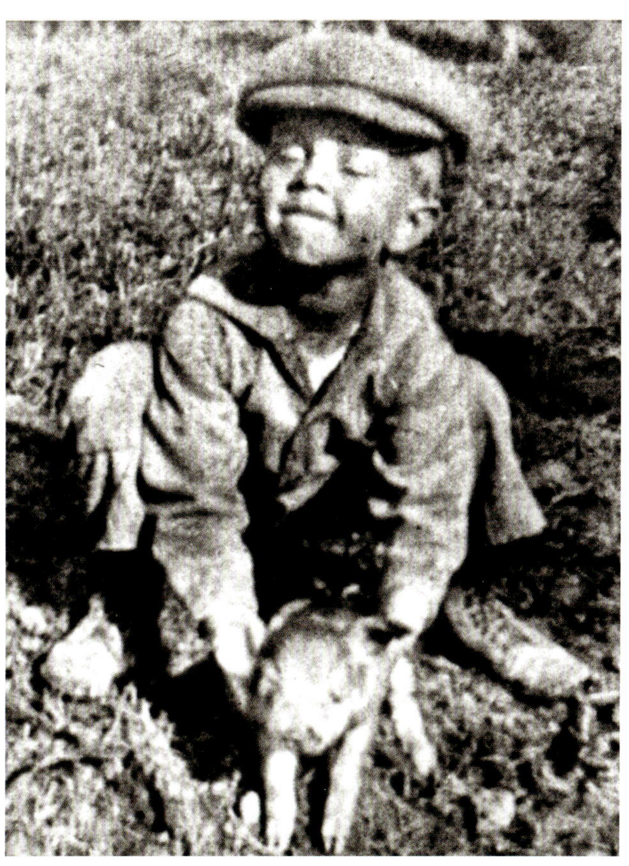

[FIGURE 1.4]
John Clemmer with his pet pig Sandy, Ascension Parish, Louisiana,
ca. 1925, *Clemmer Family archive*

grandparents moved the family to New Orleans in search of work for themselves and schooling for my father and his two younger sisters. As for his early artistic activities, my father simply described himself as "always drawing." The last documented instance of artistic accomplishment in the family occurred more than a century before his birth: his mother's great-great grandfather was the celebrated folk art wood carver Pierre Joseph Landry.[2]

My father's early instruction in art did not extend beyond basic classes at Fortier High School. My grandfather, John F. Clemmer Sr. **[FIGURE 1.5]**, pulled strings to obtain a commission for his son to attend the United States Coast Guard Academy in Connecticut, following in the footsteps of my father's late half-brother, William Lee Clemmer.[3] My father rejected the offer out of hand and declared his intention to pursue a career in art. His family's response was, quite understandably, one of disappointment and dismay. To them, it was tantamount to embracing the prospect of a lifetime of poverty and, at best, marginal respectability.

Despite his family's misgivings, following his graduation from Fortier in 1939 my father enthusiastically embraced the New Orleans art world and the vibrant bohemian French Quarter scene **[FIGURES 1.6 AND 1.7]**. It was a momentous time in the cultural history of the city's gaslit historic district, and its colorful denizens would indelibly shape the artist my father was to become.

Two important local institutions—the Arts and Crafts Club of New Orleans and Tulane University—were to play major roles in my father's life. His association with the former began at the age of eighteen when he received a scholarship to attend classes at the French Quarter–based club's New Orleans School of Art. From the family home on Magazine Street in the Irish Channel neighborhood, my father would take the streetcar down to the Vieux Carré, which he often referred to as "the Casbah," reflecting his wide-eyed view of the fabled neighborhood and its picturesque demimonde. His instructors at the New Orleans School of Art included Paul Ninas, Julius Woeltz, Xavier Gonzalez, and Enrique Alférez. It was Ninas, director of the school from 1932 to 1942, who became my father's mentor and lasting friend. My father also grew close with Gonzalez, and the Spanish-born artist became something of a father figure for him. He assisted Gonzalez with mural projects in the city,

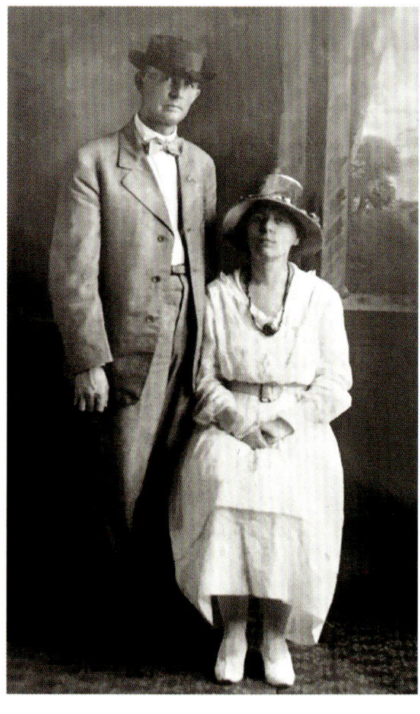

[FIGURE 1.5]
John Franklin Clemmer Sr. and Marie Landry Clemmer, ca. 1925, *courtesy of Dorsey Family archive*

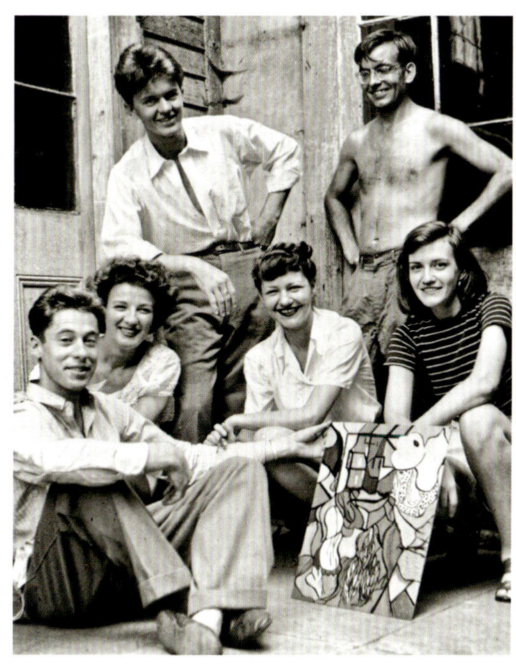

[FIGURE 1.6]
John Clemmer (standing, left) with friends in the French
Quarter, ca. 1940, *John Clemmer archive*

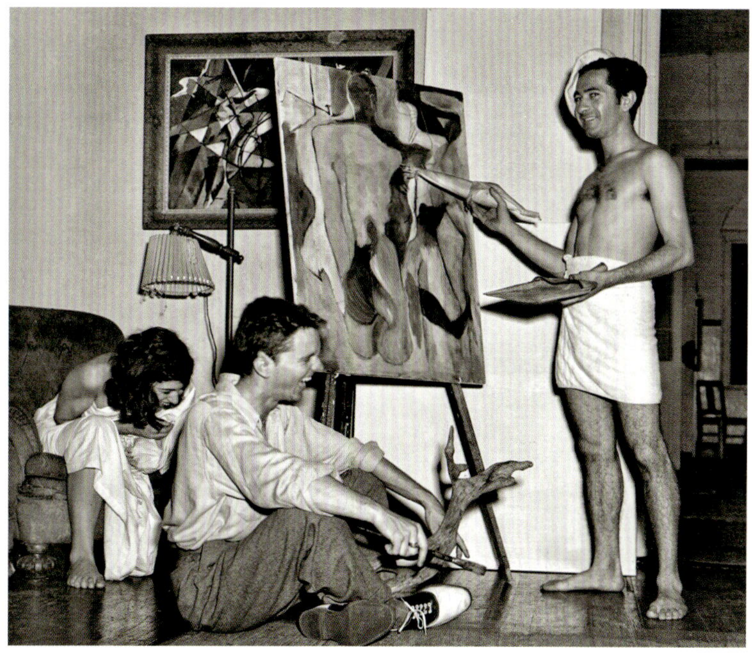

[FIGURE 1.7]
John Clemmer (seated on floor) with friends in the French Quarter,
ca. 1946, *John Clemmer archive*

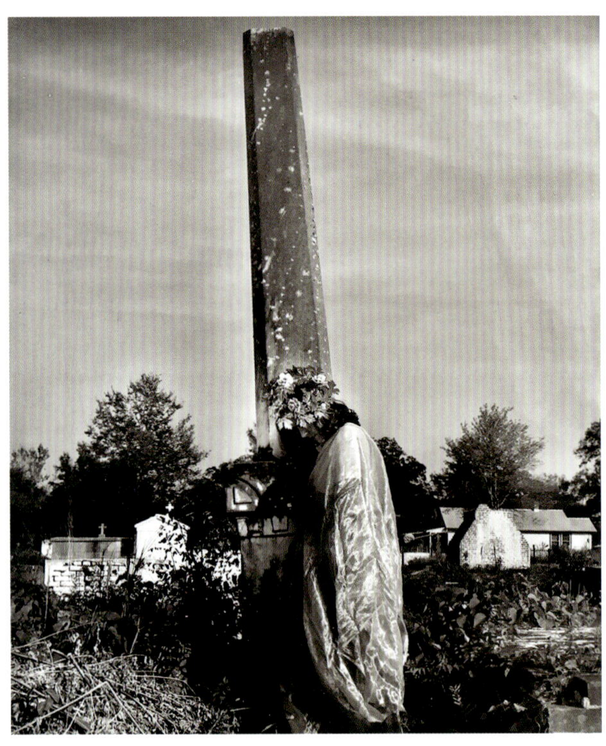

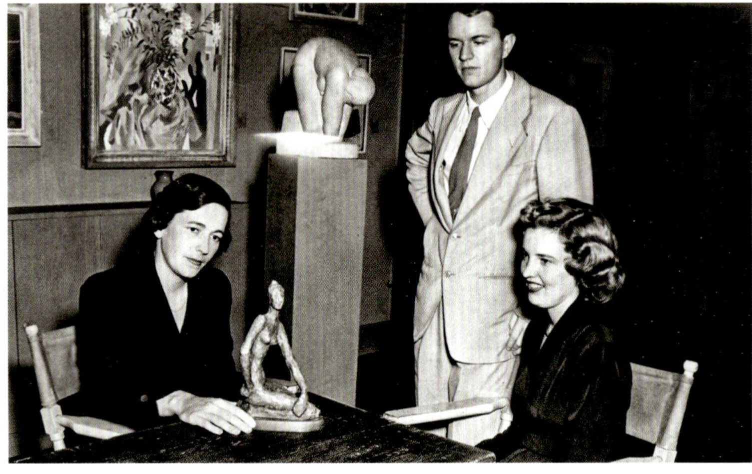

[FIGURE 1.8]

Elegy for a Leaning Column (Nancy Rathborne at Plattenville Cemetery), 1947, gelatin silver print, by Clarence John Laughlin, 9 ¼ x 7 ¾ in., *courtesy of David Clemmer, Santa Fe, NM*

[FIGURE 1.9]

John Clemmer with Nancy Rathborne (left), and Betty Stevens at the Arts and Crafts Club, 1949, photograph by J. H. Daspit; *The Historic New Orleans Collection, 1993.36.18*

[FIGURE 1.10]

John Clemmer and Litza Scoville Clemmer in the French Quarter, 1948, photograph by the *Times-Picayune*, *courtesy Capital City Press / Georges Media Group, Baton Rouge, LA*

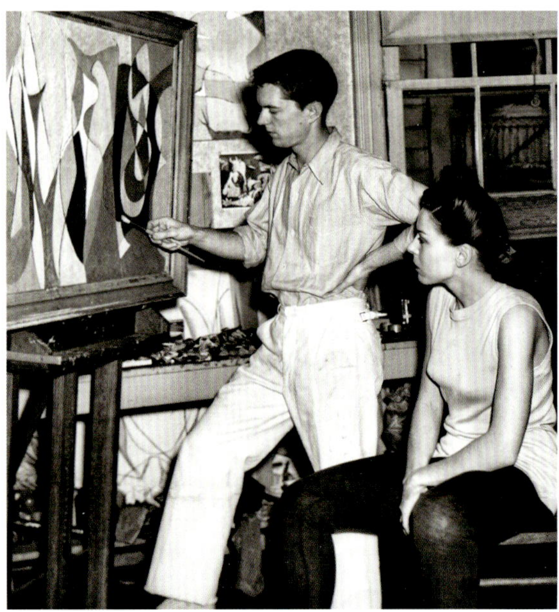

experiences that served him well when he received his first public commission in 1948 for a mural in the International Trade Mart building, then located at the corner of Camp and Common Streets.

Late in life, my father compiled a comprehensive list of the notable people he befriended and socialized with during his French Quarter days. The list enumerates some two hundred names ranging from Walt Disney to William Faulkner to the street performer Barbara "Banjo Annie" Lee. My father's anecdotes from this period included wild stories of Enrique Alférez and his trigger-happy pet monkey, photographic excursions with the volatile Clarence John Laughlin [FIGURE 1.8], and swamp tours with Max Ernst. Among the volumes on my father's bookshelves were titles with dedications from the photographer Elliott Erwitt,[4] critic Robert Rosenblum,[5] and novelists Henry Miller and Evelyn Waugh.[6]

In the first half of the 1940s, my father married his first wife, Marjorie Fischer—a union that produced two children.[7] To make ends meet, my father painted landing craft and PT boats for the wartime shipbuilder Higgins Industries at its plant in City Park. In January of 1944 his involvement with the Arts and Crafts Club and the French Quarter art scene was abruptly suspended when he was inducted into military service. Despite his absence, my father remained very much tuned into the goings-on, artistic and otherwise, back home in New Orleans. In 1945, during his second year of service, he was awarded first prize in the Arts and Crafts Club's annual exhibition—his first formal recognition as an artist. Upon his discharge from the US Army Air Forces, in 1946, my father picked up where he left off, and he became an instructor at the Arts and Crafts Club. Ultimately, he would also serve as executive secretary and director—the only person in the club's history to have been engaged with the organization in all such capacities [FIGURE 1.9].

When the club's benefactor, Sarah Henderson, passed away in 1950, its days were numbered. The organization sold the building that it had occupied since 1933 (the Bienvenu-Thomas House, at the corner of Pirate's Alley and Royal Street), where my father lived on the top floor with his second wife, Litza Scoville, a dancer and model [FIGURE 1.10]. The club carried

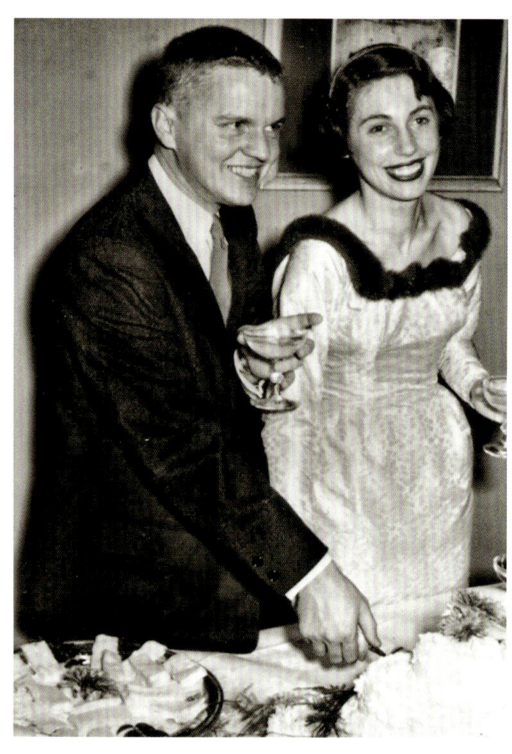

[FIGURE 1.11]
John and Dorothy Clemmer at their wedding
reception, New Orleans, 1953, *John Clemmer archive*

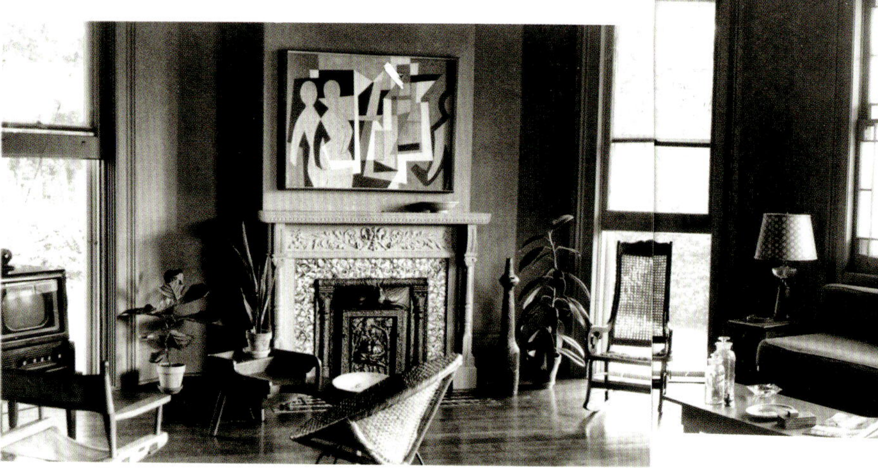

[FIGURE 1.12]
Photomontage of the front parlor at the Clemmer home, Foucher Street,
New Orleans, ca. 1955, photographs by Dorothy Clemmer, *John Clemmer
archive*

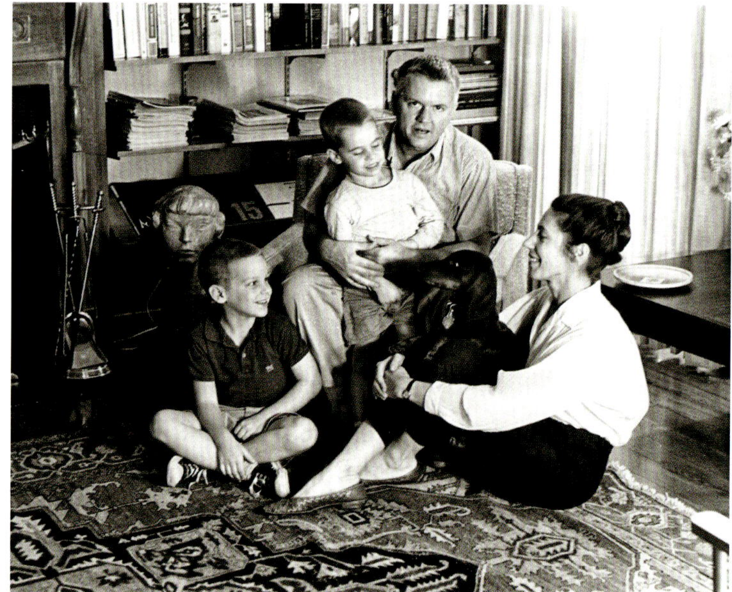

[FIGURE 1.13]
The Clemmer family at their Foucher Street home,
New Orleans, ca. 1965, *John Clemmer archive*

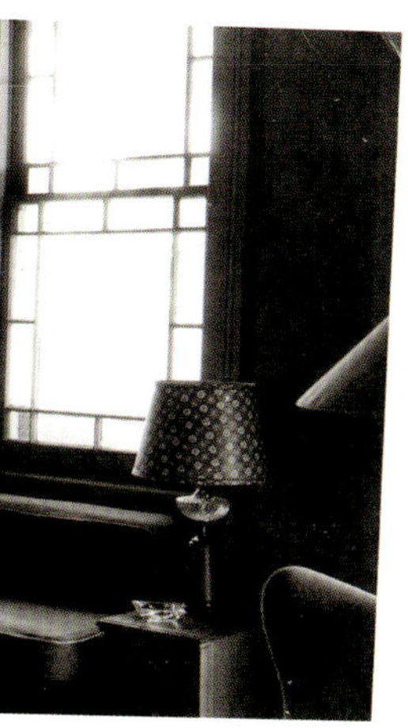

on for a few months longer at its new location a couple of blocks farther down Royal Street, ultimately closing its doors permanently in March 1951. But, as is often the case, the end of one thing heralded the beginning of another—1951 was also the first year of what was to become my father's thirty-five-year association with Tulane University.

My mother, the former Dorothy Iker of Chicago,[8] recalls first catching a glimpse of my father at a party in the French Quarter in 1948. Her Ursulines Avenue apartment was on the floor above sculptor Lin Emery's,[9] and as she was on her way up the stairs she saw my father through Lin's open door, sitting alone on the floor with his knees drawn up under his chin. She met him formally in 1949 when she and her husband were enrolled in night drawing classes taught by my father at the New Orleans School of Art. By May of 1950 my mother was mailing letters to her parents in Arts and Crafts Club envelopes that she described as being given to her by "a friend of mine who moved and now has almost 500 useless ones with his old address." Both of my parents were divorced from their respective spouses by early 1953, and they were married in December of that year [FIGURE 1.11].

Marriage to my mother and his new job at the Tulane School of Architecture teaching drawing, color theory, and model making helped to bring a degree of stability to my father's life that he had not previously known. The final element in this new era fell into place in 1955 when my parents purchased a house on a large lot at the corner of Foucher and Laurel Streets on the uptown edge of the Irish Channel [FIGURES 1.12 AND 1.13]. The property included a small outbuilding that had been built by a previous owner as a doctor's consulting room; it became my father's first studio outside of the French Quarter.

Initially hired as an instructor in the School of Architecture, my father progressed to assistant, associate, and finally, in 1974, full professorship. During his tenure at Tulane he influenced, and was in turn influenced by, generations of students. Throughout the 1960s and '70s my parents' students—my father's from the uptown campus and my mother's from the Tulane School of Medicine down in the Central Business District—were an ongoing presence in our family life. My parents' engagement with their young students brought the unprecedented tumult of the times home to us, but within the sanctuary of his studio my father sought, and reliably found, order and serenity.

One uniquely New Orleanian aspect of my father's career was his long involvement with the production side of Mardi Gras. Carnival is a home-grown industry, and throughout most of its history the parade floats, masks, costumes, and assorted accoutrement have been produced in local workshops. In the late 1940s, my father made the acquaintance of Murray Himler, a transplanted New Yorker who owned a costuming business that catered to several of the old-line krewes, including Rex, Babylon, and Momus. My father had previously found occasional work painting back-drops for Mardi Gras balls, but through his association with Mr. Murray (as he was known to my brother and me) he found steady, if seasonal, work making masks of molded buckram that were baked in a special oven, indi-vidually decorated, and dipped in paraffin [FIGURE 1.14].[10] My father worked as a contractor for Mr. Murray until the early 1960s, when his Tulane income finally allowed him to forswear the mask business. But the two remained good friends, and we would occasionally drop by the narrow pink stucco building on St. Charles Avenue just uptown from Lee Circle. My dad would have a drink and a chat with the old man in his tiny front office while my brother and I played in a heap of discarded costume trim-mings, pushed into a big pile off to one side of the large cutting table in the main room. On Mardi Gras mornings, Mr. Murray's open-house party was always our destination as we walked down St. Charles along the thronging parade route.

My father's first solo exhibition was presented at the Arts and Crafts Club in 1948, and from then on he regularly exhibited his art at venues around the city and across the South. He showed at the 331 Gallery in the mid '50s and later in the decade became a member of the co-op Orleans Gallery—the city's premier contemporary art venue from 1956 until its closure in 1972 [FIGURES 1.15 AND 1.16].

By the late '60s my father had grown weary of the obligations of the gal-lery scene and the interpersonal politics it inevitably entailed. He began

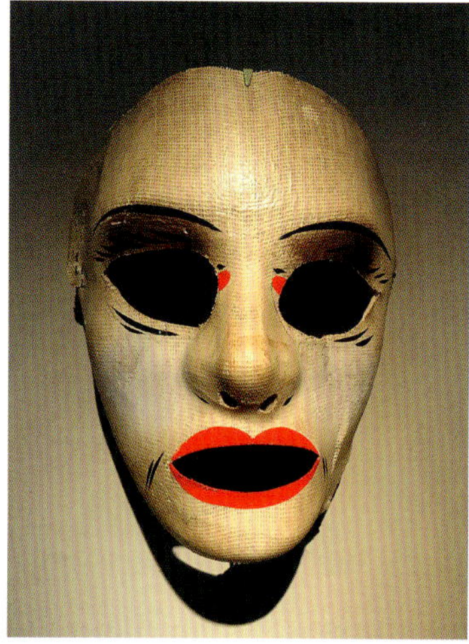

[FIGURE 1.14]
Mardi Gras mask made by Clemmer, 1959, photograph by David Clemmer, *courtesy of 3618 Studio, LLC, New Orleans, LA, collection of Don Fuson*

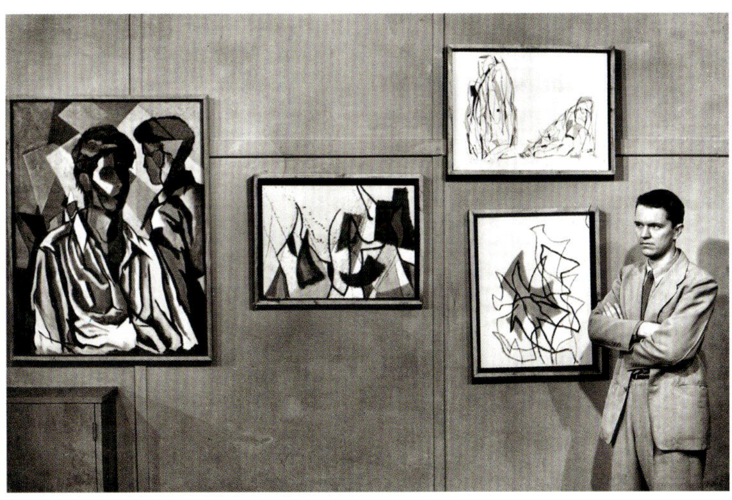

Clemmer at one of his early solo exhibitions, 1949, *The Historic New Orleans Collection, gift of John F. Clemmer, 1993.36.9*

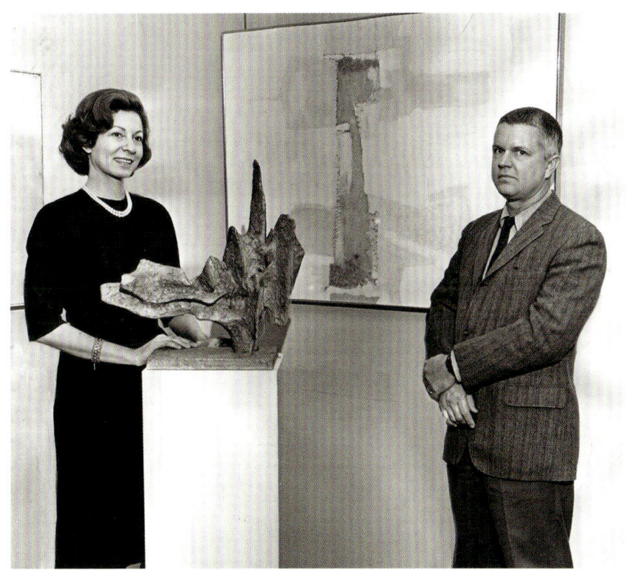

John Clemmer and Lin Emery at the Orleans Gallery, 1964, photograph by the *Times-Picayune, courtesy Capital City Press / Georges Media Group, Baton Rouge, LA*

exhibiting his new work in our family home, which fortunately provided a generous expanse of wall space. Between 1968 and 1978, he mounted five solo exhibitions on Foucher Street, the openings for which I recall fondly as crowded, smoky, boisterous affairs, which spilled out of the house onto the veranda and into the garden.

In 1978, my father was appointed to be the chairman of the Department of Art at Tulane's Newcomb College. The increased demands on his time impacted his creative output, though he did manage to complete several large sculptural commissions during this period. As he approached his mid-60s, he began to look forward to his retirement from academia, and in 1986 he stepped down from his position at Newcomb with the honor of professor emeritus of art.

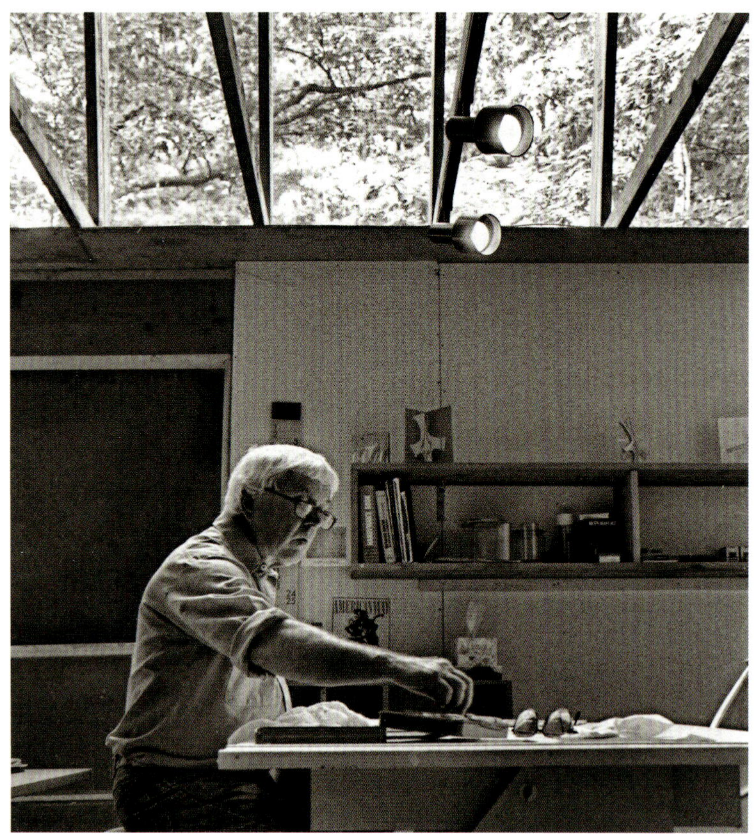

[FIGURE 1.17]
John Clemmer in his Black River, Wisconsin, studio, ca. 1998,
photograph by Curt Knoke, *John Clemmer archive*

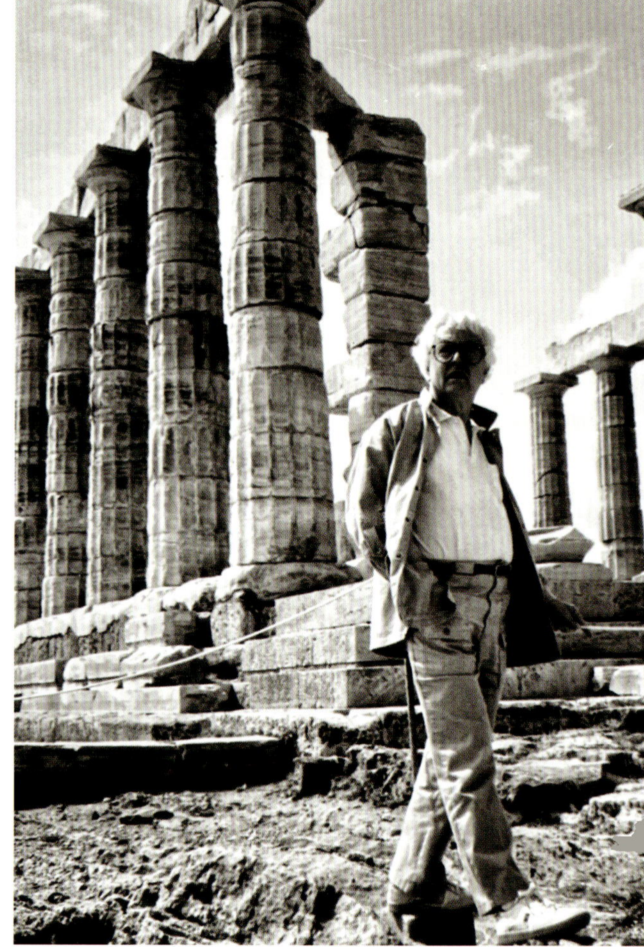

[FIGURE 1.18]
Clemmer at the Temple of Poseidon, Cape Sounion, Greece,
ca. 2006, *John Clemmer archive*

During his years at the School of Architecture, my father had maintained a studio on campus in addition to his Foucher Street space. In the 1980s, he built another studio in the densely wooded Black River area of Sheboygan, Wisconsin [FIGURE 1.17], where my mother's parents had purchased a summer cottage in 1937. My mother retired from the Tulane School of Medicine in 1989, and from then on my parents began dividing their time more or less equally between Louisiana and Wisconsin. Eventually they built a house designed by my father on the site of the original Iker family cottage. Impressions of the birch, oak, and beech woods and the shores of Lake Michigan, just down the street, became increasingly prominent in the work my father produced in his Wisconsin studio.

In the late 1980s my father embarked upon a period of sustained productivity that continued through the first decade of the next century. He began showing his work with regularity again, and in October 1999 the New Orleans Museum of Art honored his sixty years as a mainstay of the local art scene with the comprehensive retrospective *John Clemmer: Exploring the Medium, 1940–1999*.

My parents traveled extensively during their sixty-one years of marriage—throughout the United States, Canada, Central and Latin America, Europe, and the Middle East. These many journeys became a primary source of inspiration for much of my father's work. My parents traveled to Greece and Italy on multiple occasions, and my father found particular resonance with ruins of classical antiquity such as the Temple of Poseidon at Cape Sounion, southeast of Athens [FIGURE 1.18], and medieval towns like San Gimignano in Tuscany. Imagery from locales such as these heralded the beginning of a new representational phase in my father's work at the beginning of the 1990s [PLATES 31, 32, AND 33]. But their travels weren't always inspiring: When ocean liners began docking in New Orleans, my parents (by this time living in a condominium on St. Charles Avenue) decided to escape the Mardi Gras hordes one year by booking a Caribbean cruise. Driven to distraction by the Muzak piped everywhere on the ship twenty-four hours a day, my father had to work mightily to overcome the impulse to jump overboard. This particular excursion inspired no artwork.

Regardless of the frequent travel and the long summer sojourns in Wisconsin, there was never any doubt that New Orleans was home. Like many conscientious people, my father had issues with his hometown, and he looked ruefully upon many of the changes, generally promoted as "progress," that he had witnessed over the decades. The redevelopment of the old French Market into an open-air tourist mall of t-shirt shops and knickknack emporia remained a source of endless dismay and rueful head shaking, decades after the fact. The devastation wreaked by Hurricane Katrina and its aftermath was particularly distressing to him, and it seemed he went into a period of mourning for his hometown as he watched the shocking real-time television coverage of the cataclysm from the safe remove of the family home in Wisconsin. (His studio, located in the "sliver by the river," fortuitously escaped damage.[11]) Despite his occasional grumbling and years of musing about the possibility of leaving the Crescent City, there is no doubt in my mind that he loved New Orleans. This love might not have been overtly manifest—he simply wasn't that kind of artist, sentimentality having no place in his work—but undoubtedly it was always present.

In the spring of 2013, when my father was ninety-one years old, my parents sold their St. Charles Avenue condo and relocated permanently to Wisconsin. In his last months, during a record-breaking "polar vortex" winter in which Lake Michigan froze from shore to shore, my father longed terribly to return to New Orleans. The LeMieux Galleries presented an exhibition of his recent work in January 2014, and my parents made two treks south—for the opening reception and again for a gallery talk in early February. He visited his beloved Laurel Street studio on the afternoon of February 9, rearranged the paintings hanging in the front room, and sat by the open back door with my mother, reading the *Times-Picayune* and eating chocolate chip cookies with a glass of milk. Reluctantly, my father returned to Wisconsin after both trips, and in late March he suffered a debilitating stroke. He passed away peacefully in Milwaukee on the morning of April 11, 2014, three months shy of his ninety-third birthday.

IT IS NOT INFREQUENTLY the lot of the artist of note to become popularly associated with a signature visual motif or format. Be it a wide-eyed dog of unusual azure hue or paint flung and dripped across an expansive canvas, once such an association has caught hold in the critical and public mind it may become either a boon or a burden to its author—or both simultaneously. My father was not destined to become one of those artists.

If there is anything resembling an overarching theme in his work, it might well be its diversity of style and subject matter. This is not to suggest that his oeuvre is lacking in consistency. In addition to the undeniable continuities of brushwork, palette, compositional sense, and choice of media in his work are the number of conceptually cohesive bodies of work he produced over the course of his life at the easel. These series consisted of formal themes my father typically explored over a span of years, produced simultaneously with other works not related to any specific series.

In the past several years, with the completion of a detailed inventory of my father's work (if such an undertaking is ever truly "complete"), a comprehensive overview of his oeuvre has become fully accessible. Begun by my mother in the 1980s, this database was initially unable to support images in addition to the relevant verbal data. A complete cataloging of the contents of my father's studios in 2010 and the integration of decades of photographs produced in a variety of formats—35mm prints, Polaroids, transparencies, slides, and digital photographs—has finally made the database into a powerful tool with which to appreciate and assess the cohesiveness of his artistic output. Now containing over 1,550 entries, the database will certainly continue to grow as gaps are filled in and more work is documented.

The first documented examples of my father's work date to the early 1940s and his days as a teenaged student at the New Orleans School of Art. Not surprisingly, they are primarily the product of life drawing classes along with numerous sketches of my father's first wife, Marjorie. The classroom sketches display the young artist's innate facility, but the drawings of Marjorie are more telling. My father's emotional engagement with his subject in a setting outside of the art school seems to have had a beneficial effect on his work;

these drawings are more confident and deftly executed than those of classroom models (most of whom were male). Also notable for their charm and assuredness are sketches of batture camps [FIGURE 1.19], the result of excursions to the levee above Audubon Park with Paul Ninas. Works on paper predominate in my father's student days, as materials such as oil paints, canvas, and stretchers were extravagances generally beyond his limited means.

Prevalent in these early drawings is a technique of dense crosshatching [FIGURE 1.20]. Drawings from this period are executed almost exclusively in ink, but the few documented works in pencil also exhibit crosshatching as opposed to shading, indicating my father's preference for this technique over other options. The crosshatching remains consistent in works on paper throughout the 1940s (including during my father's service in the military) and in some of his paintings. Crosshatching gradually becomes less prominent in the 1950s as his facility with line drawing becomes progressively more self-assured.

When my father began his employment at the Tulane School of Architecture, in 1951, he bought his first Rapidograph technical pens, which draw extremely fine lines. With these new tools, my father made his most articulate and intimate figurative drawings. He produced fewer drawings in the 1960s—due, at least in part, to time constraints. Around this time, my mother also grew more reluctant to model for him (she worried that she was no longer of "art object" status). Then in the late 1960s, he returned to his drawing table and embarked on a series of highly detailed abstractions built up entirely from intensive crosshatching. Many of these pieces relate to his paintings of the period, specifically the *Topographia* series [PLATES 18, 19, 20, 22, AND 23].

At some unknown date, most likely in the mid-1950s, my father built four silkscreens fashioned from salvaged window frames. The screens depict straightforward but fairly charming French Quarter genre scenes featuring characteristic architecture along with horse-drawn buggies and street sweepers. By the late 1960s he was selling copies of these prints to the Thunderbird Motel on Tulane Avenue for $13.75 apiece, frequently being called upon to supply replacements when they were pilfered by guests [FIGURE 1.21]. These silkscreens constitute the only known examples of artwork

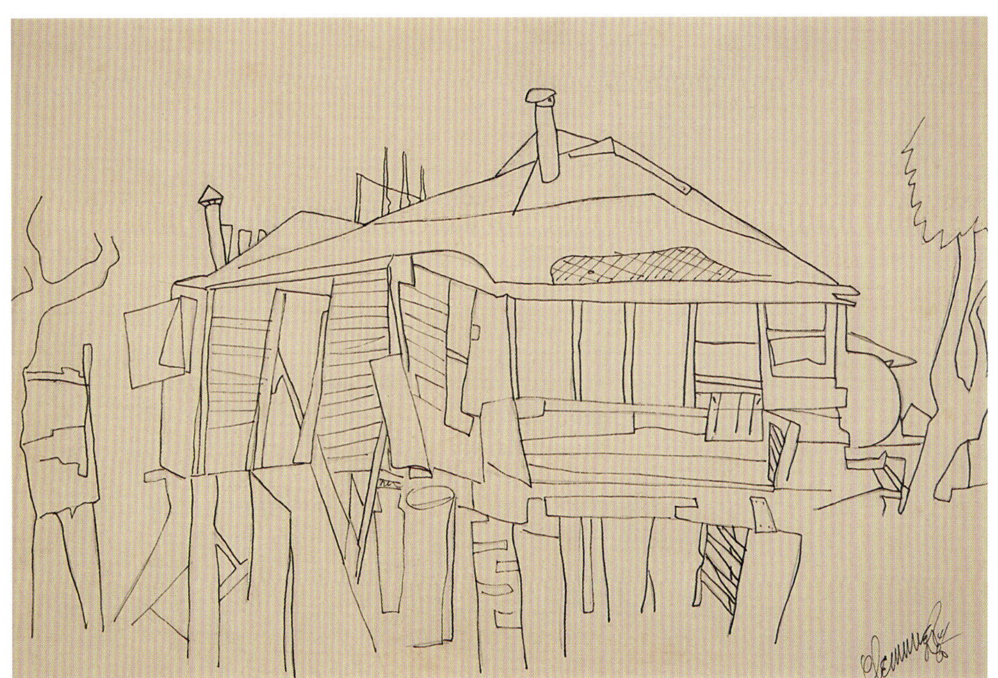

[FIGURE 1.19]
Batture Dwelling, 1941, ink on paper,
by John Clemmer, 9 ¾ × 14 ¾ in.,
courtesy of Don Fuson

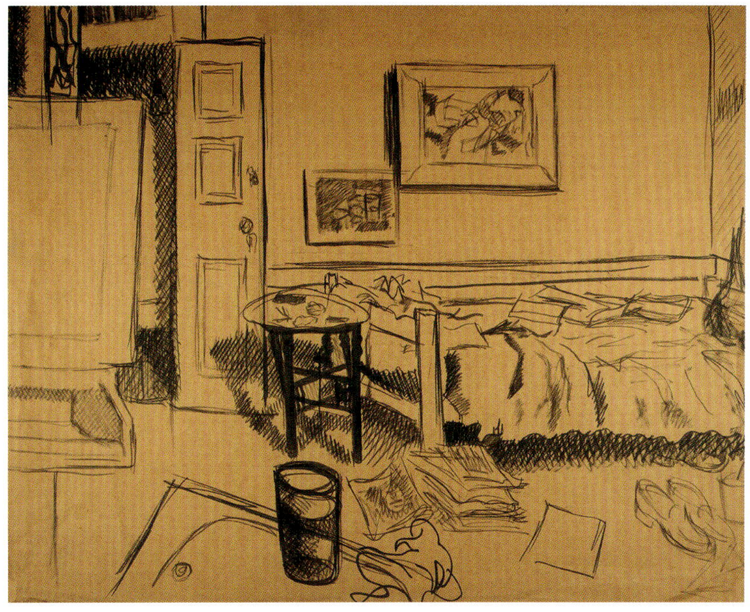

[FIGURE 1.20]
Interior, 1940s, ink and ink wash on paper, by
John Clemmer, 19 ¾ × 24 ¼ in., courtesy of 3618
Studio, LLC, New Orleans, LA

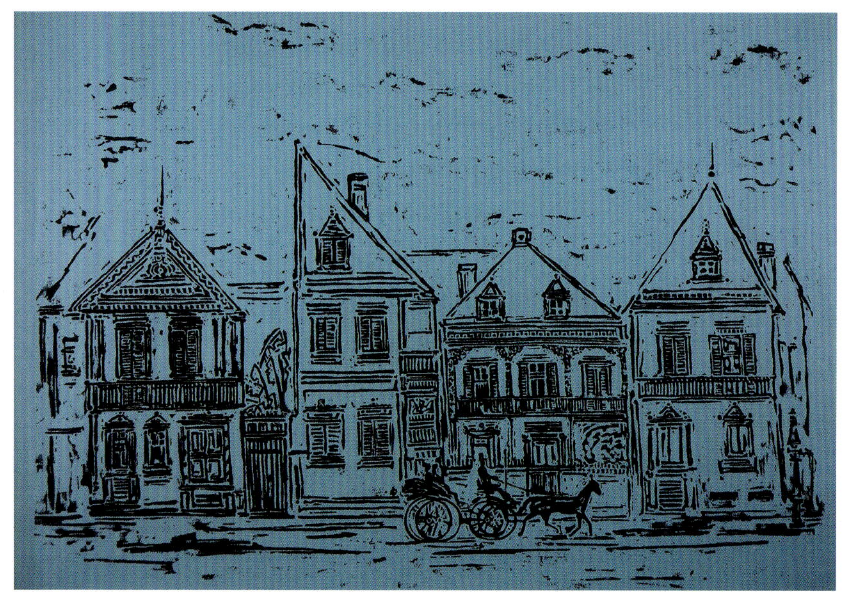

[FIGURE 1.21]
Untitled (French Quarter Scene), 1969,
silkscreen on blue paper, by John
Clemmer, 20 × 26 in., courtesy of 3618
Studio, LLC, New Orleans, LA

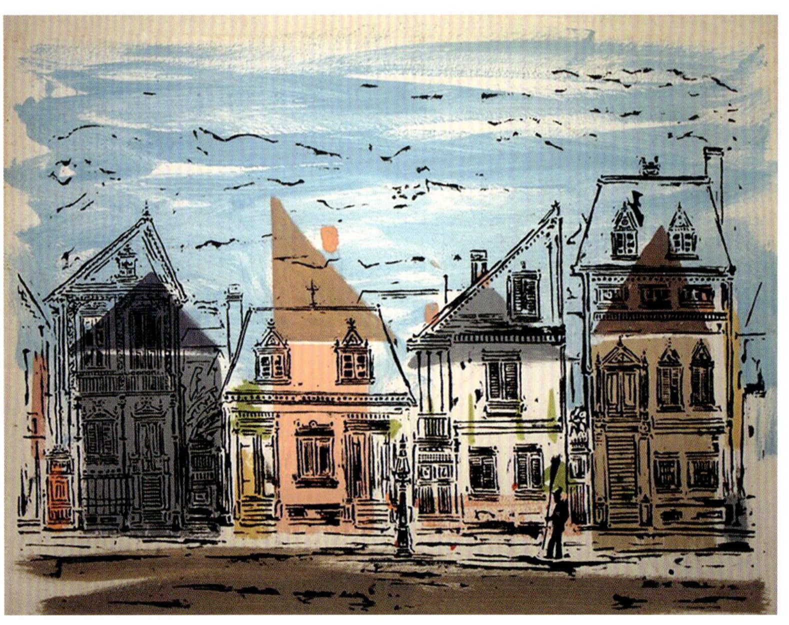

[FIGURE 1.22]
Untitled (French Quarter Scene), ca. 1960s,
silkscreen on board, by John Clemmer, 18 ¾
× 24 in., collection of Elizabeth and Fred
Laborde

that my father produced with specifically commercial intent. And though they were targeted to the tourist trade, he could not resist occasionally meddling with the formula by overprinting multiple screens and disassociating color from line [FIGURE 1.22].

In 1957, my father began producing abstract silkscreen and linoleum block prints, some of which incorporate multiple passes through the press or screen, hand coloring, and collage [PLATE 12]. This body of graphic work remained essentially unknown to me until I began cataloging the contents of his New Orleans studio in 2010. I could find no evidence that he had exhibited these prints, and I had never seen any examples of them in his studios or displayed in our home. He executed his prints on expensive, heavyweight deckle-edged art paper, signed the majority of them, and stored them away carefully. It may have been the expense of framing that discouraged my father from showing his prints: in his early French Quarter days he was employed in the Gresham Gallery frame shop, and from thereon he framed almost all of his paintings on canvas and panel himself. Works on paper under glass were a different matter, however. Whatever his reason for keeping his prints to himself, it is a strong and engaging body of work that both informs and is informed by his work in other media.

My father returned to printing in 2000 and again in 2006 to work with the monotype process at Hand Graphics in Santa Fe, New Mexico, in sessions with Santa Fe artist Mark Spencer and master printer Michael Costello. He also pulled at least three additional small-format monotypes, working with improvised equipment in his studio. In total, the inventory documents approximately eighty-five prints—a significant number constituting an essentially unknown body of work.

Painting materials were hard to come by for my father during his impoverished student days. Over the course of the 1940s, he produced only twenty-three documented paintings, thirteen of which are oils on either canvas or panel. The additional ten are works on paper executed in either gouache, watercolor, or mixed media. Twelve of these twenty-three paintings are fully abstract, and the rest are either representational or cubist-influenced figurative works or landscapes.

Though his own father was purportedly an ardent agnostic, my father was born into an otherwise observant French Catholic family. He converted to Judaism in 1953, just prior to marrying my mother. He was not rigorously observant of any organized religion, but spirituality in its many forms was consistently important to my father. This is apparent in his work from the very beginning: Entry number 0001 in his inventory is the sketch for his 1942 painting *How Men Their Brothers Maim* [PLATE 2]—a cubist depiction of the suffering Christ in his crown of thorns. The title of the piece is a quote from Oscar Wilde's *Ballad of Reading Gaol*, an indication of the twenty-one-year-old artist's literary interests intersecting with spiritual concerns in the early days of America's involvement in the Second World War.

Religious themes—Christian, Jewish, and otherwise—constitute a subtle but continuous thread throughout my father's work. Moreover, his paintings of the 1940s and the first half of the '50s consistently display a compositional motif of strong black lines that delineate the figures and forms, rather in the manner of the leading in stained glass. In 1955, he did in fact design stained-glass windows for the St. Bernard United Methodist Church in Chalmette. This structural concept gradually dissipates through the mid-'50s, and by 1957 areas of color that were once tightly constrained are allowed to soften and breathe. His work becomes steadily looser and more expansive. By the time he painted *Vertical View* [FIGURE 1.23], in 1959, the transition was essentially complete, and color was now fully freed from line. The size of his works also began to expand, from pieces that were comfortably easel sized to those that were thirty-six by forty-eight inches, forty-eight by forty-eight inches (a preferred format), and often larger.

Beginning in the early 1940s, my father occasionally worked on the smooth side of Masonite panel—an inexpensive, easily prepared surface that handles paint much differently than canvas. By the early 1960s, Masonite became his support of choice, and some of his paintings had gotten genuinely large, culminating in the eight-foot-square oil painting titled *Aureola* (circa 1965) [FIGURE 1.24].[12] The loosening of the forms in his paintings had reached its apogee by this time, and in works such as *Valle I* and *Almedia* (1962) [PLATE 14], *Naranja* (1963), and *Siloé* (1964) [PLATE 15], any remnants of

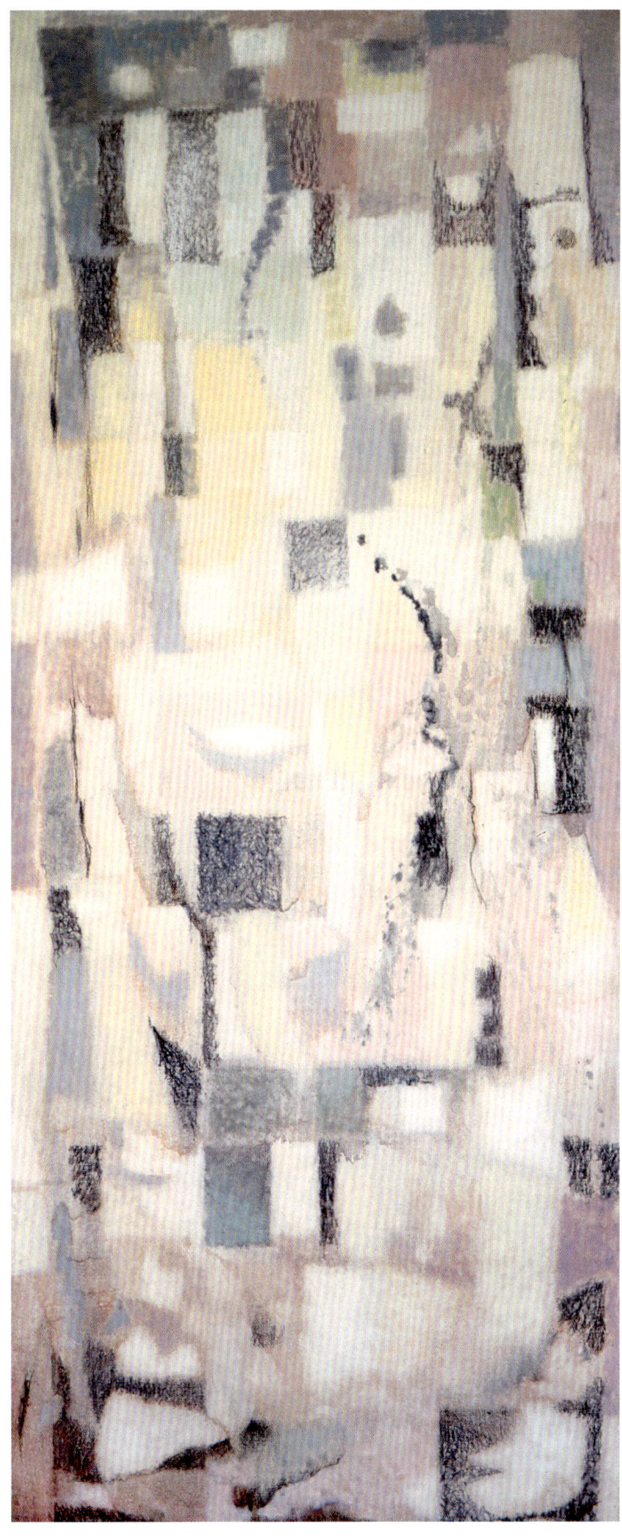

[FIGURE 1.23]
Vertical View, 1959, charcoal and oil on canvas, by John Clemmer, 60 × 24 in., *image courtesy New Orleans Museum of Art, photograph by Judy Cooper*

geometric form had dissolved into almost pure atmospheric effect.[13] Having arrived at this juncture, it seems that my father found himself at a turning point: Where to go from here?

His direction forward can be traced to a small painting titled *Summery—Season II* (1964) [PLATE 16]. If my father had been searching for a strategy that would allow him to step back from the sublime void, as it were, yet keep moving forward, he found the answer with this unassuming twenty-by-twenty-inch oil painting on Masonite. The basic compositional concept is the essence of simplicity: a circle within a square. In *Summery—Season II* the internal fifteen-inch square is centered on the panel, and a circle fifteen inches in diameter is centered inside of that. The circle, square, and the surrounding border are further subdivided into regular sections. Overall, the panel contains twenty soft-edged segments, some of which are dominated by a single hue; others contain combinations of the gold-yellow, variegated blues, and cream-whites that suggest the painting's title. The geometry serves to organize it all, but does not entirely constrain the color forms, which, particularly in the circular area, flow from one section to another [FIGURE 1.25]. The painting's format applies a level of discipline to the hazy, irregular forms he had developed—an architecture that would impart order but allow freedom.

Through the mid-'60s, my father continued to produce loosely formed abstractions, often incorporating elements of collage and, occasionally, hard-edged geometric forms. In 1969, though, he returned to the circle-in-a-square concept of *Summery—Season II* and initiated a group of paintings based on the format: the *Topographia* series. Comprising eleven named paintings and more than a dozen studies and related works [PLATE 21], the *Topographia* series was a significant breakthrough that indicated the direction that my father's painting was to take for the next fifty years. From 1969 onward, with only occasional exceptions, his paintings and works on paper would be typified by a meticulously calibrated internal architecture—sometimes overt, other times very subtle—that served to organize the composition, whether abstract or representational.

In a rare statement, composed for a 1971 exhibition of the *Topographia* series, my father stated that the paintings contain "not observations but

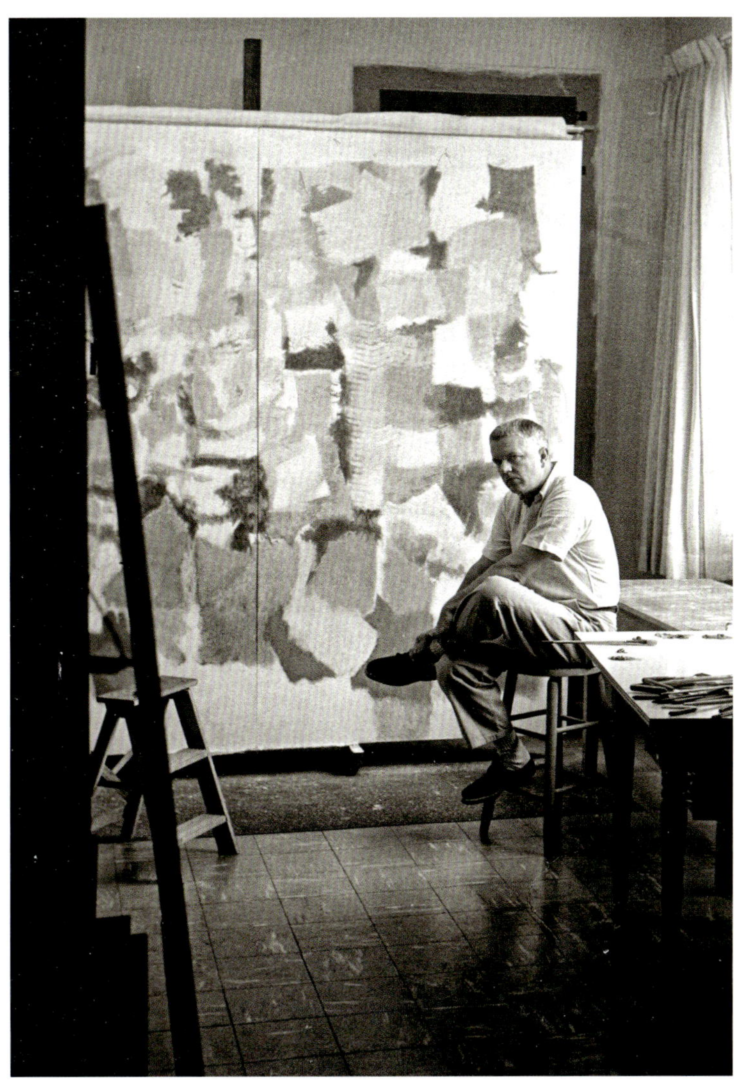

[FIGURE 1.24]
John Clemmer with *Aureola* in his Foucher Street studio,
New Orleans, ca. 1965, photograph by Milton Scheuermann Jr.,
John Clemmer archive

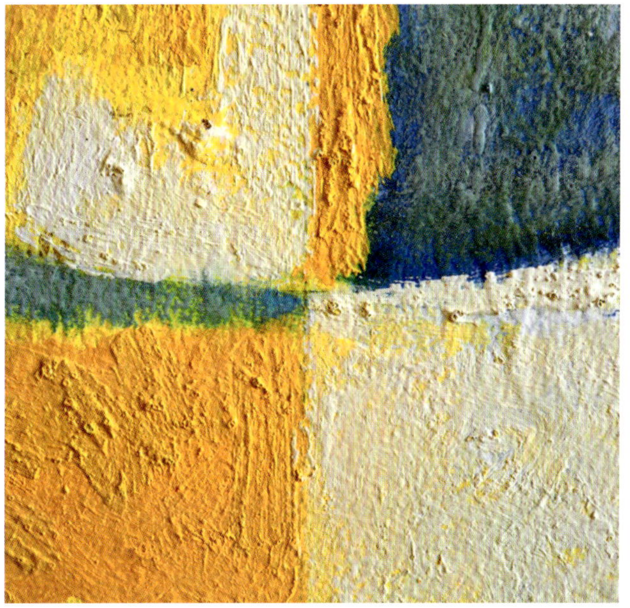

[FIGURE 1.25]
Detail of *Summery—Season II*, 1964, oil on panel, by
John Clemmer, 20 × 20 in., *courtesy of David Clemmer,
Santa Fe, NM*

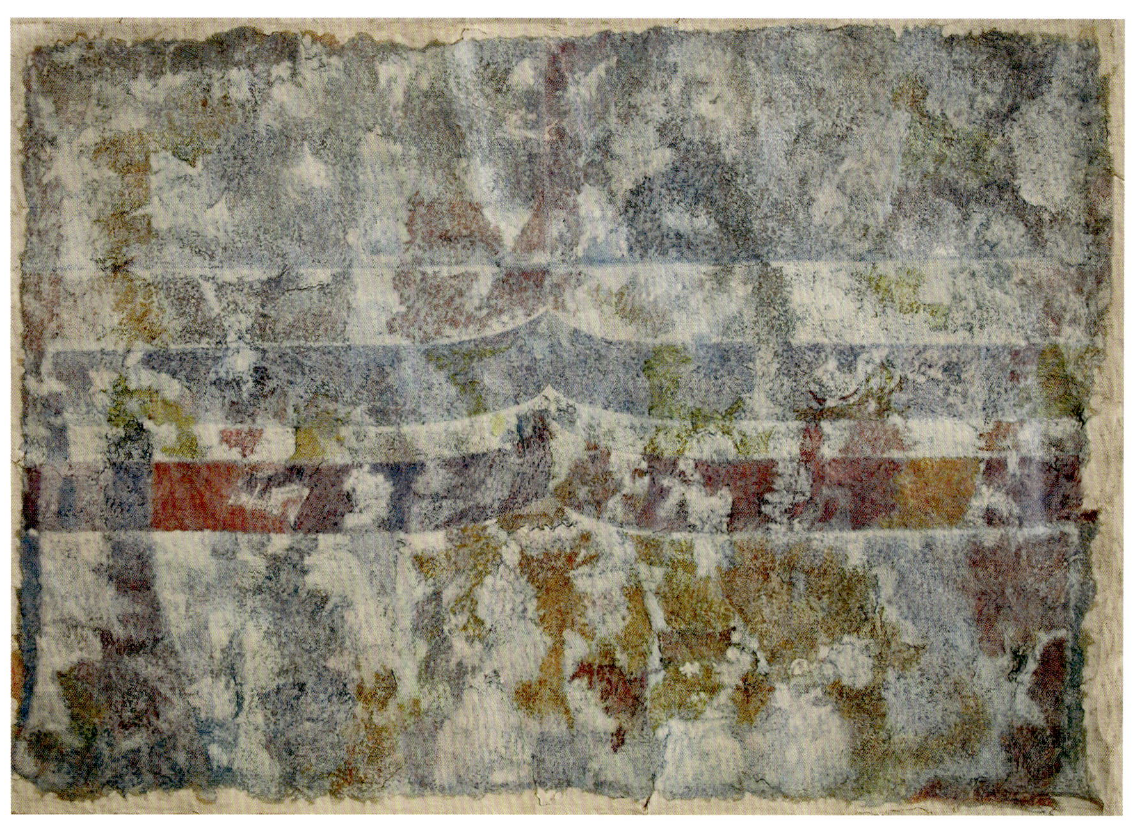

Estuario, 1985, mixed media on papel de amate, by John Clemmer,
17 × 25 in., *courtesy of 3618 Studio, LLC, New Orleans, LA*

perceptions of place, expressions of the quality of light, air, color, movement, constancy, variability, time and timelessness. They encompass variety of place. Istanbul, Crete, Mexico, Guatemala, the moon; in each there
is the development of a geometry peculiar to place as an expression of the
unity of man and the universe." The manner in which my father listed the
moon along with earthly locales to which he had traveled made me wonder
if perhaps he hadn't visited there too. (The year prior to the beginning of
the *Topographia* paintings our family had gone to see Stanley Kubrick's epic
2001: A Space Odyssey in the theater—an experience that made a profound
impression on both my father and me.)

The *Topographia* paintings concluded in 1973 with the masterful
Topographia V—Capricorn [PLATE 23], the largest piece in the series, at sixty
by forty-eight inches, and the only one to diverge from the square format. My
father recognized the importance of the *Topographia* paintings in his oeuvre
and held onto several of them, displaying them prominently in our home.
Regardless, when he felt that he had accomplished what he had intended
with the series, he moved on to other ideas.

While on a family trip to Mexico in the mid-1970s, my father came across
a shop selling large sheets of paper made from pulped tree bark. This handmade paper, which has a cork-like texture and a wavy, highly variegated surface, is known as papel de amate. My father was taken with its unique qual-
ities and brought a roll of the sheets home. He liked to say that he worked
with a surface, not *on* it, and he conceived of his approach to his work as
interactional, as a free-flowing conversation between artist and medium.
Papel de amate offered him something distinctly different from the uniform
panel, canvas, and commercially made paper that he typically used. Allowing
the irregularities of the paper to suggest forms and color choices, he produced about three dozen works on it between the late 1970s and the early
2000s, including some of his most lyrical and intuitive smaller abstractions
[FIGURE 1.26].

The 1970s and '80s constitute the middle period of my father's
career. After the breakthrough of the *Topographia* paintings, his work of
these decades became fully abstract, with only a handful of exceptions.

(Throughout his career he had enjoyed painting floral still lifes, and he produced over a dozen of these during the 1970s.) A theme in his work that had originated in the early 1960s continued to gather momentum: atmospheric abstractions inspired by impressions of specific locales—Louisiana, Wisconsin, Latin America, and Europe. Paintings and works on paper named for specific towns and regions accounted for over half of my father's output in the 1980s, a decade for which his inventory records eighty-three works. This number gives an indication of how his academic commitments impacted his studio time: in the 1990s, following his retirement from Tulane, the tally of inventoried pieces increased to 250.

In the early 1990s, my father began to apply geometric formats to landscape and still life subjects. In paintings such as *San G. I* and *La Giudecca* (1991) and *Temple of Poseidon I* (1992) [FIGURE 1.27], he divided his canvas into vertical sections, some of which are dominated by a single hue. In most cases there are three primary sections, but in some instances he included two narrow rectangular elements at either side of the scene, which function as framing structures. My father was partial to views through doors and windows—a compositional device often used by Pierre Bonnard, Henri Matisse, and Richard Diebenkorn, all artists that he admired. He painted dozens of such scenes between 1947 and 2013 and frequently used the terms "portal," "window," "view," or combinations thereof, in his titles. Perhaps most significantly, though, the 1990s signaled a return to representation: the majority of his works on canvas and panel from this point onward are either figurative or representational landscapes.

The tripartite composition proved to be enduring in my father's work. He employed it consistently over the course of three decades, including a series of abstract works on paper executed in oil crayon (the *Trilogy* series [PLATE 34]) and a bold group of large abstractions on canvas (the *Triunity* paintings [PLATE 36]) made in the mid- to late 1990s. In 1988 my father and I visited the nondenominational Rothko Chapel in Houston, Texas, in which nine of Rothko's fourteen monumental abstractions are arranged in triptychs. The significance of the triptych in relation to the traditional Christian altarpiece would not have been lost on my father. He was baptized in Ascension

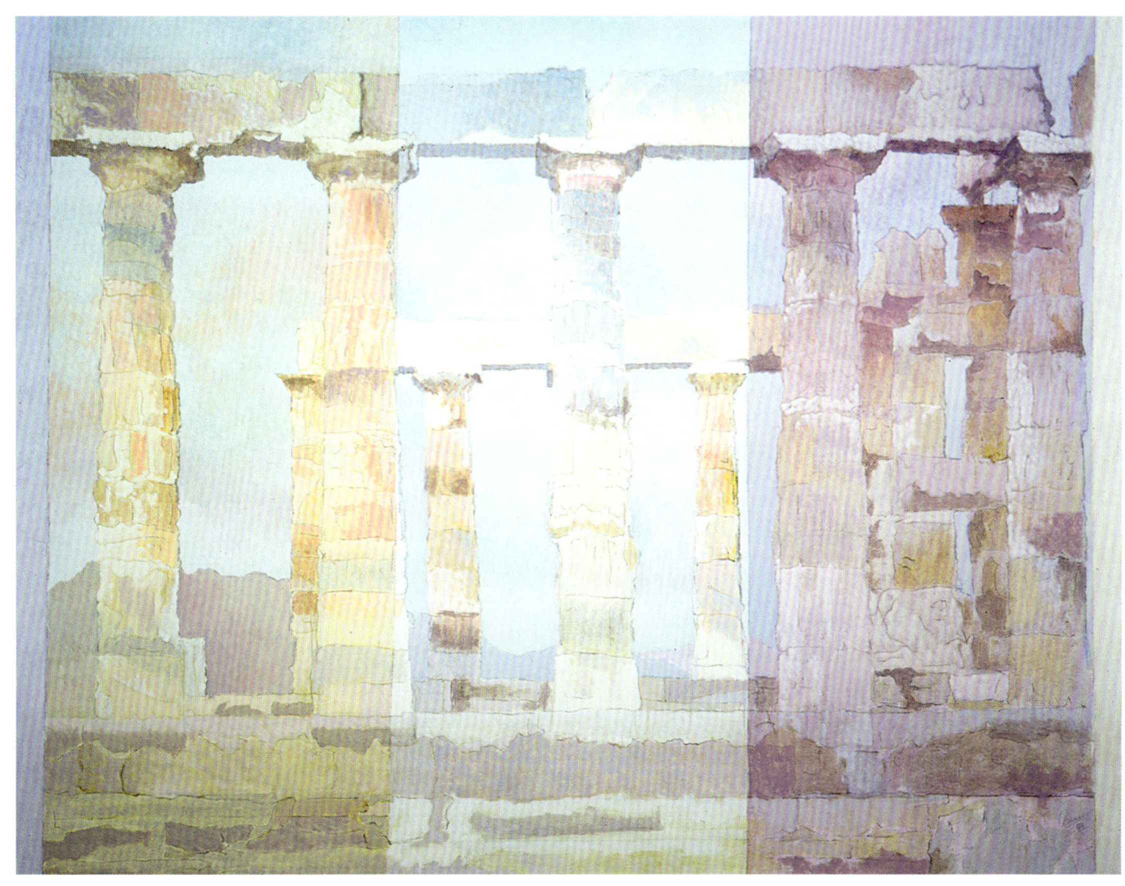

Temple of Poseidon I, 1992, mixed media on canvas, by John Clemmer, 60 × 54 in., *image courtesy New Orleans Museum of Art, photograph by Judy Cooper*

Church in Donaldsonville and spent his early childhood in predominantly Catholic rural Louisiana. On our family travels we spent untold hours wandering through cathedrals, churches, and chapels and in museums filled with the great religious art of Europe. Furthermore, my father had been commissioned to create an altar or altarpiece for St. Anthony of Padua Catholic Church on Canal Street, most likely in the late 1950s or early '60s. It would be entirely fitting with the nature of the man and his artwork that this subtle motif should become a primary expression of spirituality.[14]

Contrary to the humorously dismissive assertion, often attributed to Ad Reinhardt, that "sculpture is what you bump into when you back up to look at a painting," my father approached sculpting with the same seriousness and dedication that he applied to his work on canvas, panel, and paper. His earliest documented sculptures date to 1961, when he began to produce wall panels utilizing the sandcasting technique. In the early 1970s, he received the first of a series of commissions to produce large sculptural fountains—projects that were too ambitious in scale for his modest Foucher Street studio. He rented a storefront a few blocks downtown on Magazine Street (shared with artist Jamie Allen, who worked with plexiglass) to fabricate these complex pieces, which integrated welding, oxyacetylene brazing, and sand-casting [FIGURES 1.28 AND 1.29]. Then in the mid-'70s he acquired a double shot-gun house on Laurel Street, adjacent to the Foucher Street property, which provided space sufficient to accommodate both his painting and his large sculpture projects.

The sculptural medium that my father explored in the greatest depth was sandcasting [FIGURE 1.30]. The technique was popularized by the Sardinian artist Constantino Nivola.[15] Sandcasting involves creating negative impressions in dampened fine-grain sand inside of a shallow form lying flat on the ground or on a table. Plaster is then poured carefully over the damp sand to a depth of several inches and allowed to dry. When the layer of hardened plaster is lifted away, it presents a positive relief of the impressed design, the surface of which is covered with a layer of sand. In order for the process to work properly, all of the elements—the consistency and dampness of the sand, the fluidity of the plaster, the velocity with which the plaster is poured—must be in perfect sync. It is a delicate process that requires patience and long hours of trial and error to master.

In addition to straight sandcastings, my father produced hybrid pieces that incorporated sandcast elements with fabricated metal and painted panels. He created several architectural installations of sandcastings [PLATE 25], the most ambitious of which incorporated fifty-six individual panels. Overall, his inventory lists approximately 130 sandcast pieces, although there were certainly many more than this. He frequently gave away small examples of

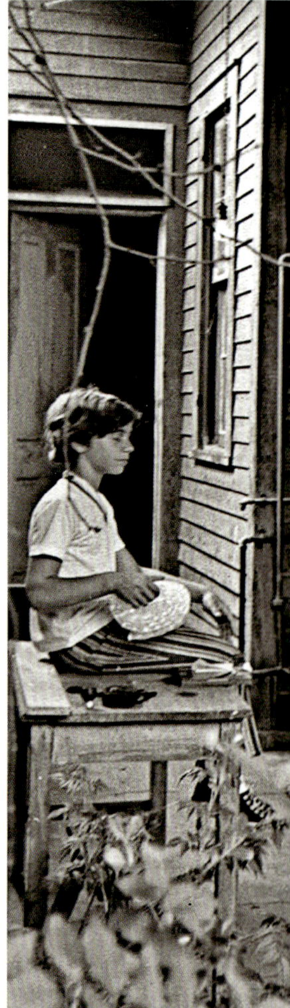

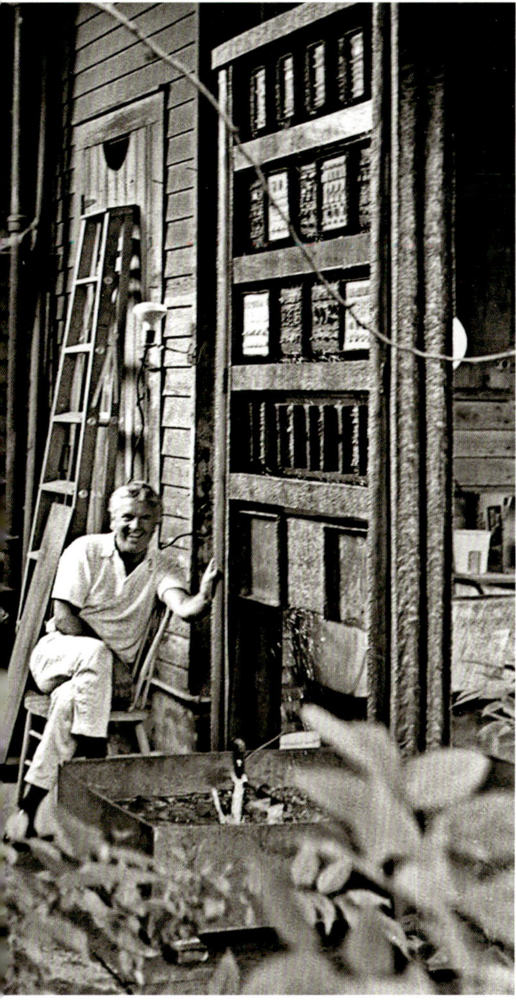

[FIGURE 1.28]
John Clemmer and David Clemmer with *Coleman Fountain* (in progress) at his Magazine Street studio, New Orleans, ca. 1973, photograph by Harold Trapido, *John Clemmer archives*

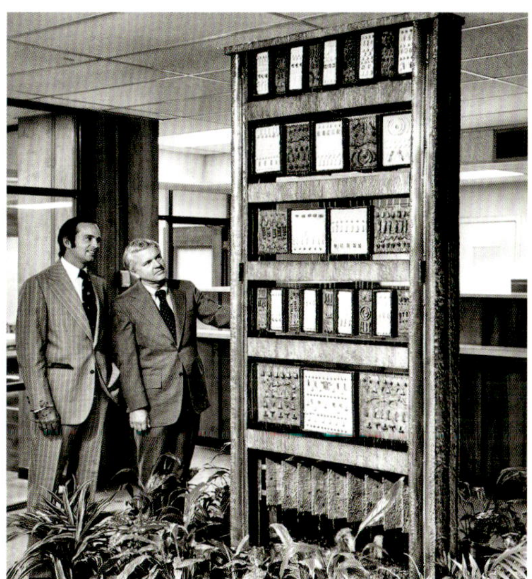

[FIGURE 1.29]
John Clemmer and Thomas B. Coleman with *Coleman Fountain*, New Orleans, 1973, photograph by the *Times-Picayune, courtesy Capital City Press / Georges Media Group, Baton Rouge, LA*

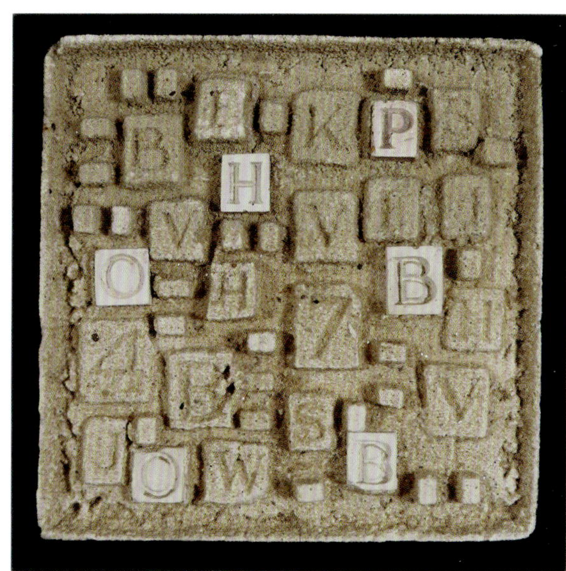

[FIGURE 1.30]
Untitled, ca. 1960s, sandcasting, by John Clemmer, 8 ½ × 8 in., *courtesy of 3618 Studio, LLC, New Orleans, LA*

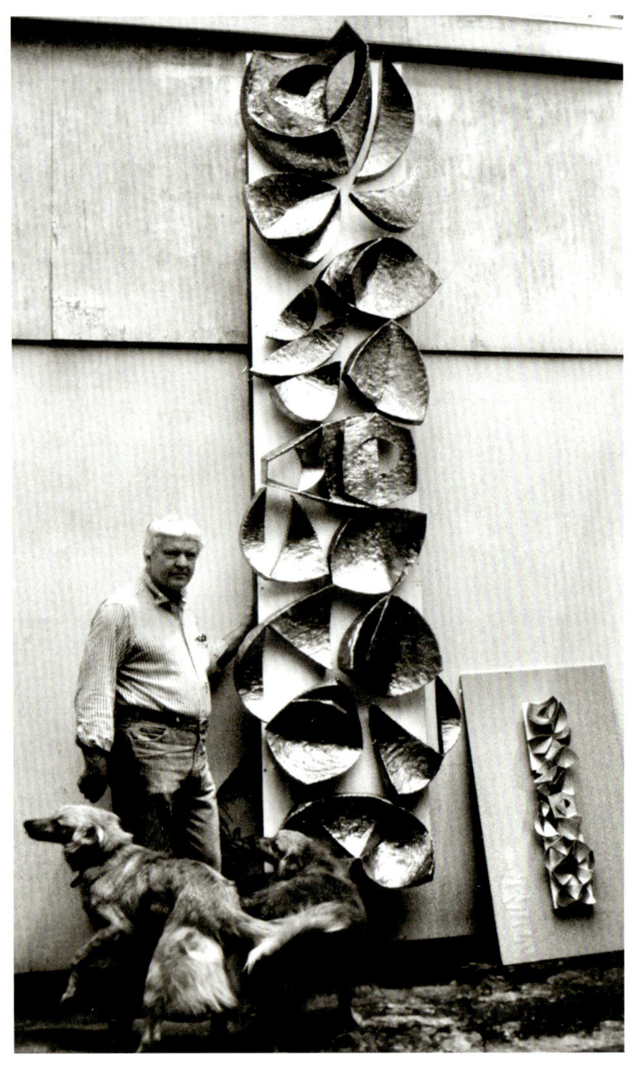

[FIGURE 1.31]
John Clemmer with *Sculpture* and maquette, Laurel Street studio,
New Orleans, 1986, photograph by Dorothy Clemmer, *John
Clemmer archive*

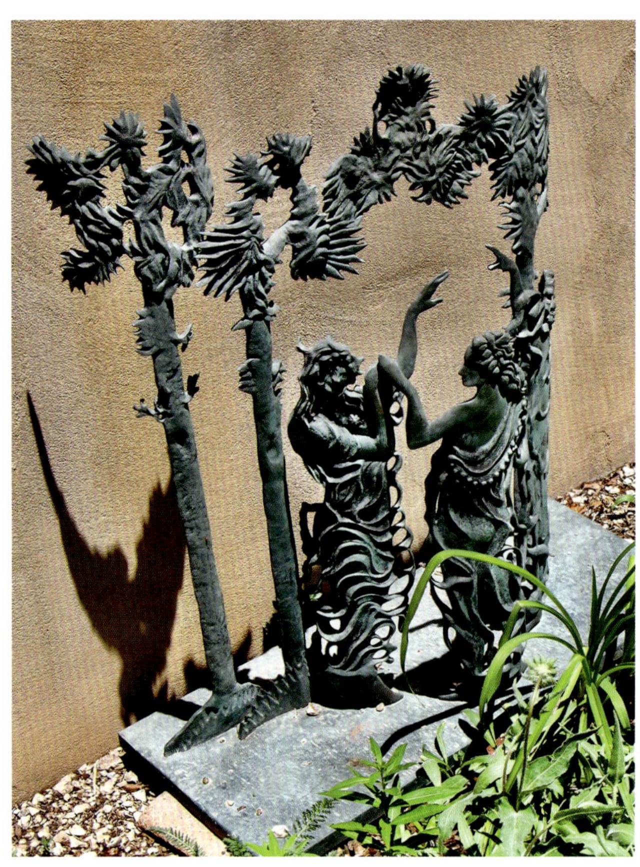

[FIGURE 1.32]
Primavera, 1993, bronze, by John Clemmer, 36 × 32 × 13 in.,
photograph by David Clemmer, *courtesy of 3618 Studio, LLC,
New Orleans, LA*

his work without recording them, and many of his commissioned works were not documented for his inventory. He found great range and expressiveness with the sandcasting technique, producing pieces as small as five inches square to more than seven feet wide. Ours was a family that loved a good beach, and there was always an element of play involved in my father's sandcast work. He often co-opted small toys from my brother and me to utilize in the process, including a plastic three-bowl pipe for blowing soap bubbles, impressions of which appear in many of his sculptures.

My father's work in metal [FIGURE 1.31], most often in combination with sandcasting, was typically executed in copper or Monel, with bronze and nickel silver finishes applied by oxyacetylene brazing. He also produced one piece in cast bronze—a garden sculpture inspired by the figures of the three Graces in Botticelli's painting *Primavera* [FIGURE 1.32]. His documented large-scale commissioned works, both public and private, number approximately twenty-five, and there are drawings and maquettes for several more unrealized projects.

In the 1990s, my father began working extensively with colored pencils. He was a superb draftsman and had always loved to draw, but up until this point his drawings had been uniformly monochromatic. By the mid-1990s, though, the drawing tables in his New Orleans and Black River studios were heavily populated with tin cans full of Prismacolor and Faber-Castell pencils in every conceivable hue. As before, he continued to paint on canvas and panel, but from the turn of the millennium onward the majority of his work was executed on paper—colored pencil, watercolor, ink, collage, monotype, and mixed media. Most of this work was abstract, while his paintings still tended toward the representational. He had begun to gather fallen leaves from the woods surrounding his Wisconsin studio and to collage them into his work, producing lovely geometric abstractions on both canvas and paper.

By the time my father turned ninety, he had begun to slow down considerably and was experiencing problems with excessive daytime drowsiness, particularly in the morning when he sat down in his studio to re-engage with works in progress. Sleep apnea was diagnosed, and the appropriate measures were taken to address it, but the problem persisted. My father was frustrated

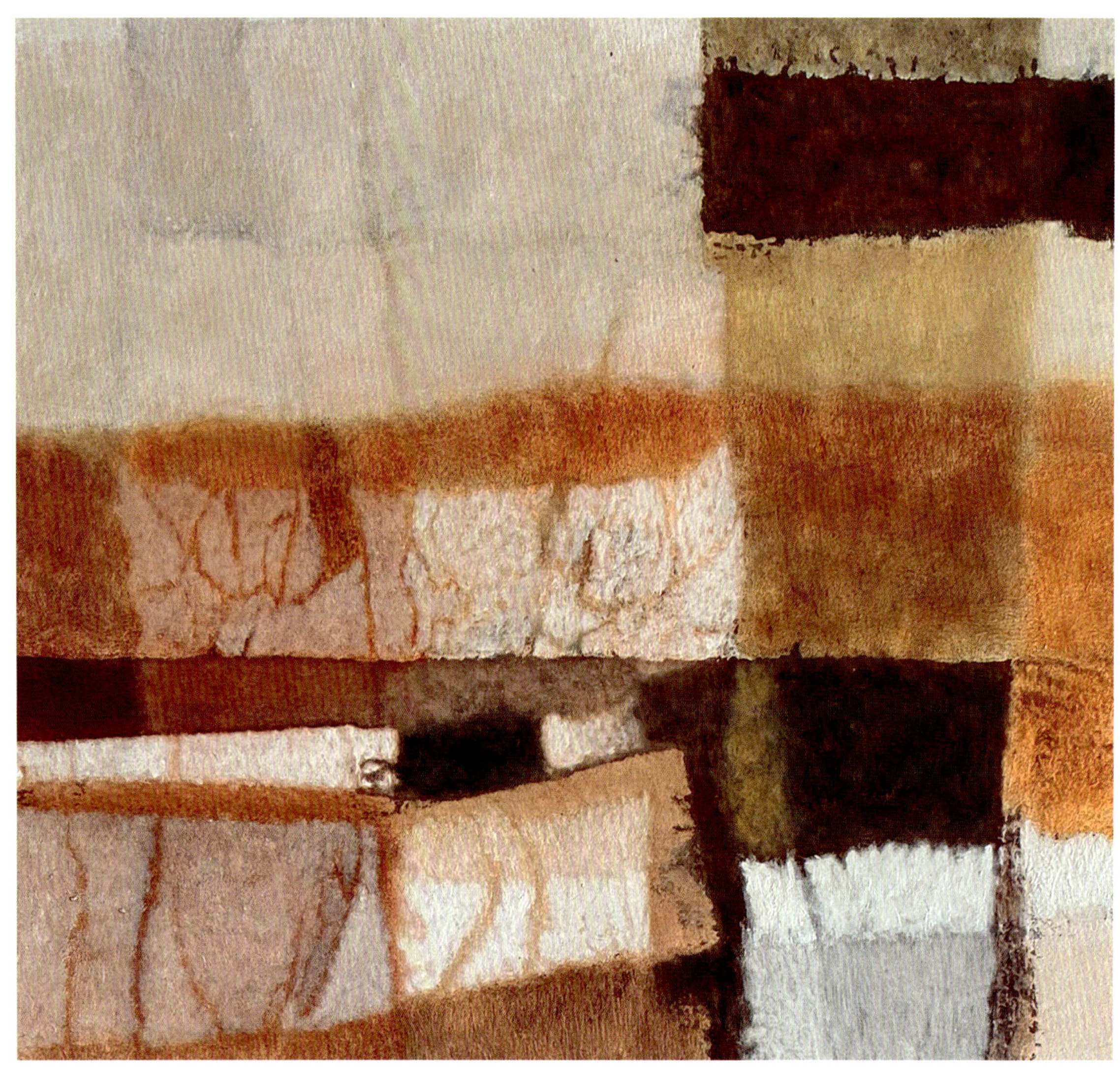

Detail of *Siloé*, 1964, oil on panel, by John Clemmer, 47 ⅝ × 42 in.,
courtesy of David Clemmer, Santa Fe, NM

by these obstacles, but every day he returned dutifully to his studio to try again. Between 2010 and 2012 he completed several bold abstractions on canvas in his New Orleans studio. In his Black River studio, he produced a series of lyrical abstract watercolors on variously colored art paper during the summer of 2013. He was pleased by my enthusiastic response to these works when I visited Wisconsin that September. He signed and dated all twenty sheets, and we selected a group to put aside for framing. These watercolors were to be his final works.

UNDERTAKING THIS EXHIBITION has been made easy for me by one simple fact: I am an unabashed fan of my father's work. I have been living with it since I was born, and I have always believed in the integrity of both the art and the artist. My father had an uncompromising dedication to his work and little interest in competition or self-promotion. He pursued his work for its own sake, and there is not an insincere gesture to found anywhere in his oeuvre.

I believe my father's signature achievement as an artist to be the singular abstract paintings of what I regard as his "heroic" period—the early 1960s through the mid '70s—masterworks such as *Siloé* [FIGURE 1.33], *Almedia*, the *Topographia* paintings and *Circles—Homage to JMWT* [PLATE 24]. Many of them are comfortingly familiar to me, yet in some ways they remain mysterious. There are so many questions that I want to ask my father, but I'll have to make my peace with not knowing all the answers. Perhaps that's the way it should be.

Ultimately, though, I find pleasure in every phase of his work. His art is one of nuance and subtlety—two commodities perpetually in short supply. My father might never have declared himself to be "at war with the obvious" (to quote another southern-born artist, the photographer William Eggleston[16]), but he was at least engaged in a lifelong skirmish with it. I'd like to think that he won. □

NOTES

1   Mark Rothko, "The Romantics Were Prompted," *Possibilities*, no. 1 (winter 1947–48): 84.

2   Pierre Joseph Landry (1770–1843) emigrated from France to Louisiana in 1785 and became a prosperous sugarcane planter. He raised a regiment to fight alongside Andrew Jackson in the Battle of New Orleans and began carving his remarkable sculptures around 1833. In 2015 the New Orleans Museum of Art presented an exhibition of all eleven documented carvings by Landry.

3   Lieutenant William Lee Clemmer died in 1939 at the age of thirty-four when the Coast Guard flying boat that he was commanding crashed in the Atlantic during a rescue mission.

4   Elliott Erwitt had exhibited his work at the Arts and Crafts Club as a teenager in 1947. In correspondence with my father from February 1948, he discussed his ambitions as a filmmaker and his desire for another show. Erwitt's portrait of my father is one of my favorites.

5   Robert Rosenblum's inscription to my father in his book *Modern Painting and the Northern Romantic Tradition* reads "John: Greetings from the northern romantic to the southern romantic."

6   Evelyn Waugh visited New Orleans in March 1949 to speak at Loyola University. He was introduced to my father by the socialite Nancy Rathborne, a close friend and a benefactor of the Arts and Crafts Club.

7   Trina Marie, born in 1942, and Erik Patrick, born in 1945.

8   My mother had moved to New Orleans in 1947 with her first husband, Frank Lossy—an intern at Touro Infirmary.

9   My mother had met Lin Emery in 1944 when they were both students at the University of Chicago. My father met Lin in New Orleans in the years just after World War II and the two artists became good friends and great admirers of each other's work.

10   Three articles regarding my father's mask-making business were published in the local papers in the early to mid-'50s, a primary theme in two of them being his profound dislike for the venture. My father held onto one mask—the last one he made, he claimed—as a memento of his days in the Carnival business and a reminder of his resolve never to return to it. Pie Dufour, "Here's the Way Masks Rex Cast Will Wear Mardi Gras Are Made," *New Orleans States*, March 2, 1957, p. 6; Joe Carmichael, "The Face Behind the Faces," *Times-Picayune*, February 28, 1954; Elsie Brupbacher, "No Mask for Man Who Paints Them," *New Orleans States*, February 14, 1953.

11   While my father's Laurel Street studio was not impacted by Katrina, artwork owned by many others, elsewhere in the city and on the Gulf Coast, suffered damage or destruction in the storm.

12   In the mid-1990s my father decided to destroy *Aureola* along with at least five other large abstract works on Masonite dating from the mid-'60s to the mid-'70s, apparently for lack of storage space. John Bullard, then director of the New Orleans Museum of Art and a longtime family friend, had tried to dissuade him from this, but sadly, to no avail.

13   My father typically used a paint roller to prime his works on panel, and he sometimes integrated the forms left from this process into the painting, as seen in *Valle I* and *Almedia*.

14   For an insightful discussion of spirituality and its symbology in my father's work, see Gridley McKim-Smith and Leo Costello, "Crafting the Intangible: The Art of John Clemmer," in *John Clemmer: Exploring the Medium, 1940–1999* (New Orleans: New Orleans Museum of Art, 1999): 21–29.

15   Constantino Nivola (1911–1988) immigrated to the United States from Italy in 1939. He exhibited with the Leo Castelli Gallery in New York City and received acclaim for his sandcast decorative panels at the Olivetti showroom on Fifth Avenue, executed in 1953.

16   William Eggleston, *The Democratic Forest* (New York: Doubleday, 1989): 173.

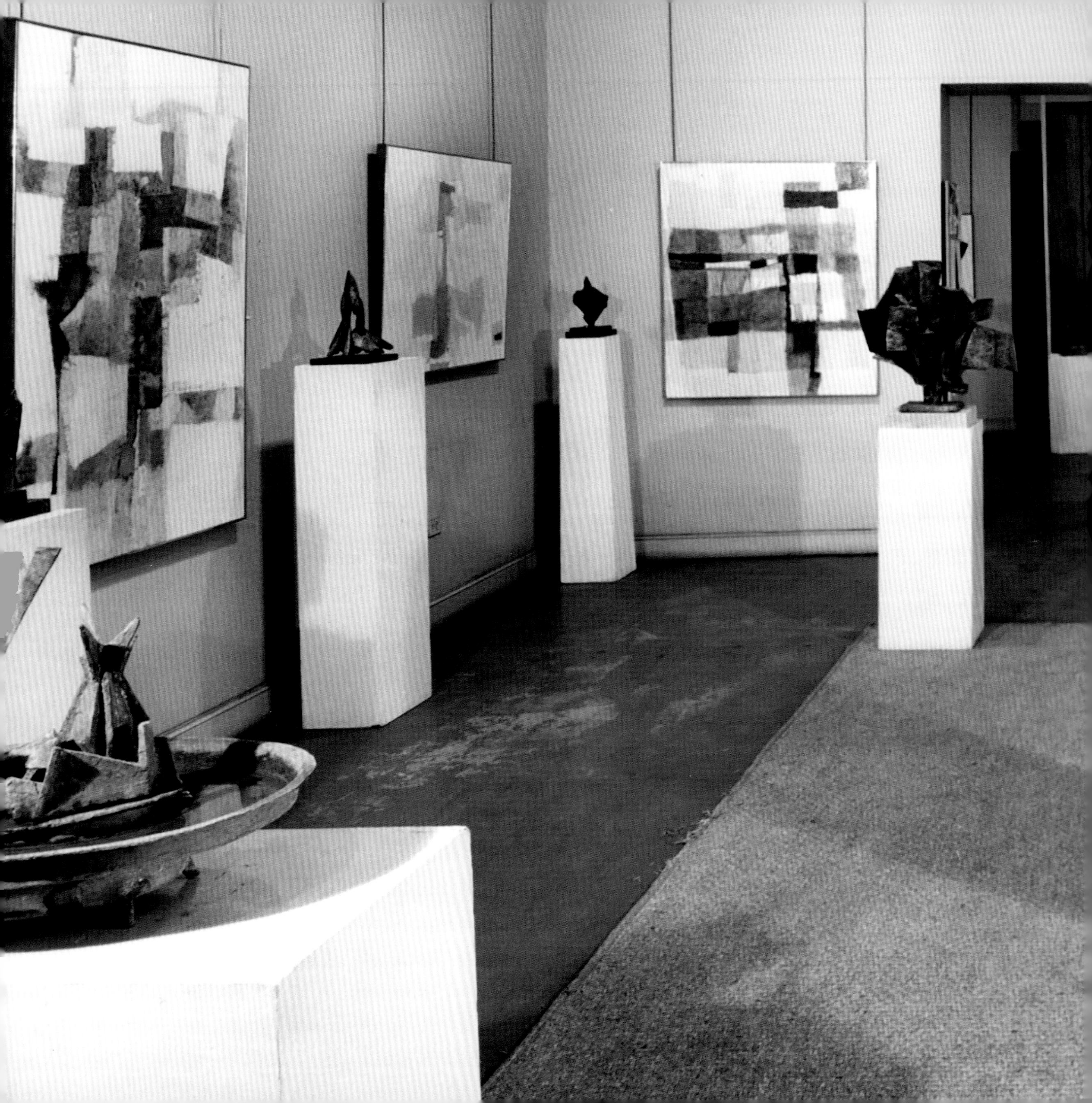

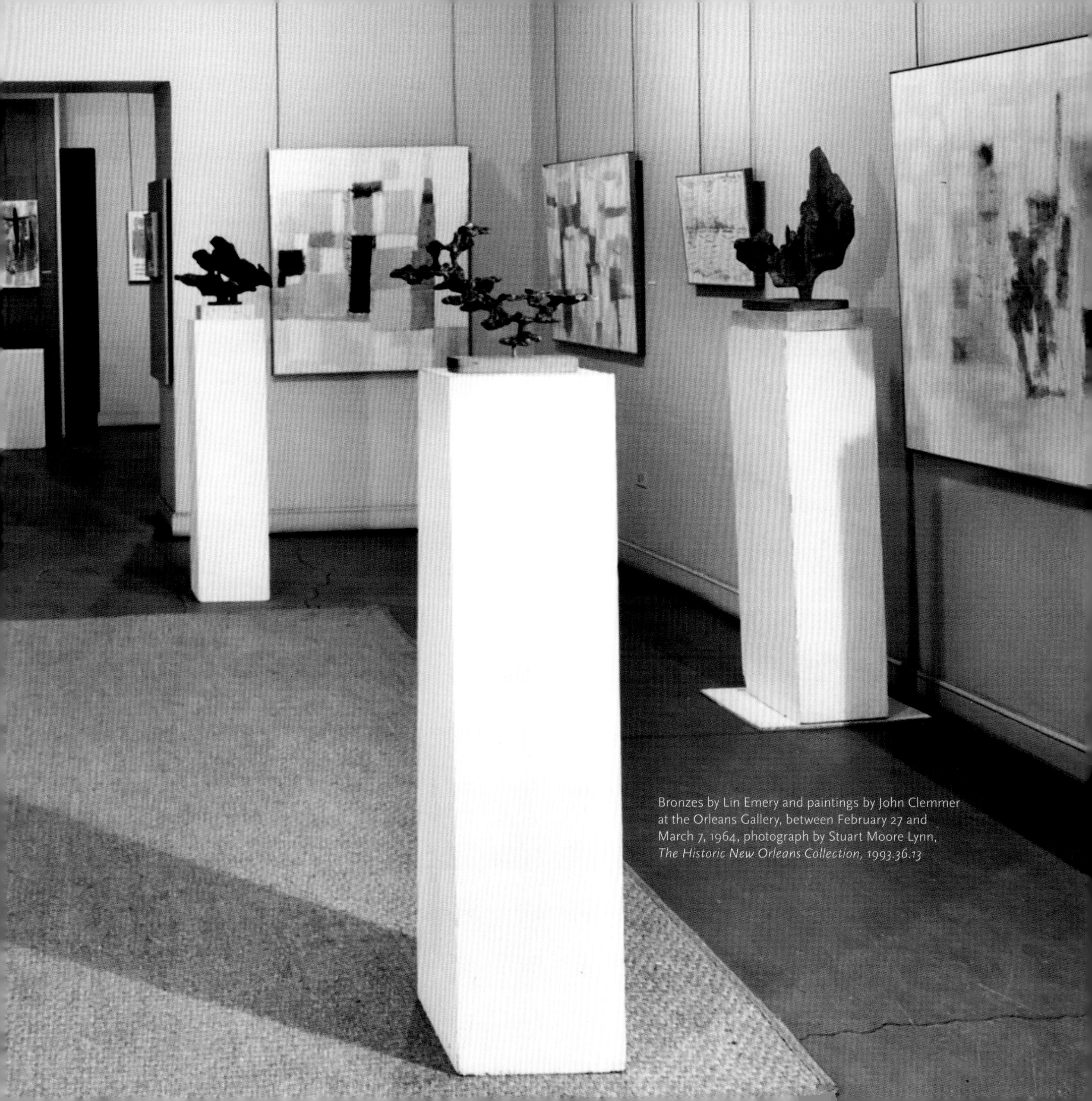

Bronzes by Lin Emery and paintings by John Clemmer at the Orleans Gallery, between February 27 and March 7, 1964, photograph by Stuart Moore Lynn, *The Historic New Orleans Collection, 1993.36.13*

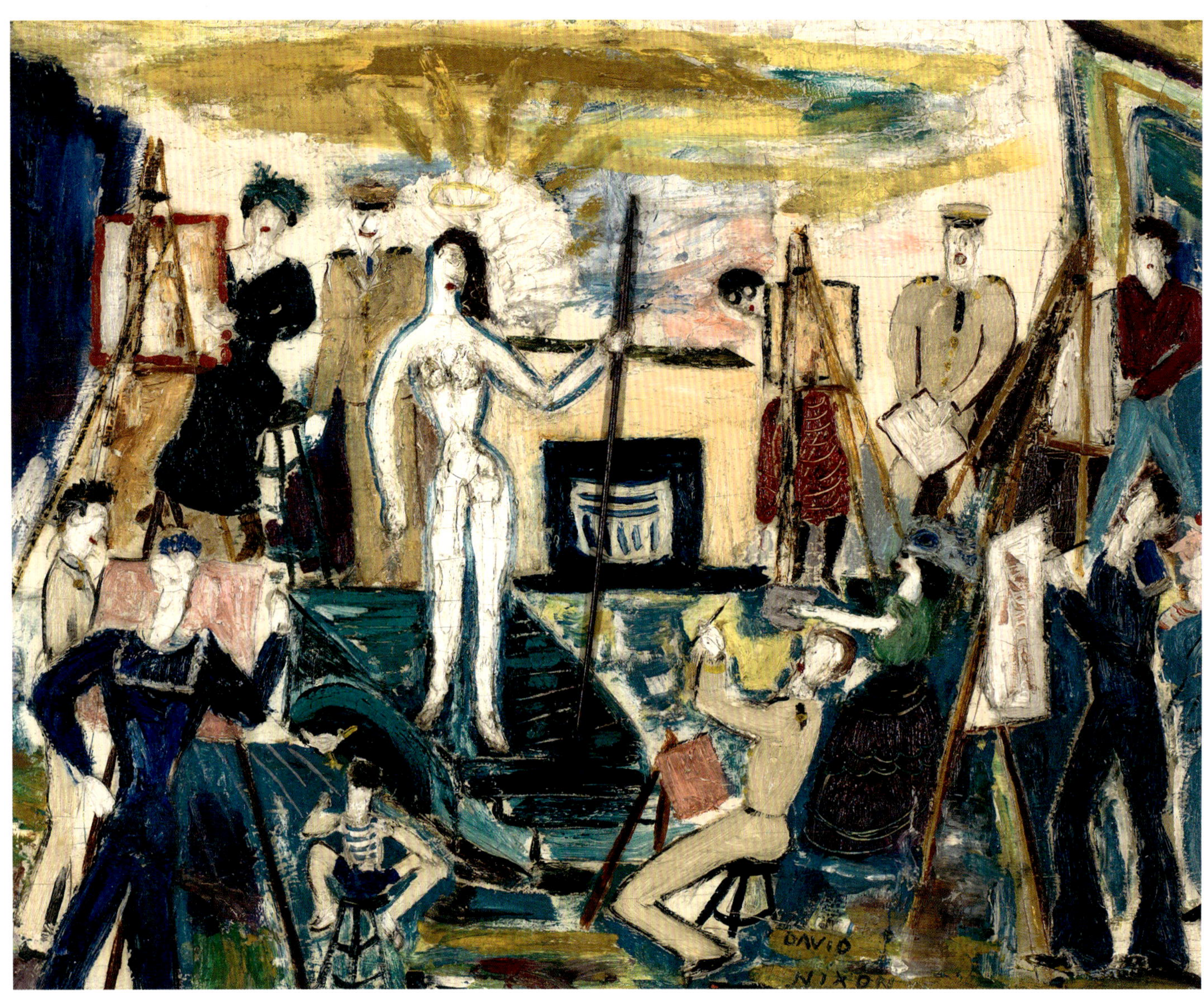

[FIGURE 2.1]

The Night Life-Drawing Class at the Arts and Crafts Club,
between 1942 and 1945, oil on board, by David Sinclair Nixon,
20 × 24 in., *The Historic New Orleans Collection, gift of Evelyn
Gladney Witherspoon, 1983.129*

Clemmer's Circle: Modernism in New Orleans

by Judith H. Bonner

OVER THREE-QUARTERS OF a century, from his student days at the New Orleans School of Art through his career at Tulane University and to his last years in his Wisconsin studio, John Clemmer produced a diverse body of paintings, drawings, prints, and sculptures. His mature works are well-planned compositional arrangements characterized by precision, orderliness, and an underlying cerebral conception not immediately perceivable by the uninitiated. These range from figural art to abstract and non-objective subjects, as well as three-dimensional works, including religious sculptures for synagogues. His modernist techniques attracted a wide range of collectors, galleries, and museums.

Clemmer produced a body of work based on Wisconsin rural scenes and his European travels, particularly to Greece and Italy. Although he rendered few scenes of New Orleans, his life in the city was central to his work. His French Quarter experience makes it particularly fitting that this exhibition of his art be held at The Historic New Orleans Collection, two blocks from where his career began at the Arts and Crafts Club of New Orleans [FIGURES 2.1, 2.2, AND 2.3]. Clemmer is the only artist to have been a student, teacher, and director of the Club's School of Art. After its demise in 1951, he taught at the Tulane University School of Architecture and then chaired the Newcomb Department of Art. A reserved man possessed of a generous spirit, he provided transformative opportunities for many people, including this author, throughout his life.

The success of an artist depends largely on the artistic training received and the expertise of the teachers. Pre–Civil War New Orleans saw a flourishing of the arts—primarily by European-trained artists and accomplished artists from the eastern seaboard—which experienced a hiatus during the Civil War through Reconstruction. In the late nineteenth century, the establishment of the Artists' Association of New Orleans provided for artistic training and exhibitions. Few women found opportunities for art studies until the H. Sophie Newcomb Memorial College for Women offered classes in 1886. Still, there was no program available for young men to study art under the aegis of a school unless they wished to study architecture at Tulane University, which did not parallel Newcomb's art offerings.

In the early twentieth century, the French Quarter was decadent in appearance, and many well-heeled residents moved elsewhere. By 1917, Ellsworth Woodward (1861–1939), the prominent director of the Newcomb School of Art, and visiting painter Will Henry Stevens (1881–1949) advocated the formation of an arts organization in the Quarter to attract artists to the city. Thanks largely to the efforts of painter Alberta Kinsey (1875–1952), Newcomb painter-teacher Gertrude Roberts Smith (1869–1962), and other artists and literati, the Arts and Crafts Club and New Orleans School of Art opened formally on November 2, 1922, at 520 Royal Street (now a campus of the Historic New Orleans Collection).

Upon its founding, the Arts and Crafts Club and its school had no comparable institution in the South. The organization gained immediate success with Charles Bein (1891–1966), a graduate of Tulane University and Columbia University, as its director. Many of the city's best-known artists of the first half of the twentieth century were associated with the Club.

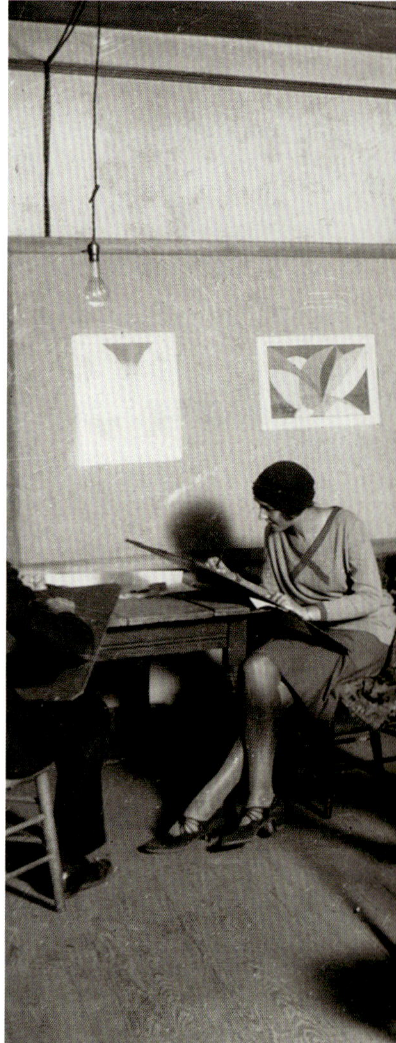

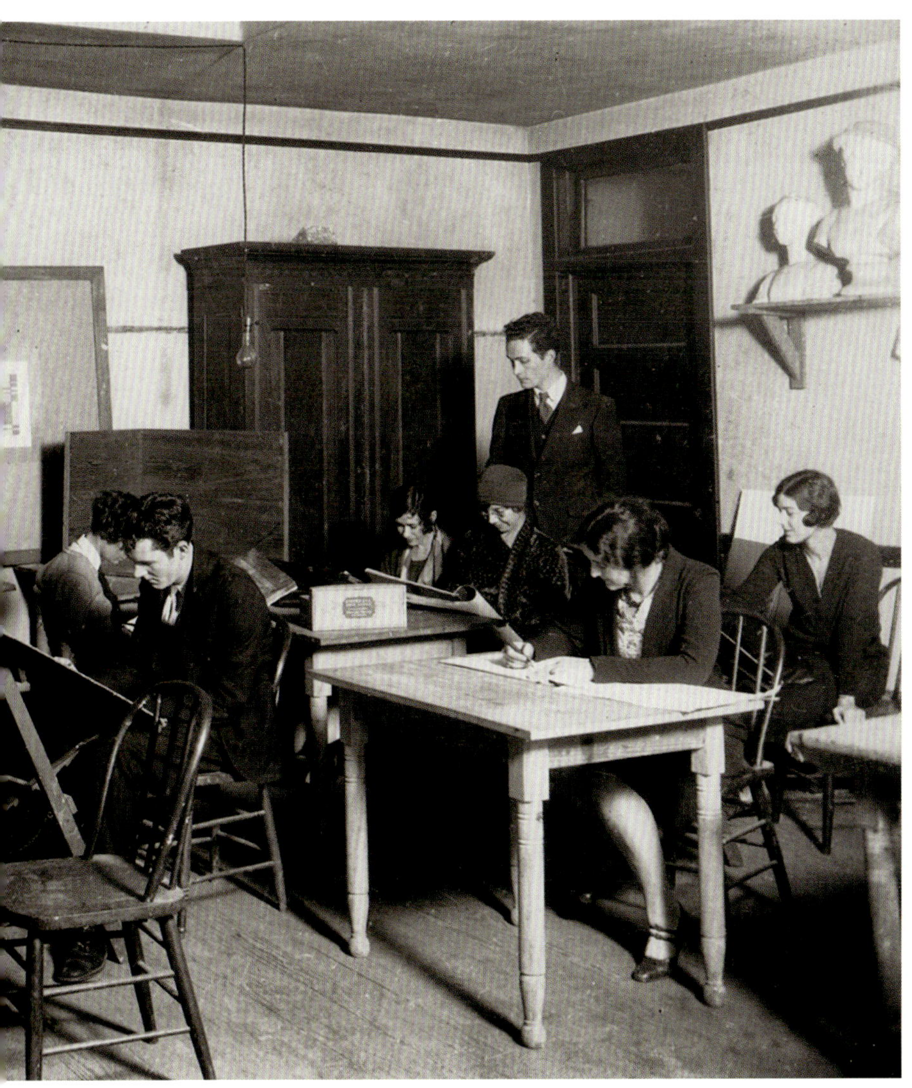

Sketch class at the Arts and Crafts Club, ca. 1927, photograph, *The Historic New Orleans Collection, gift of John F. Clemmer, 1991.116.1*

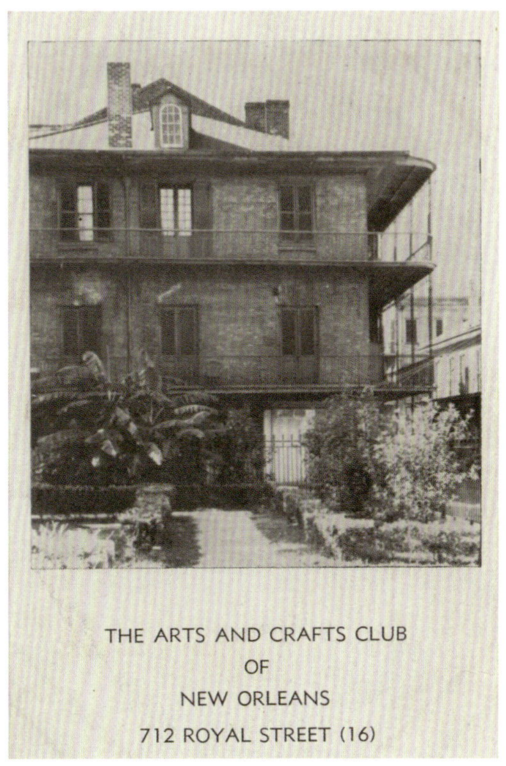

Postcard of the Arts and Crafts Club, ca. 1935, ink on paper, *The Historic New Orleans Collection, gift of Boyd Cruise, 1958.85.172*

From its inception the Club hosted local, national, and international exhibitions and provided awards and scholarships for students. In 1939 Fortier High School student John Clemmer received one such scholarship, which afforded a golden opportunity for the budding artist.[1] As the only formal art training Clemmer received, the Arts and Crafts Club prepared him successfully for a lifetime of achievement in art. Later in life Clemmer would speak emphatically of the accomplishments of the school, its teachers, and its students.[2]

Based on the guiding principles of the international Arts and Crafts movement, the Club offered courses on painting, drawing, printmaking, sculpture, and pottery. After students learned the basics of composition, the principles of design, and excellence in craftsmanship, they were encouraged to explore artistic expression through non-traditional art movements. Architecture classes based on the teaching methods of the École des Beaux-Arts in Paris rounded out the available curriculum. Children's classes were also offered as a foundation for future students.[3]

Clemmer benefited immeasurably from his experiences at the Club and its New Orleans School of Art. Despite not having a collegiate degree in art, he trained under some of the best-known artists of the day, particularly Paul Ninas (1903–1964), Xavier Gonzalez (1898–1993), Enrique Alférez (1903–1999), and Julius Woeltz (1911–1956) [FIGURE 2.4]. The faculty of the school during the 1920s and 1930s reads like a Who's Who of twentieth-century Louisiana art, including Caroline Durieux (1896–1989), Angela Gregory (1903–1990), Weeks Hall (1894–1958), John McCrady (1911–1968), Clarence Millet (1897–1959), Gideon Townsend Stanton (1885–1964), Will Henry Stevens, Helen Maria Turner (1858–1958), and Daniel Webster Whitney (1896–1965).

When Clemmer arrived at the school, although some of these notables had departed, their reputations were lauded among students and artists associated with the Club. When the Club exhibited artworks by these luminaries, Clemmer studied them with a keen eye. The annual exhibition schedule included noted national and international artists, including Braque, Picasso, Calder, Cézanne, Dalí, Dufy, Kandinsky, Magritte, and Renoir. Additionally,

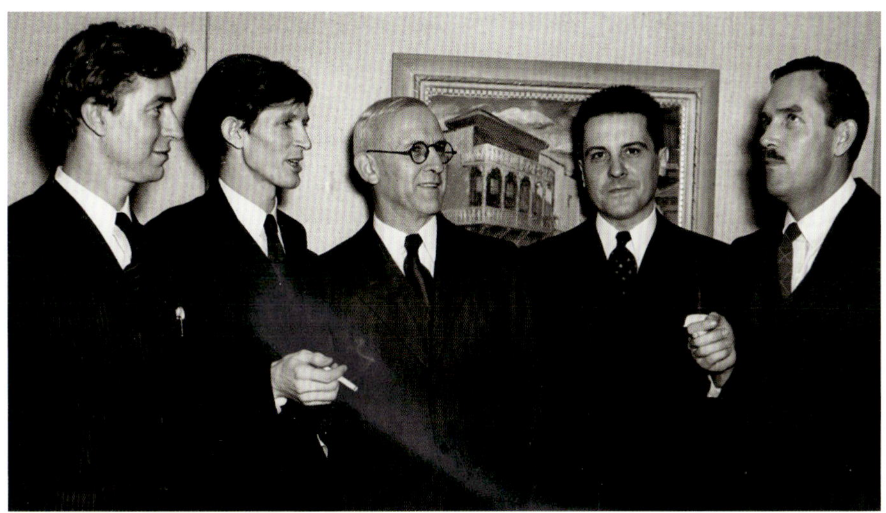

[FIGURE 2.4]
Rudolf Staffel, Julius Woeltz, Richard Koch, Albert Lieutaud, and Paul Ninas, ca. 1940, gelatin silver print, *The Historic New Orleans Collection, gift of John F. Clemmer, 1991.116.2*

the Club introduced Georg Jensen silver, Orrefors crystal, and Steuben crystal to the city.

The Club and its School of Art achieved considerable success during its first eleven years under Bein's leadership, but it would truly fulfill its goals under Paul Ninas's directorship. Ninas assumed charge in 1932. He had abandoned engineering studies at the University of Nebraska–Lincoln to study in Paris at the Académie des Beaux-Arts and Académie Lhote. At the latter, the philosophies of Andre Lhote (1885–1962), a major proponent of cubism, profoundly affected Ninas's artwork and his teaching.

Ninas had an undeniably romantic and worldly status—he reportedly went to sea at age fourteen, hitchhiked across the United States, and rowed down the Mississippi River in a leaky canoe. He traveled extensively through Europe, North Africa, the Middle East, Mexico, and the Caribbean.[4] His work generally focused on subjects associated with the locations in which he lived. His 1939 series of four murals in the Sazerac Bar in the Roosevelt Hotel depicts scenes of local life, including one featuring local artists and city officials, with the figures set against St. Louis Cathedral.

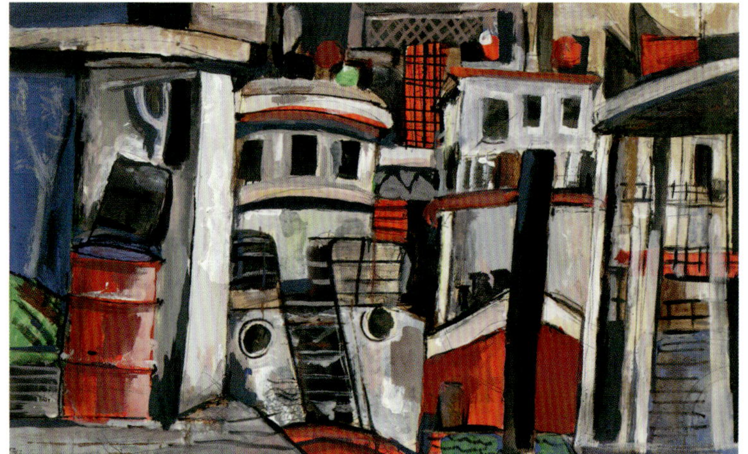

Heralded as the "Dean of New Orleans Artists," Ninas served as director of the Arts and Crafts Club during a critical time in the development of the modernist art movement during the 1930s. He espoused a progressive modernistic aesthetic. His oeuvre reveals that he stayed abreast of emerging artistic trends, a priority that had been initiated at the School's founding and continued with Ninas at its helm. The concepts—exploration, experimentation, and modernism—proved to be guiding principles for the serious-minded Clemmer throughout his career.

Ninas's training abroad and his extensive travels had a lasting effect on his work. Generally, his paintings and drawings are immediately recognizable. Rather than typical early cubist works with fragmented angular shapes reassembled and rendered in somber monochromatic shades, Ninas emphasized simple planes with heavily outlined contours that had the effect of flattening his subject. His works, which are frequently rendered in bright saturated colors, vary from cubist non-objective to modernistic representational works [FIGURE 2.5].

During Ninas's tenure, the Club was home to a close-knit network of talented artists, many of whom had a clear influence on Clemmer, for they

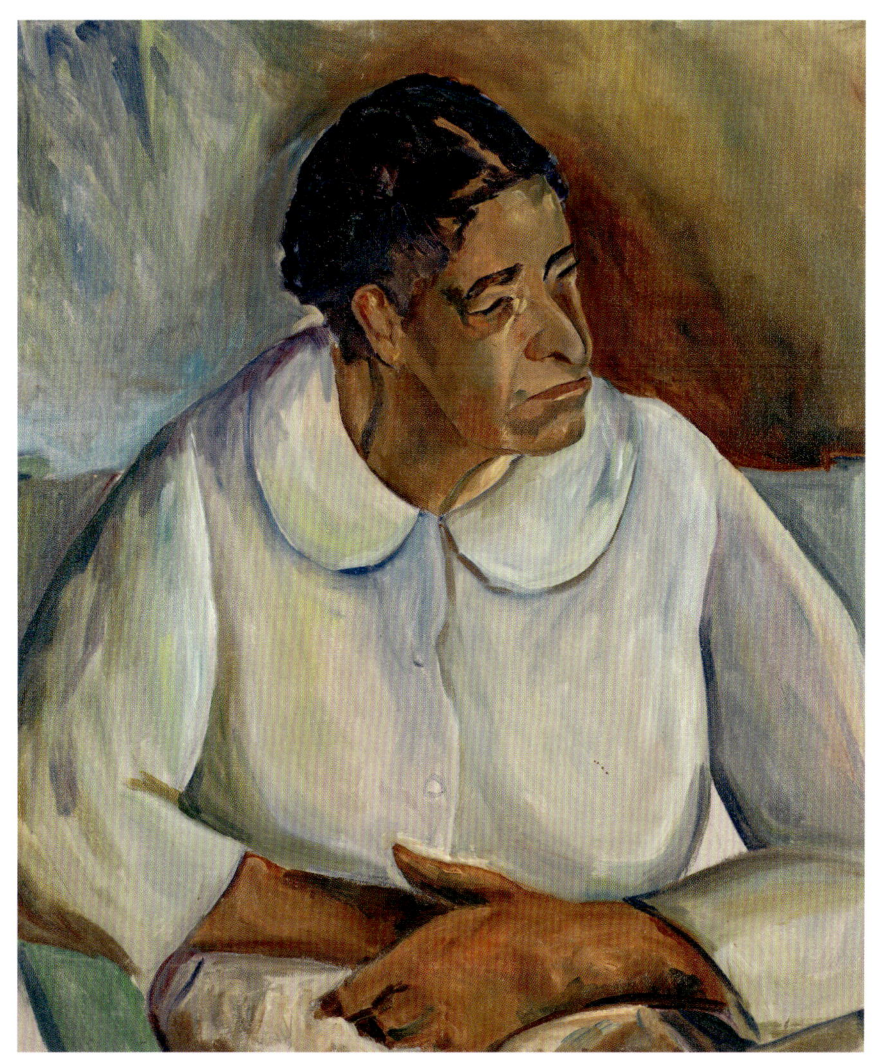

Portrait of Francis Gains, between 1928 and 1935, oil on canvas, by Josephine Marien Crawford, 24 ¾ × 20 in., *The Historic New Orleans Collection, bequest of Charles C. Crawford, 1978.23.12*

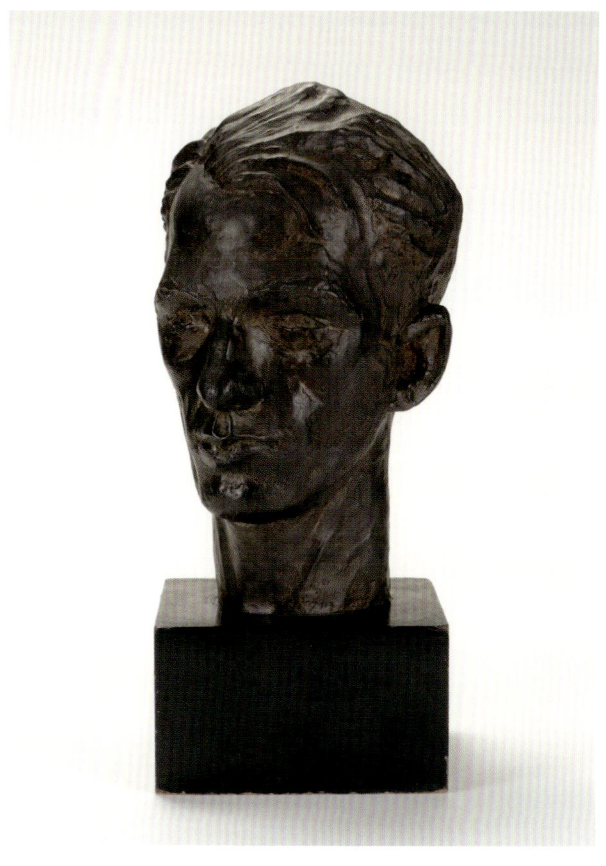

John Edmond "Jack" Sparling, 1938, bronze, wood, paint, by Angela Gregory, 15 × 8 ¼ × 6 ¾ in., *The Historic New Orleans Collection, gift of the Estate of Angela Gregory, 2006.0156.3*

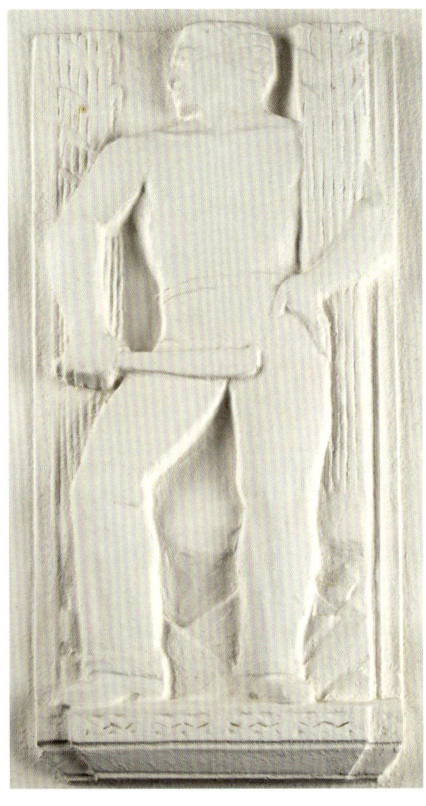

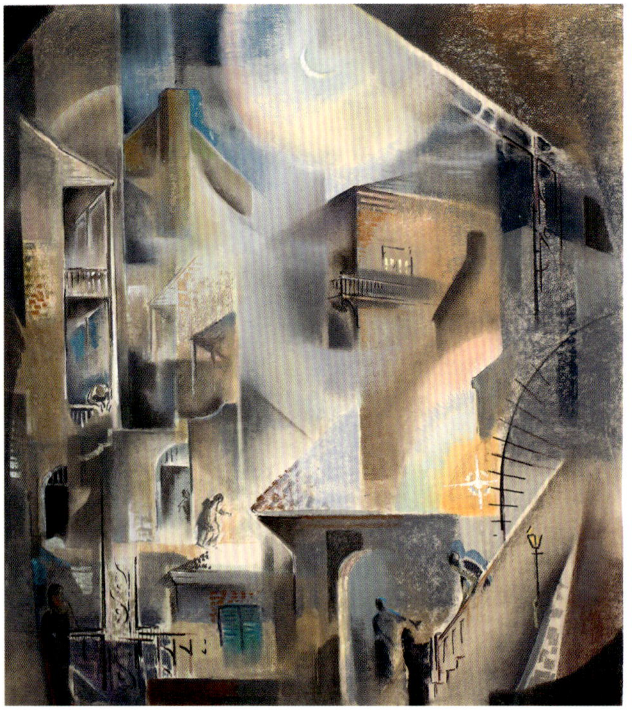

intensified his awareness of international ideas and openness to emerging
artistic developments.

Josephine Marien Crawford (1878–1952) [FIGURE 2.6] had trained at the
New Orleans School of Art under Bein's leadership before studying in Paris
with Lhote. Upon her return home Crawford abandoned the traditional
artistic style she learned previously and moved toward flat geometric planes

depicted in a monochromatic palette, generally in shades of gray. Her canvases became increasingly simplified and minimalist with strategically placed fine lines to delineate the subject and emphasize an overall flatness of the composition. Crawford introduced cubism into the city in 1928 in a joint exhibition at the Club with Angela Gregory [FIGURE 2.7], who returned at the same time from her Parisian studies under Antoine Bourdelle (1861–1929).

Gregory studied in Paris at the Parsons School of Design after initial studies at the School of Art under William Woodward (1859–1939), founder and head of the Tulane School of Architecture.[5] Woodward, a painter, taught himself sculpture in order to teach the intensely determined fourteen-year-old Gregory.[6] Gregory's horizons widened again when Gertrude Roberts Smith, a member of the executive committee of the Arts and Crafts Club and watercolor painting instructor at Newcomb, invited her to assist at the School of Art, where German sculptor Albert Rieker (1886–1959) [FIGURE 2.8] taught. Rieker, who studied in Munich, Stuttgart, and Italy, instructed Gregory in the traditional method of constructing an armature, applying clay to this essential foundation for modeling a three-dimensional figure, and casting a relief. Gregory had a bold, energetic sculptural style that was unusual for a young woman and brought immediate commissions on public buildings.

Rieker sculpted likenesses of many political and civic leaders in the 1930s. His commissions include sculptures for the state capitol in Baton Rouge, notably a sculpture of Jean-Baptiste le Moyne, sieur de Bienville, the founder of New Orleans and colonial governor of Louisiana. In 1950 Gregory received a sculptural commission to commemorate Bienville for the city of New Orleans. She produced a massive three-figure monument depicting him with the monk who traveled with him, as well as a seated Native American man meant to represent the Bayagoula Nation that met Bienville when he first set foot on land in the area that is now the French Quarter. Gregory achieved greater recognition for her monument than Rieker did for his single figure of the city's founder.[7]

Will Henry Stevens [FIGURE 2.9] was another Arts and Crafts Club luminary whose work influenced Clemmer. Stevens, an Indiana native, taught at the Newcomb School of Art and also served as an instructor at the New

Orleans School of Art. He was one of the original members of A New Southern Group, an offshoot of the Arts and Crafts Club that included several of its members. Stevens created striated abstract compositions, often divided into three or more horizontal or vertical bands and populated with floating geometric or amorphic shapes from his personal repertoire of motifs. Recognizable shapes, including birds, fish, trees, clouds, and mountains, merged into harmonious, well-constructed designs in which all the varied compositional elements share equal gravity. He also produced sylvan views of the forested hills and valleys of the Appalachian region, and he often exhibited his representational works alongside his non-representational compositions. Stevens's compositions frequently employ tripartite divisions, which could be equally pleasing whether vertical or horizontal, a motif that is frequent in Clemmer's later works.

Clemmer at times exceeded this limitation of three divisions, particularly in his sandcastings—some of which have multiple divisions, with the highest number being a grouping of fifty-six square panels. Like Stevens's canvases, Clemmer's later compositions manifest an atmospheric sense of depth combined with a lyricism reminiscent of works by Russian painter Wassily Kandinsky (1866–1944) and Swiss-born painter Paul Klee (1879–1940). Kandinsky is generally credited as the pioneer of abstract art, while Klee combined elements of cubism, surrealism, and expressionism. Many of Clemmer's two-dimensional works indicate an awareness of these elements. His small sculptures and sandcastings, however, display an orderliness that differs from some of Kandinsky's constructivist sculptures.

Clemmer found inspiration in the work of another instructor of note, Enrique Alférez, who sculpted numerous reliefs for parks, buildings, and landmarks in the city, including the facade of Charity Hospital, numerous sculptures and bridges for New Orleans City Park through the Works Progress Administration, and *Molly Marine* at Canal Street and Elk Place— the first American sculpture to depict a woman in military uniform. His *Fountain of the Four Winds* [FIGURE 2.10] of the late 1930s remains a landmark at the New Orleans Lakefront Airport (formerly Shushan Airport). It was Alférez who in the late 1940s reassembled and mounted one of

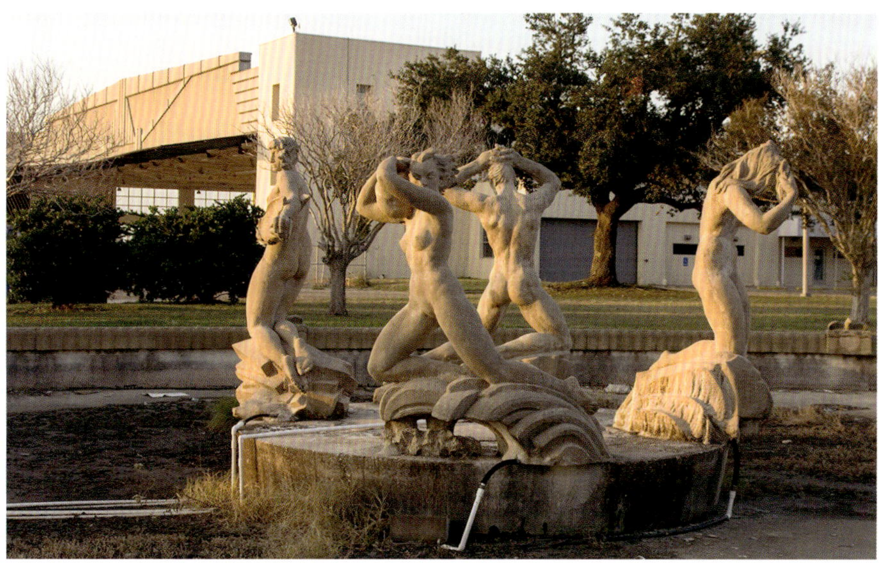

Alexander Calder's innovative sculptures for an exhibition at the Club. One of the cutting-edge art creations in the 1930s and '40s,[8] Calder's work was dramatically different from the bold, weighty forms of Alférez's sculpture. The petal-like shapes of Clemmer's ten-foot-high bronze and nickel silver *Sculpture* [PLATE 29] of 1986 suggest movement and recall the delicate, airy forms of Calder's mobiles, even though Clemmer's are mounted to a support.

Clemmer maintained a longtime friendship with his former teacher, Spanish painter-muralist Xavier Gonzalez, who also taught at Newcomb. Gonzalez's first mural won a prize at the International Mural Competition in Los Angeles in 1930. He received commissions for murals for the San Antonio Municipal Auditorium; the Hammond, Louisiana, post office; and the Tennessee Valley Authority in Huntsville, Alabama. In New Orleans, he painted murals at Newcomb and at the New Orleans Lakefront Airport [FIGURE 2.11], in which eight ten-foot-by-ten-foot panels were arranged around the second-floor balcony like the cardinal and ordinal points on a compass.

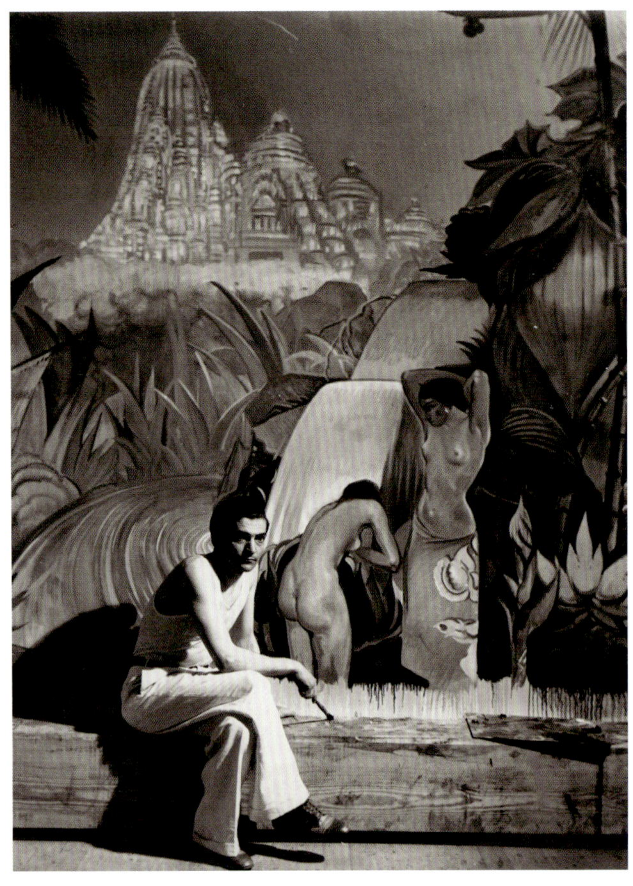

[FIGURE 2.11]
Xavier Gonzalez with one of his murals at the
Shushan Airport, 1933, photograph by Dan Leyrer,
*The Historic New Orleans Collection, gift of F. Lee
Eiseman, 1991.114.32*

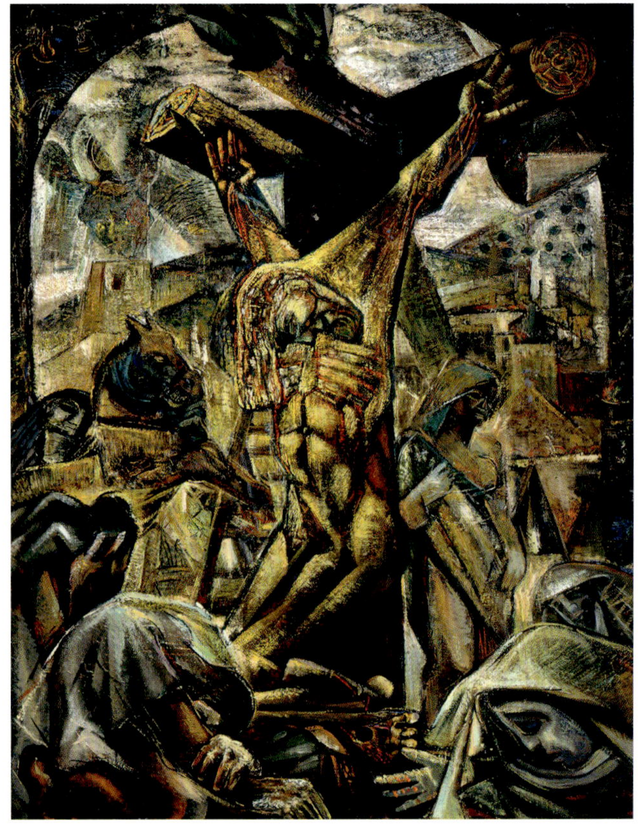

[FIGURE 2.12]
Crucifixion, 1947, oil on Masonite, by Xavier Gonzalez, 48 × 38 in.
(framed), *New Orleans Museum of Art, Museum purchase, 50.3*

Clemmer, who admired the well-traveled Gonzalez, especially appreciated the navigational arrangement of these murals. This may have influenced the paintings in his *Topographia* series, developed in the late 1960s and '70s, which feature a circle within a square.

The paintings in the *Topographia* series [PLATES 18, 19, 20, 22, AND 23] reflect the nautical and cartographical references to the compass rose, the points that were originally used to indicate the directions of the wind and referred to as the "wind rose" or "rose of the winds." Alférez conceived his *Fountain of the Four Winds* according to this directional orientation, but he refers only to the four principal points of the compass: north, south, east, and west. Clemmer extends this concept of the compass rose to the historical practice when apprentice seamen learned the thirty-two directional points perfectly; the accomplishment was known as "boxing the compass,"[9] an obvious reference for Clemmer's works exploring the circle within a square. Further, his *Topographia* works reference geography and constellations: some are subtitled *Cosmas, Atitlan, Guatemala, Capricorn,*[10] and *Luna.* This series was also informed by his interest in illuminated Byzantine manuscripts, which he developed in coursework in early Christian and Byzantine art that he took at Newcomb.[11] He was particularly drawn to two ninth-century reproductions of a manuscript by sixth-century Alexandrian scholar Cosmas Indicopleustes and second-century mathematician-astronomer Ptolemy.

In many early works, Clemmer explores cubism with both representational and abstract subjects rendered in a restricted palette of somber colors rather than bright colors. Clemmer's *Swamp Fire* [PLATE 6], painted the same year as Gonzalez's *Crucifixion* [FIGURE 2.12] and exhibited in the Orleans Gallery, glows with warm yellow and orange tones tempered by sepia and white highlights. Carefully placed black lines provide cohesiveness to the composition and suggest blazing architectural structures or cypress trees.

Though Gonzalez often depicted figures in broad shapes reminiscent of those painted by Mexican muralist Diego Rivera (1886–1957), he explored cubism in many of his early works. A 1949 cubistic portrayal by Clemmer, *Two Figures—Macbeth* [PLATE 8], recalls the angular shapes of Gonzalez's

1947 painting *Crucifixion*, rendered in shades of brown. Clemmer's painting, however, differs in its warm yellow, orange, red, and green tones. Clemmer's 1942 *How Men Their Brothers Maim* [PLATE 2] can also be compared to *Crucifixion*. This somber cubist work, painted by Clemmer during the early years of World War II, shows the jester-like figure of a crucified Christ with a distorted face. Clemmer's emphasis on the psychological and physical pain inflicted by fellow humans parallels Gonzalez's *Crucifixion* in its psychological impact. From his earliest works, Clemmer explored themes related to literature and mythology, as well as spiritual and religious themes—including both Christian and Jewish subjects.

John McCrady [FIGURE 2.13], a native of Canton, Mississippi, left the University of Mississippi after his second year to study at the New Orleans School of Art. McCrady abandoned his early style of painting with thickly applied impasto for a dramatically different smooth painting style influenced by local and national artists and focused on southern scenes, often with religious themes. Like Stevens, McCrady was a member of A New Southern Group. He taught at the New Orleans School of Art before opening his own school in 1942, together with his wife, Mary Basso McCrady (1911–1994). The John McCrady School of Art, which operated on a much smaller scale, was a mainstay in the French Quarter for four decades. After McCrady's death in 1968, Mary McCrady continued to operate the school until 1983.

In 1948, Clemmer held his first solo exhibition at the Arts and Crafts Club. He served as director of that organization until it closed its doors on March 24, 1951, following the death of its benefactor, Sarah Henderson. For thirty years the Arts and Crafts Club had offered an environment in the French Quarter in which the camaraderie of the artists was integral to the organization. The closing of the Arts and Crafts Club left a void for arts education and artistic exhibitions, for there were no commercial galleries in the city.

It was into this vacuum that a group of seven accomplished artists came together in 1956 to form the Orleans Gallery. The first artists' cooperative gallery in the city, it opened at 527 Royal Street in a building now owned by The Historic New Orleans Collection. The Orleans Gallery's seven founders were sculptor Lin Emery (1926–2021), painter Shearly Grode (1925–2003),

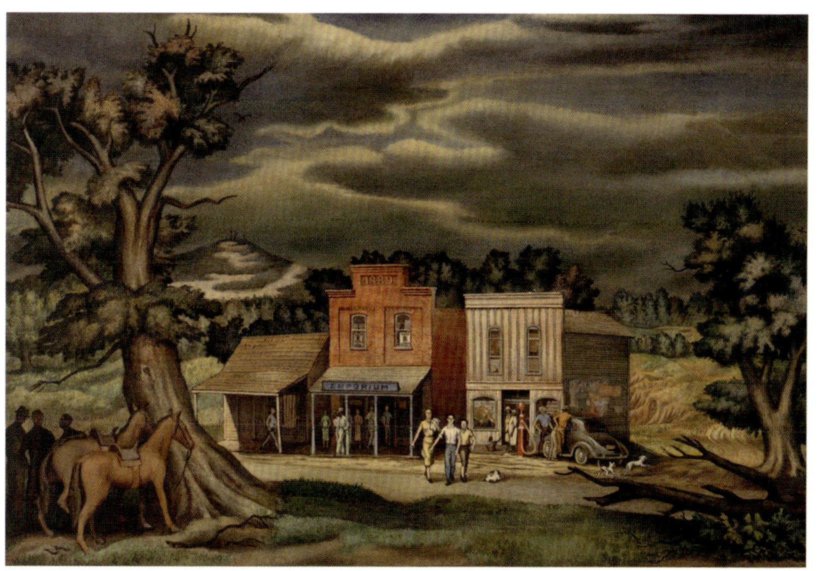

[FIGURE 2.13]
The Emporium, 1946, tempera and oil on canvas, by John McCrady, 36 3/16 × 47 3/16 in., *The Historic New Orleans Collection*, 1975.129

painter Robert Helmer (1922–1990), sculptor-painter George Dunbar (b. 1927), painter-sculptor Jack Hastings (ca. 1926–2013), painter Jean Seidenberg (b. 1930), and painter-architect James Lamantia (1923–2011). Membership requirements included an initial payment of $100.00, a ten-dollar monthly fee, and a 10 percent commission on any artwork sold through the gallery. Clemmer enjoyed membership in the Orleans Gallery and served as an officer for the organization.

Organized as a nonprofit gallery, the group aimed to produce a national awareness of the city as a cultural center for creative art. In addition to exhibiting works by its permanent members, the Orleans Gallery exhibited guest artists, students, and artists of national and international acclaim. After fifteen years, a lack of financial support caused the Orleans Gallery to close its doors in 1972, twenty-one years after the demise of the Arts and Crafts Club. Both organizations espoused modernity and individualist artistic voices, tenets that were important for Clemmer's artistic development and his continued explorations in artistic trends.

In 1964 Clemmer and sculptor Lin Emery held a joint exhibition at the Orleans Gallery, in which his paintings reveal his evolving essays through cubism. This exploration subsequently gave way to an orderly style that evolved into precisely controlled systematic works, some of which would be suggestive of well-defined architectural shapes.

A native of New York City, internationally acclaimed sculptor Emery studied in Chicago, Mexico, New York, and Paris. She first relocated to New Orleans as a fashion writer for the *Times-Picayune*. She worked in clay and plaster before her ongoing studies at the New York Sculpture Center, where she explored welding and casting. Emery exhibited her work with abstract expressionist sculptor-painter David Smith (1906–1965) and others before returning to New Orleans in 1953, settling into a French Quarter apartment and a fully equipped metalworking studio. Though Emery is known today for her kinetic sculptures powered by wind, water, magnets, and motors, her early work was figurative [FIGURE 2.14] or abstract, and it was these works that she showed in her joint exhibition with Clemmer at the Orleans Gallery in 1964. In this show Clemmer, who had held solo exhibitions in the gallery in 1960 and 1962, displayed large abstract works accomplished with a paint roller and featuring geometric shapes, including *Siloé*.

Like the artists associated with the Arts and Crafts Club, the Orleans Gallery artists embraced modernist artistic styles and explored various techniques and media. Shearly Grode [FIGURE 2.15], native New Orleanian, was a graduate of the John McCrady School of Art, where she met Robert Helmer, to whom she was briefly married. Grode experimented with metal within the frame of a non-objective painting on a two-dimensional surface to produce the effect of three-dimensionality. Clemmer collected one of her works in which she applied gesso to the canvas in thick sculptural forms overlaid with gold leaf and silver leaf. Clemmer also experimented with combined media and variations in dimensionality, as is evident in his non-objective work, *Painting—Sandcasting (Ten-Piece)* [PLATE 25], which features oil paintings mounted with sandcastings—a mixture of sand and Portland cement that he highlighted with applied bronze accents.

Three of the Orleans Gallery's founders had studied at Tulane's School of Architecture and would return to teach there: James Lamantia

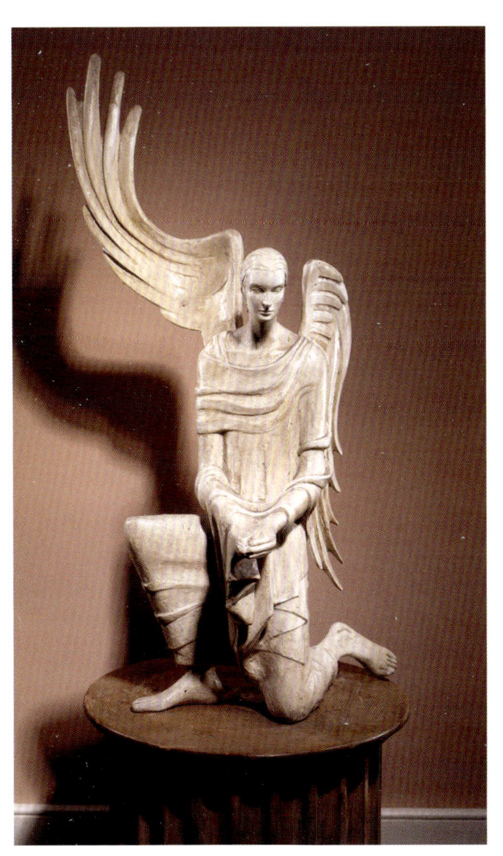

Angel, between 1950 and 1961, plaster, by Lin Emery, 34 × 15 × 15 in., *The Historic New Orleans Collection, the L. Kemper and Leila Moore Williams Founders Collection, 1961.79.1*

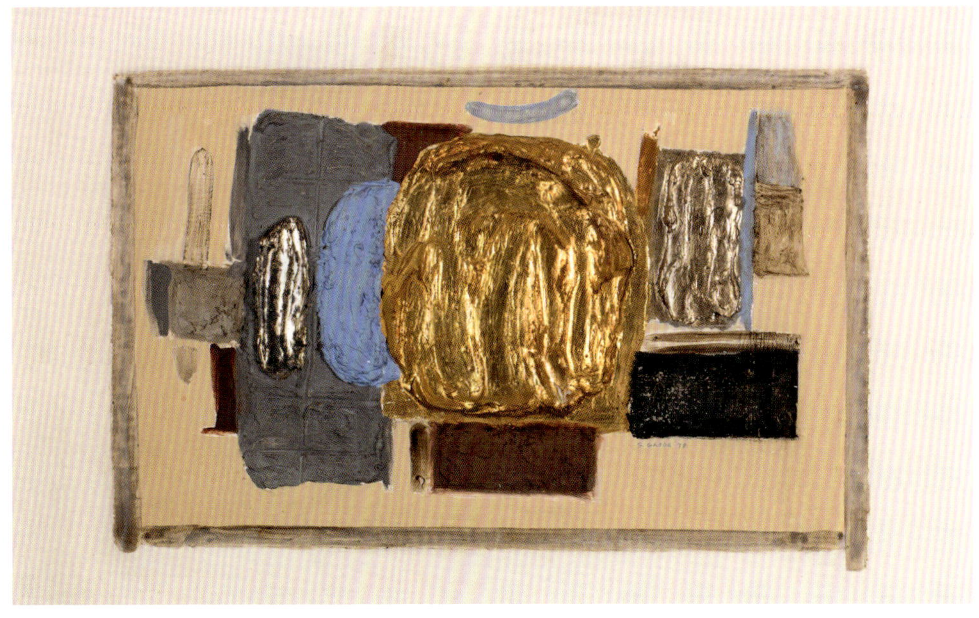

Conglomerate #2, 1978, mixed media with gold leaf and silver leaf, by Shearly Grode, 16 ½ × 24 ¾ in., *The Historic New Orleans Collection, gift of John Clemmer, 2009.0171*

[FIGURE 2.16], Robert Helmer [FIGURE 2.17], and Jack Hastings [FIGURE 2.18]. Lamantia was the recipient of the Prix de Rome and a Fulbright grant for architecture and painting in Italy. A 1943 graduate of the School of Architecture, he earned a master of science degree from Harvard University, then returned to teach at Tulane. Although he was an accomplished painter, Lamantia's contributions are seen primarily in numerous local, national, and international

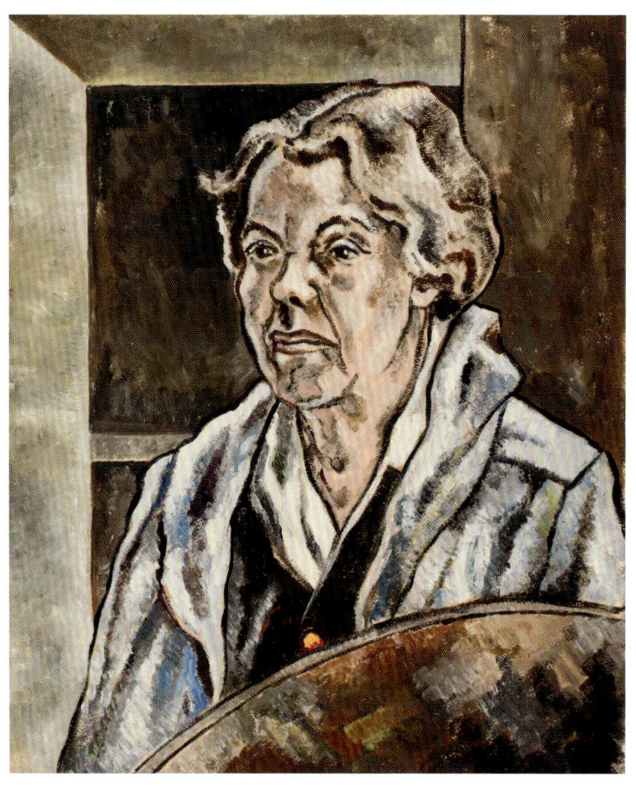

[FIGURE 2.16]

Portrait of Alberta Kinsey, 1942 or 1943, oil on paper, by James Lamantia, 20 ⅞ × 14 ⅞ in., *The Historic New Orleans Collection*, 1993.108.7

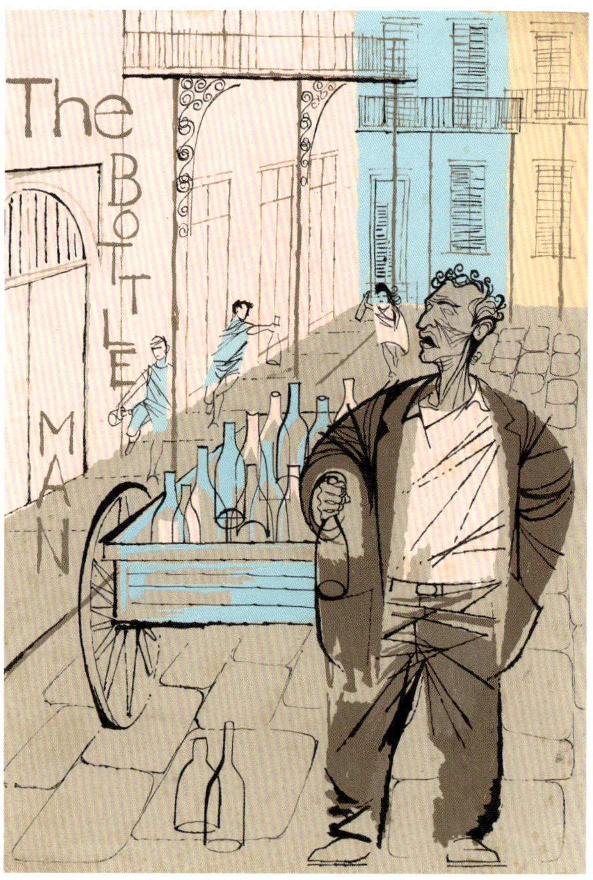

[FIGURE 2.17]

The Bottle Man, between 1954 and 1964, gouache on illustration board, by Robert Helmer, 15 ¼ × 10 ⅛ in., *The Historic New Orleans Collection, gift of John F. Clemmer*, 1991.116.19

structures and architectural details. Helmer began his studies at Tulane in 1949. He led the final season of exhibitions at the Arts and Crafts Gallery (as it had been renamed after its move to the Miltenberger House at 900 Royal Street). Helmer joined Tulane's faculty in 1952, a year after Clemmer. Hastings worked with Diego Rivera to learn the process of fresco painting. Hastings would later cast bronze sculptures in Italy, create cement

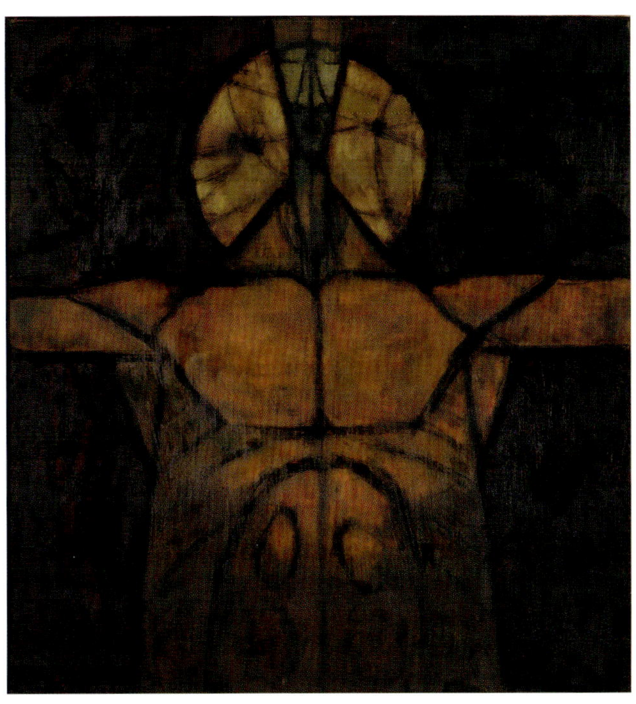

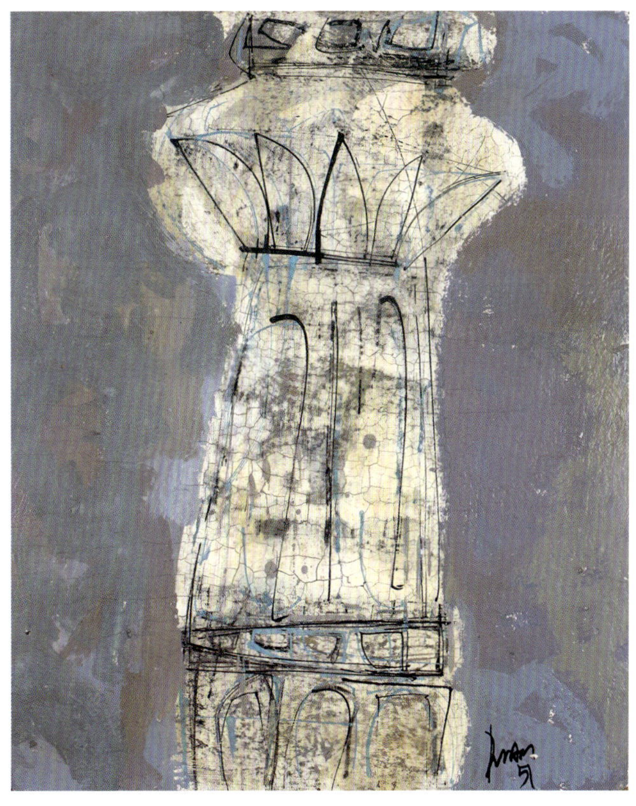

fountains and garden sculptures in Arizona, and make sculptures in New York City; in Boston, for the Nashville International Airport; and for the Chattanooga, Tennessee, headquarters of the Tennessee Valley Authority.

Another founder of the Orleans Gallery, George Dunbar [FIGURE 2.19], received a bachelor of fine arts degree in painting in 1953 from the Académie de la Grande Chaumière in Paris. He held his first solo exhibition in

59

Philadelphia that same year. He taught in New Orleans at 331 Art School in the French Quarter and at Tulane's School of Architecture. Like Clemmer, both Helmer and Dunbar explored both representational and non-representational art, but each one had a distinctive painting style. A Brooklyn native, Jean Seidenberg was active in the New York art scene before he moved to New Orleans in 1951. He is primarily considered a portraitist, but his oeuvre includes abstractions, figure studies, and genre scenes, all of which are rendered in his personal artistic style.

It was among this energetic cultural milieu that Clemmer developed as an artist. Clemmer worked alongside these talented artists, maintaining contact with many of them throughout his career. His work is varied in subject and technique, yet he revisits earlier subjects and redevelops them. His artistic evolution can be traced through selected works. His first independent painting, a 1940 still life of fruit and a spiky potted mother-in-law's tongue [PLATE 1], executed after a year's study at the New Orleans School of Art, is characteristic of work produced by artists of that time, with geometric fragmented areas in the fabric and a brown folding handheld fan. This composition, which is carefully arranged with balancing complementary colors, presents the subject naturalistically, while the background textile has crisply delineated geometric shapes. The geometric shapes of the textiles and the centrally placed spheres, ovoids, and cones point to Clemmer's future direction in art.

Four years later his *See Ungeheuer (Sea Monster)* [PLATE 4] was developed from ink sketches revealing a certainty in drawing and an economy of brushstrokes with delicate, precise cross-hatching. Here the muted tones parallel those of the work he did spray-painting camouflage on landing crafts and PT boats at Higgins Industries in City Park prior to his induction into the military in 1944.[12]

Almedia [PLATE 14], a large near-pastel 1962 abstract painting, moves from fragmented cubist elements toward muted overlapping rectangular sections with a collaged colored magazine illustration of a cracked ear. The painting makes reference to Pablo Picasso (1881–1973) and Georges Braque (1882–1963), who both moved from an analytical cubist style of disassembling and reassembling facets of a subject, toward applying wallpaper and newspaper fragments into a collaged composition in the so-called synthetic cubist style. This painting underscores Clemmer's studious approach to his artwork, particularly in allowing a painting to "rest" before continuing. He turned the painting, which originally had a horizontal format with chevron-shaped trees, to discover that it worked well in a vertical format. In this decision he paralleled Stevens's philosophy that a painting should be interesting from any viewpoint.

Almedia was also the name of a sugar plantation on the upriver east bank of the Mississippi River. Clemmer enjoyed this type of "happy acci-dent." He would continue to explore this concept in employing a Mexican paper, papel de amate, made from the bark of trees related to the fig tree. The rough texture of this handmade paper allows an artist to explore the surface for inherent designs, an experience that suited Clemmer's apprecia-tion of aleatory images.

Clemmer's late 1960s double portrait of his colleague Lin Emery and her husband, Shirley Braselman, was painted in his studio in the School of Architecture [PLATE 17]. The two sitters were unable to pose simultaneously, and Clemmer portrayed Emery standing behind Braselman with her hand resting on the back of his chair. This arrangement reflects the long-established convention of portraiture in paintings and photography with the wife stand-ing behind her husband and resting her hand on his shoulder or on the back of his chair. In this simple composition, the background behind Emery is a window, while the large white rectangle behind Braselman reveals a mod-ernistic trend toward minimalism. Here the gesture of her hand serves as a connective device rather than one of submissiveness. Other portraits by Clemmer are similarly composed, with the subject posed against a sparse background.

The vast body of Clemmer's work—whether nonrepresentational or still life—displays his interest in geometry and nature. His exploration of still life compositions throughout his career culminates in his 2008 paint-ing *Floral Circle* [PLATE 38], which developed after his *Topographia* series, and yet his interest in architecture is evident in the sharp lines and crisply delineated geometric shapes and compositional divisions. He centered the floral arrangement within a circle set in a square modified by vertical divisions and semicircular shapes. Clemmer frequently revisited past artistic themes, with *Floral Circle* recalling his 1970–71 *Topographia VIII—Azteca* [PLATE 22], in which the overall composition features a central blue orb-like form emanating from a large earth-toned circle set within a square against a backdrop of vertical stripes bordered by semicircular shapes. In his 1964 oil painting *Summery—Season II* [PLATE 16], with its earth-like circle within a square, he explores the changing seasons and nature and presages the *Topographia* series.

Many of Clemmer's mature works focus on classical structures or architectural elements, which can be seen in paintings like his 1993 *San G. II* [PLATE 32], continuing through his 2007 *Belle Grove II* [PLATE 39]. In both of these works, Clemmer's palette has lightened considerably, and the partitions suggest a progression from warm dawn through a bright midday to a cool dusk—a tripartite division that is evident in several of his paintings. Clemmer departs from his focus on architecture in these triptych-like compositions in his 1994 *Trilogy V, San Marco* [PLATE 34], with three full-length jesters shown in different stances, as though they are actors interacting in a stage play.

Overall, Clemmer's work is characterized by a sense of quiet composure and serenity, though other pieces suggest the probability of suppressed turmoil beneath the surface. He continuously developed new approaches to his art and assimilated new ideas as he developed his personal artistic voice. In doing so, he frequently revisited and reinterpreted earlier themes and subjects. Clemmer synthesized his awareness of art trends throughout the 1940s to the 1960s and his association with a wide range of working artists into a singular voice, a voice that is undeniably recognizable as his own. □

NOTES

1   Although Clemmer began his studies in 1939, it is probable that he visited the Arts and Crafts Club in 1938 and applied for the scholarship at that time. He later compiled a list of artists and literati he had met under the title "French Quarter 1938–1950."

2   Clemmer collected artworks by several artists associated with the Club, some of which he donated to The Historic New Orleans Collection, including works by Paul Ninas, Julius Woeltz, Alice Frances Goodall, Shearly Grode, Robert Helmer, and Hazel Guggenheim McKinley. He also donated a large collection of correspondence, programs, exhibition announcements, and other manuscripts collected during his years as head of the Arts and Crafts Club.

3   Judith H. Bonner, *The New Orleans Arts and Crafts Club: An Artistic Legacy* (New Orleans: New Orleans Museum of Art and the Historic New Orleans Collection, 2006), 4.

4   Judith H. Bonner, "Ninas, Paul," in *The New Encyclopedia of Southern Culture: Volume 21: Art and Architecture*, ed. Judith H. Bonner and Estill Curtis Pennington (Chapel Hill, NC: University of North Carolina Press, 2013), 394–5.

5   William Woodward joined the Tulane faculty in 1884. He worked toward reestablishing the engineering department as the School of Architecture in 1907 and designed the building in which it was housed.

6   At this point only three sculptures by William Woodward are known, all of them portrait heads of his mother, Mary Carpenter Woodward. The Historic New Orleans Collection has two of these in its permanent holdings, one executed in plaster and one in bronze. The third portrait head, executed in terra-cotta, was sold at Neal Auction Company on April 23, 2017.

7   In the late 1980s Clemmer would honor Gregory and her mother, Selina Brès Gregory (1870–1953), with a joint exhibition in the Newcomb Art Gallery.

8   In a personal conversation with the author in 1993, Clemmer discussed the Club's introduction of modernist artworks and recalled his experience with the Calder installation.

9   Bill Thoen, "Origins of the Compass Rose," GISNET, accessed March 7, 2021, http://www.gisnet.com/notebook/comprose.php.

10   Thoen, "Origins." The Chinese compass was divided into twelve major directions based on the signs of the zodiac.

11   Clemmer's statements, found in a 1971 newspaper article on his exhibition at the Louisiana State University–Alexandria and an unpaginated exhibition catalog. See also Gridley McKim-Smith and

Leo Costello, "Crafting the Intangible: The Art of John Clemmer," in *John Clemmer: Exploring the Medium, 1940–1999* (New Orleans: New Orleans Museum of Art, 1999).

12   Clemmer was inducted into the US Army on January 27, 1944.

BIBLIOGRAPHY

Bonner, Judith H. "Ninas, Paul." *The New Encyclopedia of Southern Culture, Volume 21: Art and Architecture*, ed. Judith H. Bonner and Estill Curtis Pennington. Chapel Hill: University of North Carolina Press, 2013: 394–5.

Bonner, Judith H. *The New Orleans Arts and Crafts Club: An Artistic Legacy.* New Orleans: New Orleans Museum of Art and The Historic New Orleans Collection, 2006.

Bonner, Thomas Jr., and Judith H. Bonner, eds. *Sherwood Anderson and Other Famous Creoles.* New Orleans: Pelican Publishing, 2018.

Clemmer, John, with essays by David Clemmer, Gridley McKim-Smith, and Leo Costello. *John Clemmer: Exploring the Medium, 1940–1999.* New Orleans: New Orleans Museum of Art, 1999.

Douglas, Paul Whitfield, "Paul Ninas, Dean of New Orleans Artists," M.A. thesis, Louisiana State University, 1997.

Kemp, John R. "Dean of New Orleans Modernism." *Louisiana Cultural Vistas* (summer 2000): 12–23.

Kemp, John R. "Paul Ninas." 64 Parishes. Accessed March 23, 2020. https://64parishes.org/entry/paul-ninas.

Marshall, Keith. *John McCrady (1911–1968).* New Orleans: New Orleans Museum of Art, 1975.

Martinez, Matthew J. "A Conversation on Artist John McCrady." *Xavier Review* 13 (2): 1–25.

"Orleans Gallery Collection: Inventory." Earl K. Long Library, University of New Orleans. Accessed March 23, 2020. https://libguides.uno.edu/mss046.

Thoen, Bill. "Origins of the Compass Rose." GISNET. Accessed March 7, 2021. http://www.gisnet.com/notebook/comprose.php.

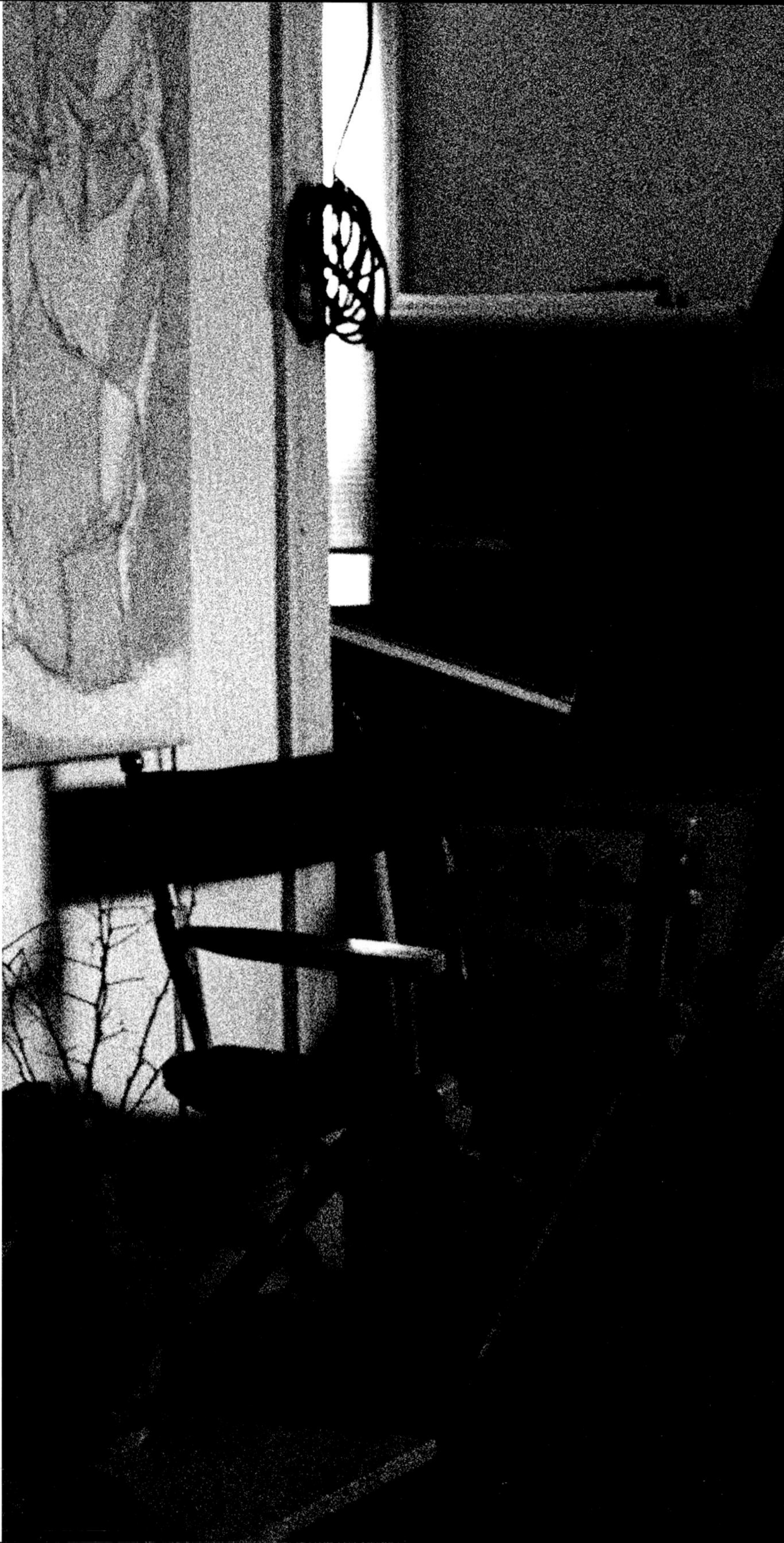

John Clemmer in his Laurel Street studio, New
Orleans, 2010, photograph by David Clemmer,
courtesy of 3618 Studio, LLC, New Orleans, LA

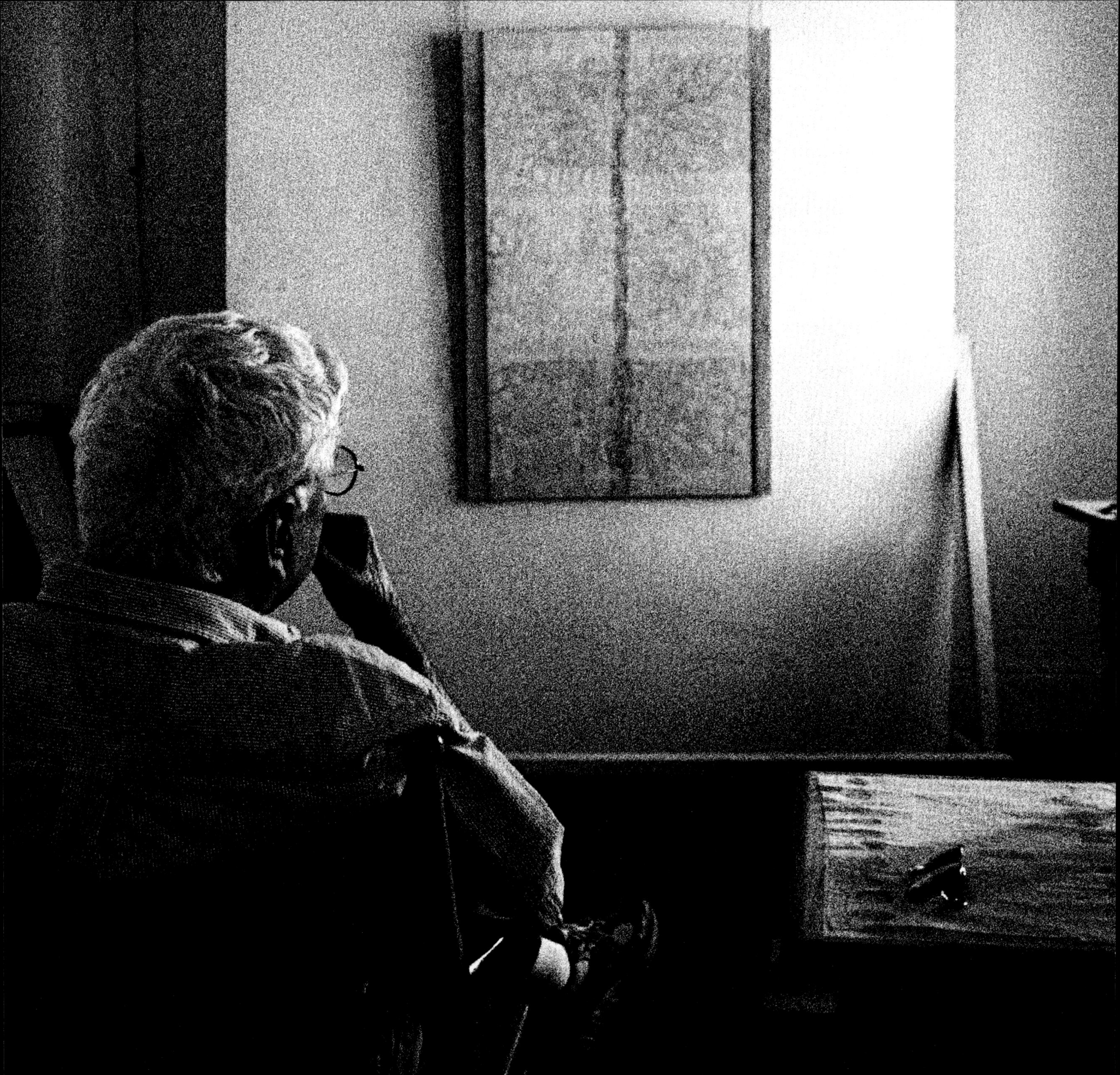

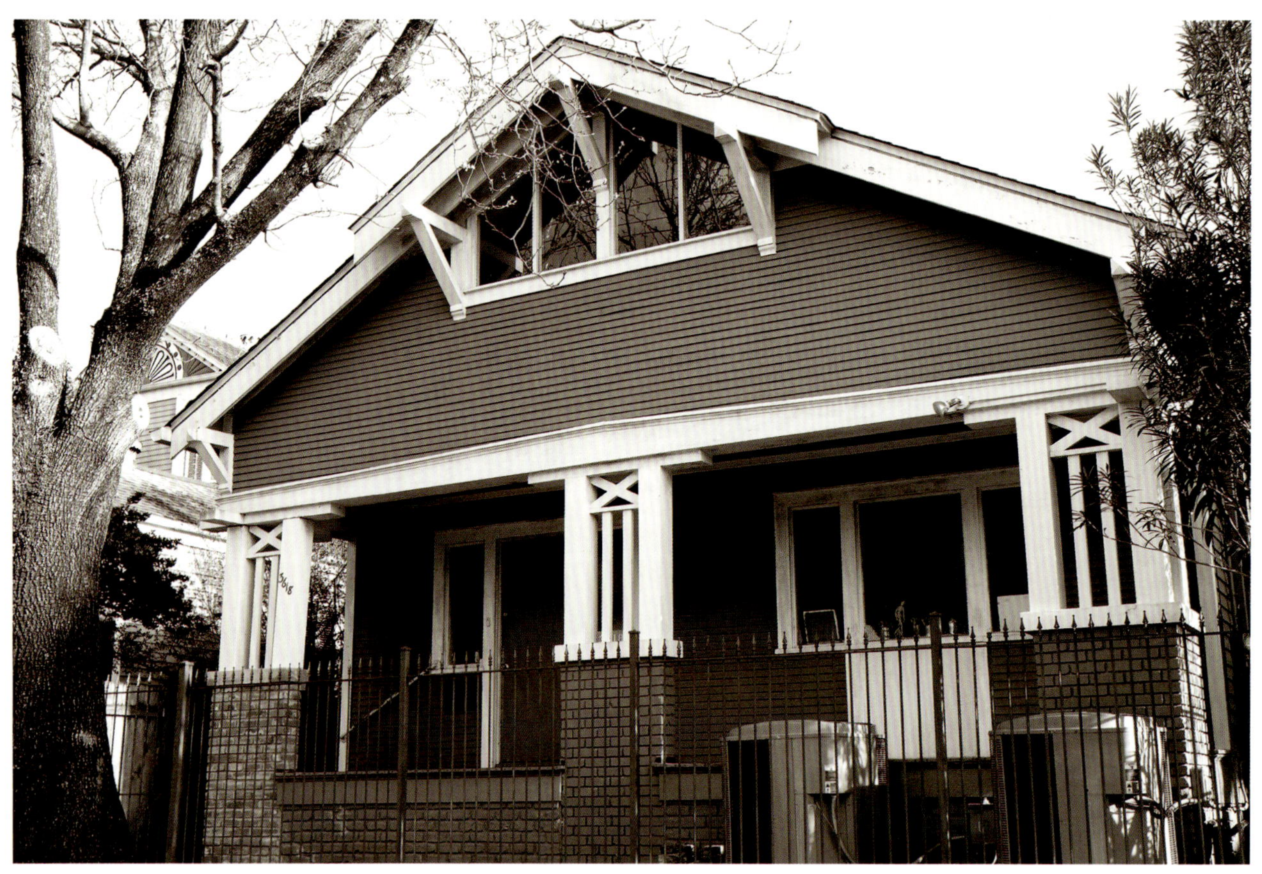

[FIGURE 3.1]
3618 Studio, New Orleans, Louisiana, 2021, photograph by David Clemmer

The Artist Remembers: Sharing a Life

by John Ed Bradley

IN THE BEGINNING, we met on Fridays for lunch. It was always shrimp po'boys and Barq's root beer from Barcia's Grocery, served in the large, light-filled room where he painted.

I'd park my old pickup in the shade of the towering cypress trees that John himself had planted years before, and I'd march over to the cottage with the little sign on the porch that said 3618 Studio [FIGURE 3.1]. Most days I carried a satchel holding a reporter's notebook, a microcassette recorder, and a plastic sandwich bag filled with tapes already labeled with his name.

I rarely had to knock. Hearing my feet thump against the board steps, he liked to greet me by rapping on the other side of the door—beating me to the punch just as I raised my fist.

"Ladies and gentlemen . . . the great John Clemmer!" I'd announce the moment he pulled the door open.

Inside, a stereo played classical music, and the smells of paint and varnish were sharp in the air. The po'boys, wrapped in white butcher paper

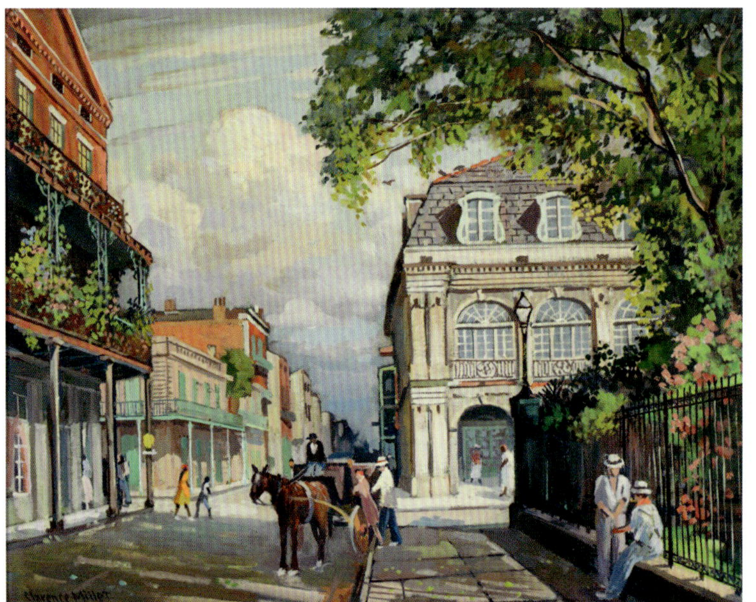

[FIGURE 3.2]

Corner of St. Peter and Chartres Streets, ca. 1940, oil on canvas board, by Clarence Millet, 15 × 18 in., *The Historic New Orleans Collection*, gift of Laura Simon Nelson, 2017.0111

stained with oil, waited on a small table positioned between two director's chairs. I removed the recorder and punched a button, then I started pitching questions:

"Was Paul Ninas as much trouble as everybody says?"

"Did you ever go to New Iberia and spend time with Weeks Hall at his plantation house like so many of the other artists?"

"What was Alberta Kinsey like?"

John answered them all, usually with anecdotes so rich in detail they carried me back decades to a time before I was born **[FIGURE 3.2]**. In my mind we were young dreamers together in the French Quarter, where "the streetlights were still gaslit," as he told me once, "and there were few automobiles, and the streets were brick and cobblestone, and, oh, the parties . . ."

He said he'd known the heirs to a sugar fortune who replaced the hood ornaments on their limousines with Degas bronzes. There were Mardi Gras and Christmas dinners at Antoine's, and one especially memorable late-night feast at Fong's with Henry Miller, who later sent him a post-card saying, "John, don't buy my new book from a store. Buy it from me, I need the money." He met William Faulkner and Max Ernst and Josef von Sternberg. And one afternoon a woman approached him on the street with a reproaching finger raised. "Communist," she yelled. Her anger startled him. Modernists like John, he believed she was saying, had no business in the old district: Why were they ruining everything?

He was eighty in the spring of 2002, when I first turned up at his door. I was forty-three, although a midlife slump had me feeling every bit his age. Some men, upon outpacing their perceived usefulness, bet the ponies or chase misery in strip clubs and gas-station casinos, but everything I had went to buying art, particularly paintings by artists who'd worked in Louisiana in the first half of the twentieth century. They were my obsession and my raison d'être, and they were why I lived in a cheap apartment with squirrels in the walls.

When I looked at the paintings in my collection, I marveled at their beauty and wondered about the people who created them. Where had they come from? How did their lives go and their stories end?

To learn more than I could find in books and old newspaper clippings, I began interviewing artists who'd worked in the state in the 1930s and 1940s. One of my first meetings took me to Wausau, Wisconsin, where I spent several days in December of 1998 with Edward Schoenberger, then eighty-three. Eddie had worked for the WPA in New Orleans, producing a mural for a public library on Canal Street and a painting that appeared in the book *Gumbo Ya-Ya: A Collection of Louisiana Folk Tales.* "What about John Clemmer?" Eddie asked, tired of my interrogation. The years had soft-ened his Yat accent, but "John Clemmer" still came out sounding more like "Joan Clemmer." "Have you talked to Joan yet? Oh, yeah, gotta talk to Joan. Joan knew everybody, and I'd bet he remembers better than me."

Most of the artists I wanted to learn about were dead. Undeterred, I arranged to meet with their surviving family members. One year I flew to Ohio for a weekend with Alberta Kinsey's cousin, Jack Kinsey, who drove me from the Dayton airport to the cemetery in West Milton where she's buried. It was cold and the ground was wet from melting snow, but seeing the modest gray slab decorated with her first name only, Alberta, dropped me to my knees. The way Jack looked at me, he must've been wondering if I'd lost my mind.

Not long after, on a muggy November afternoon, I went to see Franz Heldner at his Uptown home. We sat on patio chairs in his yard and drank warm beer as I bombed him with questions about his parents, Knute and Colette Heldner. Franz finally pointed to my notebook and said, "Write this name down. He's someone you should talk to." I got my pen out. "Clemmer," Franz said. "John Clemmer." And then he spelled it for me.

WE STARTED SMALL, with those Friday lunches at his studio, but soon graduated to long restaurant meals at Kim Son and Mr. John's Steakhouse and meandering drives around the city. There never was a day when I wasn't pushing him to remember. "Come on, John," I'd tell him. "What else?"

"What do you mean, 'What else?' Haven't I told you everything?"

One day, we parked in front of the townhouse on Esplanade Avenue where Paul Ninas had lived with his second wife, Grace Chavanne Ninas. "There was a pirogue in the courtyard that he kept filled with water, so it wouldn't shrink," John said. "Visitors would drink too much, and on this particular Saturday I went to see him, and the house was full of school-teachers, all of them drunk. One was an elderly lady named Irma, and she was sitting in Paul's pirogue. The water was up to her waist, and Irma was paddling, and the paddle was scraping the ground."

John showed me other locations from his past—the building on Poydras Street that had housed Maylie's, one of his old haunts, and the house on Magazine Street where he lived as a teenager and his mother died from injuries suffered in a kitchen gas explosion. We drove by places where he'd rented rooms and studios. Standing in front of the building at Royal Street and Pirate Alley that was the last home of the Arts and Crafts Club before it folded in 1951, John said, "There was a gallery on the first

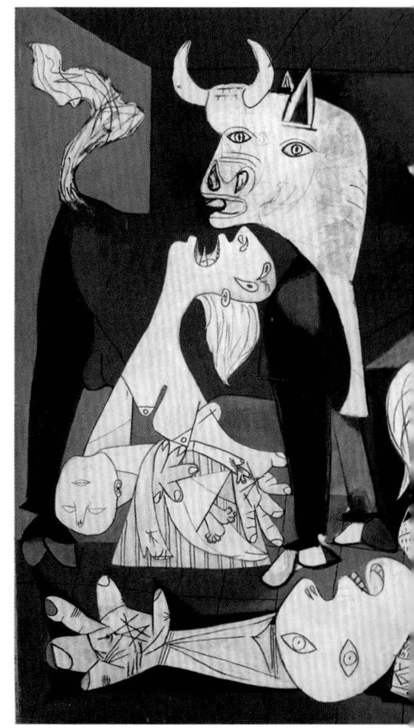

floor, the school was on the second, and I lived on the third. I was offered the building for $40,000. The real estate agent said, 'Come on, John. What about the GI Bill?' I said, 'It's not the GI Bill I'm worried about. It's the monthly payments.' You know what that building's worth today?"

Another day, I drove John to the Vincent Mann Gallery to see a sales exhibition of Françoise Gilot's work. As we searched for a place to park, he talked about Gilot's complicated relationship with Pablo Picasso, her former lover and the father of two of her children. Then he described the first time he saw a Picasso painting in person. It was the large anti-war manifesto *Guernica* **[FIGURE 3.3]**, displayed at the Isaac Delgado Museum of Art, now the New Orleans Museum of Art. "Did I imagine this, or did it happen?" John said. "I open the door, and there it is at the foot of the stairs. It might

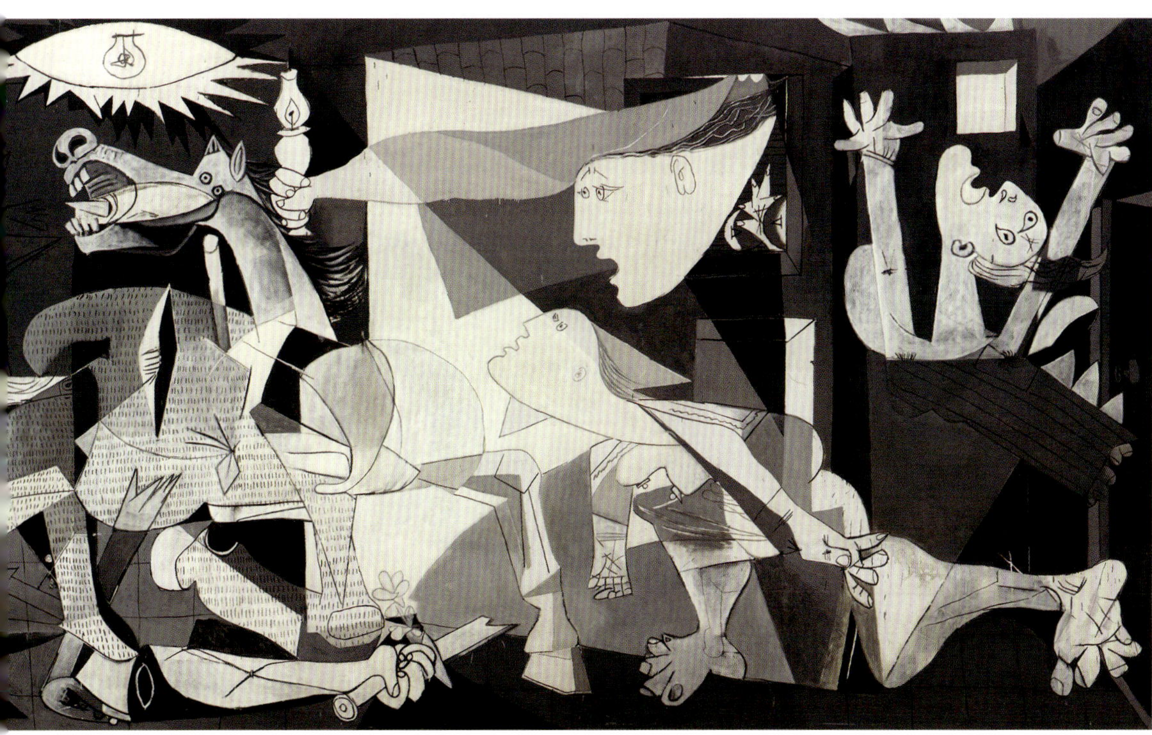

Guernica, 1937, oil on canvas, by Pablo Picasso, 137 ½ × 305 ¾ in., *courtesy of Museo Nacional Centro de Arte Reina Sofía © 2021 Estate of Pablo Picasso / Artists Rights Society (ARS), New York.*

be exaggerating to say the experience changed my life, but it did something to me. I never forgot it, and I still think about it—stepping toward it . . . *Guernica*!"

On hearing that an old friend was in the gallery, its owner, Jacob Manguno, appeared suddenly and greeted John with a long handshake. Manguno was himself an artist, and he and John started trading stories about the Quarter in the days after the Second World War. They found their way to the subject of the all-male New Orleans Art League and one of its leaders, Clarence Millet. "Clarence called a meeting at his studio, and I arrived late," John said. "I knocked softly, not wanting to disturb the important proceedings. When no one answered, I went in. The room was dark and there was a projector going. It was a bunch of men, and they were sitting in a cloud of smoke watching a dirty movie. 'Welcome, John! Come join us!' Clarence called out."

The conversation with Manguno went on for half an hour. "Oh, no," John said, glancing at his watch. There was someone expected at the studio. We'd spent time with only a few of Gilot's paintings.

"Goodbye, Jake," John said. "Terrific show."

I followed him to the door.

EMBOLDENED, I INVITED HIM to my apartment to see my collection. By now I knew that he was sensitive enough not to scoff at what I'd assembled, if it happened to disappoint. I turned the lights on and ushered him in. He shuffled from one painting to the next, inspecting works by Harry Armstrong Nolan, Noel Rockmore, Marion Souchon, and Alice Peak Reiss. He paused before a large Kinsey painting hanging over the fireplace. It showed the interior of an antique shop. "Alberta could be so self-deprecating," he said. "I remember something she told me once. She said she wasn't a real painter, not like the rest of us. She meant she wasn't modern. But look at this." John shook his head, eyes on the painting. "Marvelous."

We climbed a spiral staircase to the second floor. Over a wall of closets in my bedroom hung an oil by Knute Heldner, painted in Paris in the early

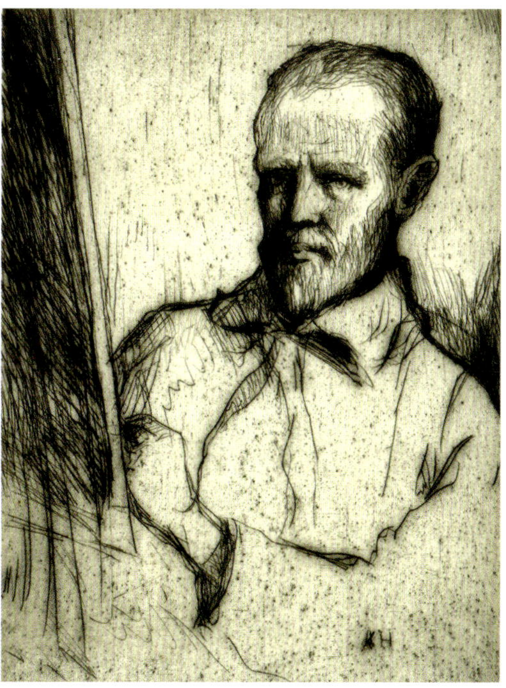

Self-Portrait, 1940s, etching, by Knute Heldner, 11 ⅝ × 9 in., *The Historic New Orleans Collection, partial gift of James W. Nelson, 2008.0216.125*

1930s. The raven-haired nude reclined on an elbow, looking away from the viewer. "He'd had quite a reputation as a young man, when he would've painted this one," John said. "But by the time I knew him he was churning out trash for tourists. He had a big indentation on his temple here, and one eye was all kooky. I said to him, 'Knute, what happened to you?' He said, 'Well, I tell you, John, I was playing golf and this man wasn't swinging right, and I walked over and offered to help'" [FIGURE 3.4].

He might've been joking about the golfing incident; I couldn't tell. Before I could question him further, John positioned himself under a landscape by Conrad Albrizio, loosely painted pine trees standing shoulder to shoulder like soldiers at attention. "Oh, sure," he said. "We should go to the train station, don't you think? See his murals?"

With John, one adventure always led to the next. Before long, it wasn't only my Fridays that belonged to him. I gave him all the other days of the week. And in return he gave me his.

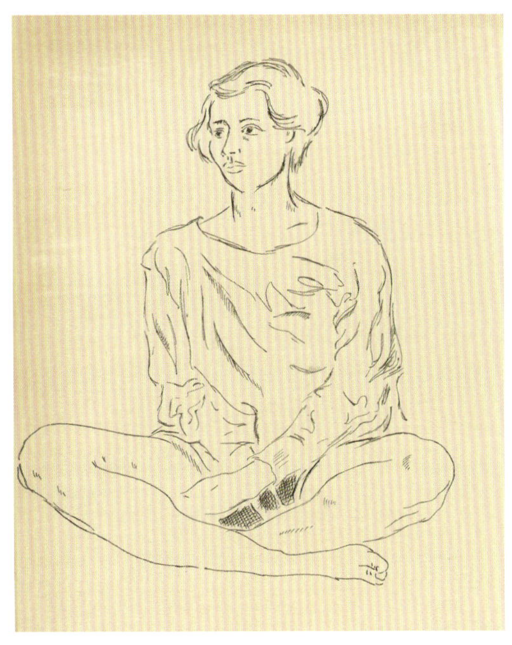

Seated Figure (Dottie), 1951, ink on card stock, by John Clemmer, 10 ½ × 7 ½ in., *The Historic New Orleans Collection, gift of Dorothy, Jonathan, and David Clemmer / 3618 Studio, LLC, in memory of John Clemmer, 2016.0041.23*

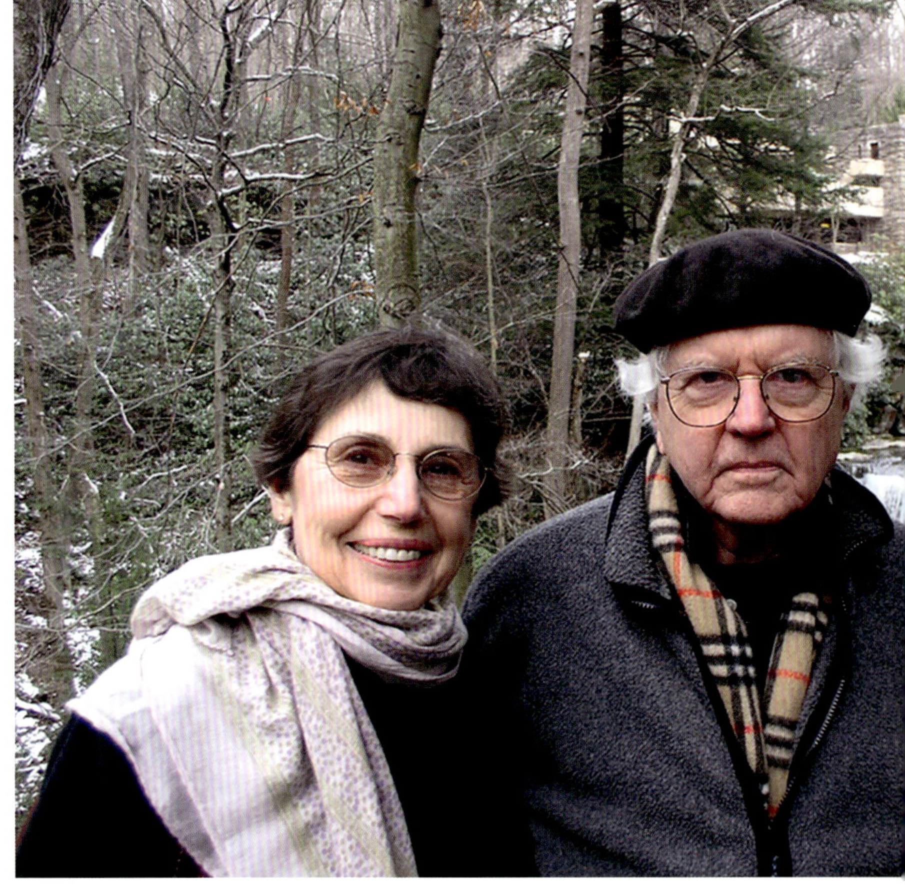

Dorothy and John Clemmer at Fallingwater, Mill Run, Pennsylvania, 2003, photograph by Jonathan Clemmer, *courtesy of Jonathan Clemmer*

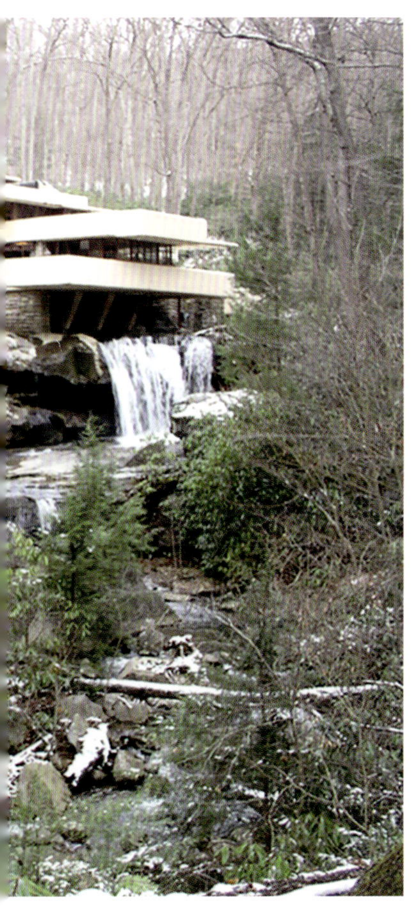

HE FAVORED BUTTON-DOWN SHIRTS, pants with lots of pockets, New Balance running shoes, and white socks that drooped a little. He might've been a bohemian in his youth, but when I knew him he had a refined, almost genteel manner. He was always clean-shaven, and he always smelled good, like soap. I made a point of telling him he looked handsome whenever I saw him with his beret on. "The artiste," his wife, Dottie, called him.

He liked to describe things as "delightful," "charming," "exquisite," "lovely," and "marvelous." John had no discernible accent despite his childhood in Ascension Parish, Barataria, and the Irish Channel. In his studio he kept shelves crowded with books about theology and history that I wouldn't have touched with a ten-foot pole. He talked about artists I'd never heard of and would have to Google when I got home.

Except for his Friday po'boy, he usually had yogurt and a banana for lunch. He made it his mission to paint every day, but I never once saw him with paint on his fingers.

For all his confidence he still exuded the humility of someone who'd feasted on failure. I never heard him boast or curse or raise his voice in anger. In photos he tends to look grumpy, but I rarely spent time with him when he wasn't happy.

He and Dottie got married in 1953, but to John she remained his "lovely bride." He would say, "Let me check with my lovely bride first." Or, "It's really up to my lovely bride" [FIGURES 3.5 AND 3.6].

He once showed me a drawing of a partially clothed young woman lying in a small bed. I assumed it was Dottie, but a moment of modesty kept me from asking him to identify her. In the picture John had included a couple of his paintings on the walls, and two pairs of shoes stood on the floor— the man's pointing toward the bed, the woman's pointing away from it. "The direction of the shoes," I said. "That says it all, doesn't it?"

"That day it did," he answered with a laugh.

John didn't seem to care about the fame and riches that some artists pursue. It was the work that mattered—doing it every day, and doing it well.

"Do you consider yourself a southern artist?" I asked him once.

"No," he answered.

"Then what kind are you?"

"No kind. Just an artist. Why do I have to be anything?"

PO'BOYS VANQUISHED, BARQ'S BOTTLES standing empty, John approached the easel holding his latest canvas and began to paint. This was a magical moment for me, watching him build his surface one careful smear at a time. At his feet, the dusty planks held a thousand colored drips that, taken together, served up as fine an example of abstract expressionism as any I'd ever seen on a museum wall. By now I'd placed him front and center on my personal Mount Rushmore of Louisiana artists, and my certainty about his greatness only deepened with the deepening of our friendship.

"Yeah, sure, go ahead," he said, as I walked toward an adjacent room where he stored his paintings in racks. I started sliding favorites out: *Two Nudes in a Landscape* (1949) [PLATE 7], *Nude on the Beach* (1950s). I ran my fingertips over the cool, grainy face of *Noon Visit* (1950) [FIGURE 3.7], yet another early classic.

"*Noon Visit*," I said. "Why did you name it that?"

"I was having a love affair with a married woman," he answered. "We would meet at noon. Her husband . . . Well, let me just say there would be bruises on her face and arms. She had wealth and social standing, and I had nothing, but when we were alone together our troubles went away. I worked on the painting but couldn't get it right. I grew frustrated and put it in a closet. Then one day I got word that her plane had crashed in the Gulf of Mexico. They were searching for her body. I started working, which is what you do to survive a moment like that. The painting had resisted me before, but no longer. I finished that same day."

Tears shone in his eyes. What do you say when the only words left are the most pedestrian, the most mundane? "I'm sorry, John."

"Sure," he said and turned back to the painting on the easel.

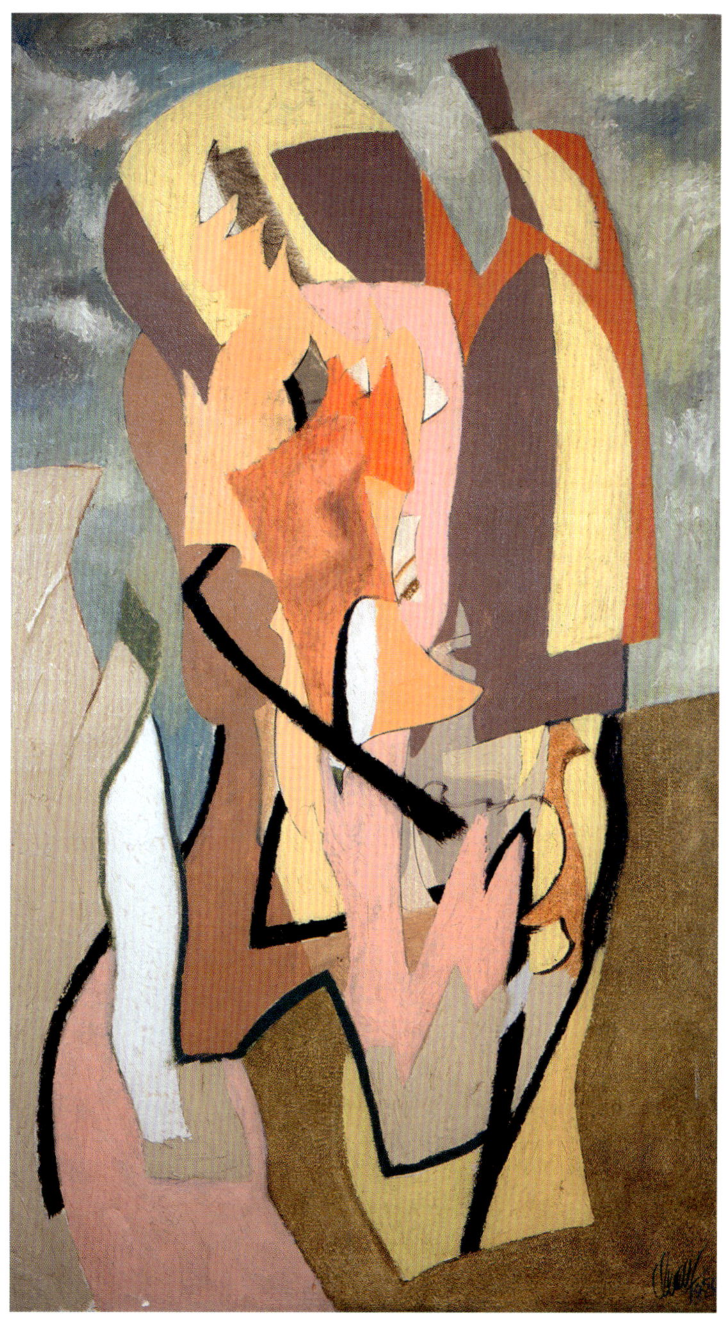

Noon Visit, 1950, oil on canvas, by John Clemmer, 38 × 21 in., *image courtesy New Orleans Museum of Art, photograph by Judy Cooper*

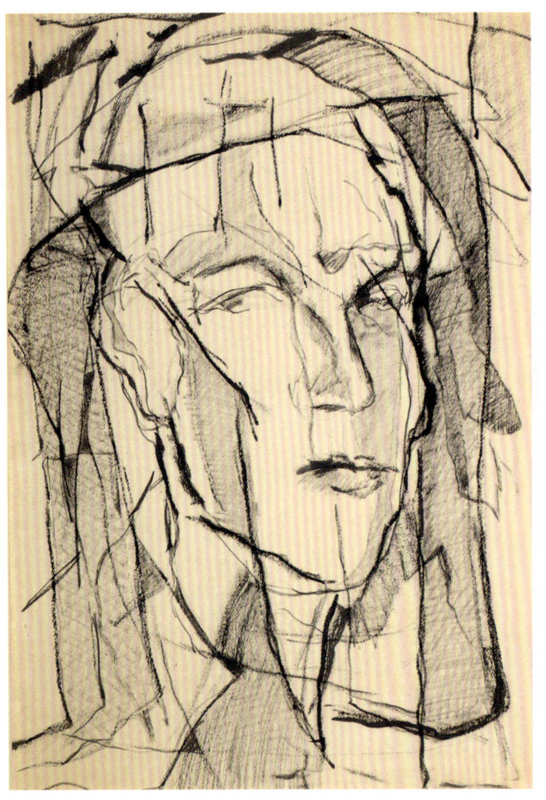

There was a cabinet filled with works on paper. I sat on the floor and
removed drawings that dated as far back as the 1930s, when John was a teenager studying at the New Orleans School of Art. Acidity had turned many
of them brown. Some were sketched on the reverse of cards used to adver-
tise exhibitions at the Arts and Crafts Club gallery. There were portraits and
nudes of lovers—one of them his first wife, Marjorie, with whom he had
two children, Trina and Erik. A large sketch on heavy paper showed a young
man looking out from a cubist field [FIGURE 3.8]. "Is this you, John?" I asked.

He didn't answer.

"It is you, isn't it?"

"No, I don't think so," he whispered, but I'd never heard a denial spoken with less conviction. The moment confused me. After his confession about the doomed affair that inspired *Noon Visit*, perhaps he didn't want to admit that he and the boy in the drawing were still one and the same.

I started placing his drawings side by side on the floor around me and soon found myself encircled. They told the story of his life, with the subject of the presumed self-portrait staring at me while the real John Clemmer, white-haired and unsteady on his feet, watched from the next room.

"When it's time," he said, "I want it to be right here." He pointed to the floor in front of his easel, and I understood that he meant it. As we both stared at the spot, he lifted his foot and banged it against the wood.

I nearly jumped out of my skin.

BEFORE JOHN AND I BECAME friends, I'd owned more than thirty paintings by Alberta Kinsey. One after another, I sold them off. I sold my Nolans and my Heldners, including the Paris nude. The Souchon, the Albrizio, the Ninas drawings from his time in Dominica. The resplendent Millet that gave a bird's-eye view of Jackson Square. It hurt to let them go, but there were bills and taxes to pay. My one consolation was knowing what John had in the racks at his studio. Better one great Clemmer, I thought, than all the others put together.

I can't say he ever expressed joy at commanding a place of such prominence in my collection. No, it would be more accurate to say he was barely moved. His bigger concern was my constant striving to add more of his art to the walls of my slatternly apartment, when I needed clothes and a couch.

John had long ago sworn off gallery representation. When I asked him why, he groused about having to give up 50 percent of sales. So it was his job now to create and sell the work, and he was much better at one task than the other. "What do you have to get for it, John?" I asked him one morning in the studio. My financial situation was on the upswing, and I'd found another beauty in the racks that I couldn't live without.

"That one?" Had he shown any less enthusiasm I would've needed to call Frank Minyard. "Where do you plan to put it?"

"On the wall, John. I'll make room."

"There's a price list around here somewhere," he said. But he never did get up from his chair. Instead of the usual soaring orchestrations, traditional New Orleans jazz was playing on the stereo, and John seemed mesmerized. "George Lewis. Slow Drag Pavageau," he said. "I used to paint to their music. I did some drawings of George. You haven't seen them in all your digging, have you?"

I knew when I'd been beaten. I returned the painting to the racks.

I sometimes wondered if he cared to sell anything at all. Once, a collector took one of John's sandcast wall sculptures on approval. Too slow in making up her mind, John had his studio assistant report to her home and retrieve the thing. The next morning, the sculpture was standing on the floor in John's studio, tipped back against the wall. "What can you do?" John said with a sigh, as if fate, rather than his own indifference, were responsible for the lost sale.

My work as a novelist and magazine writer often sent me out on the road, but as soon as I returned to New Orleans, I would go to see John. After one trip I found an unexpected check from my agent in the mail. I headed over to the studio and bought two paintings on the spot. I might've bought a third had John been willing to part with it. He'd started the painting in the 1950s, but it still wasn't finished. "They let you know when they're ready," he said. "You step back for a look: 'That's it, don't touch it.' But I'm afraid we're not there yet."

"No? You started it fifty years ago, John."

He shrugged, as if to say, "Don't blame me. It's the painting."

We celebrated my windfall by walking around the corner to Barcia's [FIGURE 3.9]. It wasn't Friday, so they weren't serving shrimp po'boys, but we did have root beer with our club sandwiches. The glass door opened and workers from the riverfront came shuffling in, their coveralls black with sweat and grime. Then the sculptor Thomas Bruno, who had his own studio nearby on Tchoupitoulas Street, showed up and started lecturing John

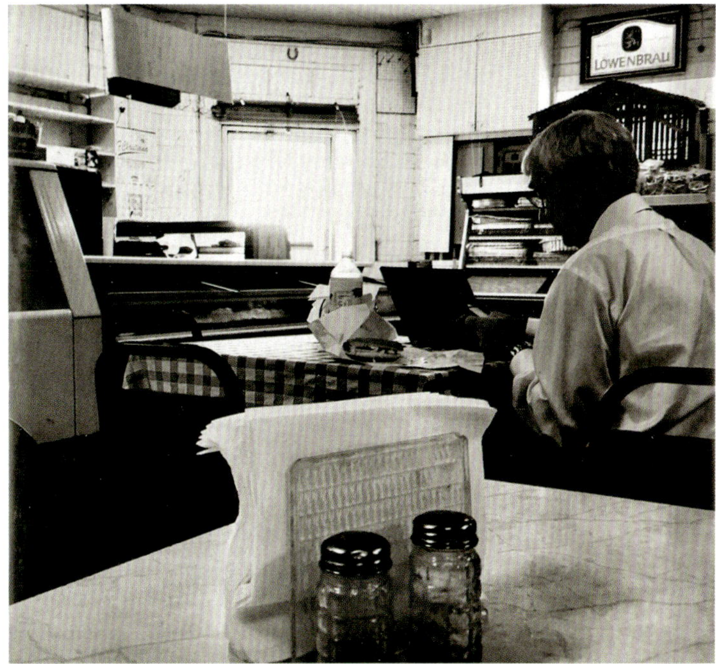

[FIGURE 3.9]
Barcia's Grocery and Po'boys, New Orleans, 2016, photograph by David Clemmer, *courtesy of 3618 Studio, LLC, New Orleans, LA*

and me about classical sculpture. His voice was so ripe with emotion that it silenced the room. John began to laugh, and I soon joined in. "What?" Tom said, pausing for a look around.

Life was good when you'd used surprise book money to land two bona fide masterpieces from the world's worst art dealer and a brilliant sculptor with a goatee was taking you to school in a busy corner grocery.

I still don't think I've ever had it better.

THEY WERE UP IN SHEBOYGAN, Wisconsin, the town on Lake Michigan where he and Dottie kept a second home and spent as many as six months each year. Dottie grew up in Chicago, and she first started vacationing at Sheboygan when she was a child. The old cottage she and John owned in

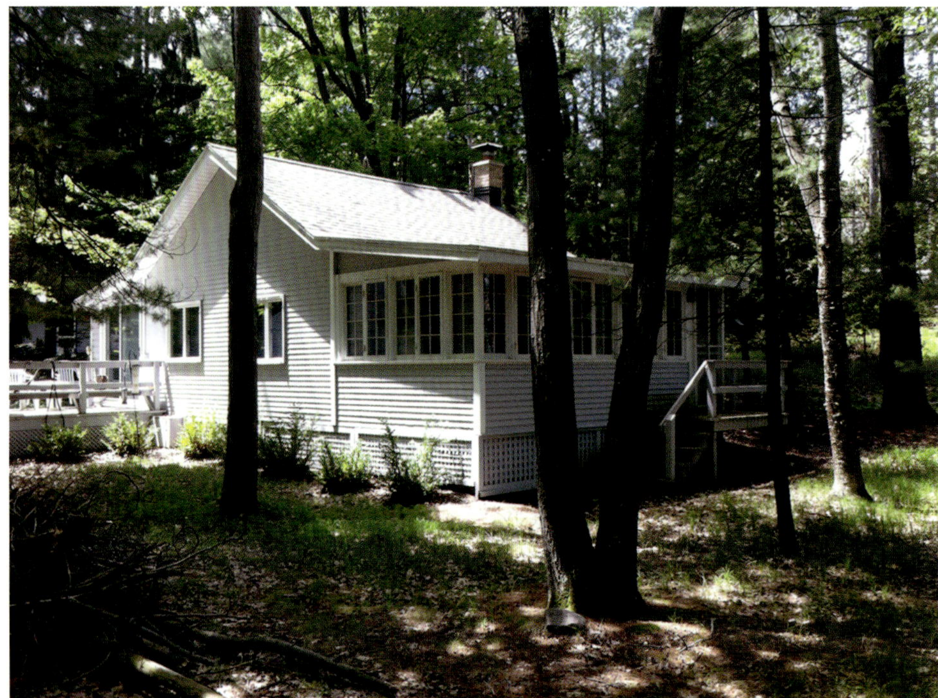

[FIGURE 3.10]
Clemmers' cottage in Sheboygan, Wisconsin, 2016, photograph by John Ed Bradley, *courtesy John Ed Bradley*

the Black River area had belonged to her parents [FIGURE 3.10], and it now was part of a compound that included a studio and a newer house that John had designed himself . The beach was a short walk away. "Why don't you come?" John said on the phone. "You'll have the cottage to yourself. We'll show you the sights." I flew to Milwaukee, rented a car, and headed north.

The new house was filled with recent examples of John's work, most of them Wisconsin landscapes. "I wish I'd come in my truck," I told him. "We could back it up to the front door and start throwing things in."

My first night there we went to dinner at Trattoria Stefano, their favorite local restaurant. Dottie radiated the same youth and beauty that John had captured in his best drawings of her, and John looked very modern in his black knit shirt and slacks, his hair combed straight forward but for the slight kick on top. He kept his hands folded on the edge of the table, not a single drop of paint on them.

I waited for him to look at me. "The great John Clemmer," I whispered. It was easier than saying what I really wanted to—what I always have difficulty saying to the people I love—and John seemed to understand this. He reached over and put his hand on my shoulder. "Me, too," he said.

The next morning, he was too tired to go out. Perhaps, if he felt better later, he could get some work done; he would like it if I joined him. So I followed Dottie down to the lake. We stood in the sand and held hands and gazed out at the huge, dark water. Clouds hung low in the sky and a blustery wind blew. I had a feeling that I should memorize everything before it was gone.

We left the beach and I hurried back to the studio, for some reason afraid to go inside. But he was standing in front of a canvas, the bristles on his brush wet with paint. "You'll be happy to know we're communicating again," he said.

"You and the painting?"

"Yes, that's right. Who else?"

He had a way of tilting his head back and looking through his old-lady glasses, his mouth slightly open, that always cracked me up.

"Hey, John, what about Alberta?"

"What about her?"

"What was she like? Come on. Tell me a story."

HE ALWAYS CALLED ME as soon as they returned to New Orleans. "I hope I'm not disturbing you," he'd say on the phone, Satie or Tchaikovsky or Mozart playing in the background. It didn't matter if I was working and had a deadline to meet. Fifteen minutes later I was parking under the cypress trees. Fifteen more after that and we'd resumed our grand tour of the local art scene.

We visited museums, frame shops, junk and antique stores, auction houses, art supply stores, art galleries, and an art school. We made mini-pilgrimages to see his paintings in private collections—a newer piece hanging in the stairway at JoAnn Greenberg's house, an older one in Herbert Halpern's shop.

One day I drove him to Pat Trivigno's house for lunch. The two retired Tulane University professors sat at a table and tossed memories around, several of them involving Mark Rothko, who in 1957 spent two months at the Newcomb Art School as a visiting artist. It was Trivigno who'd persuaded Rothko to accept the position. "Mark would say, 'Whenever you're in New York, John, call me.' So I did. I called him," John said. "He was living in a walk-up flat, close to the Modern. We had breakfast in his kitchen, and there were lines crossing from one end to the other, with baby diapers hanging from them."

"Yeah, and now for fifty million you can own one of his paintings," I said, with way too much attitude. The old artists lowered their forks. Then they turned and faced me as if only now remembering that they weren't alone.

One weekend, Dottie drove him to Opelousas to meet my family and to attend a party celebrating my recent marriage. He stepped into the small brick house where I grew up and handed my mother a gift wrapped in kraft paper: an oval-shaped ink drawing of flowers in a vase, exquisitely framed, his familiar signature shooting upward from the lower right corner [FIGURE 3.11].

"I never thought I'd own a Clemmer," Mom said as I went in search of a hammer and a nail. "Thank you, John. And thank you for being John Ed's friend."

He waited until she looked at him. "You're welcome, madam."

I noticed that he was beginning to repeat himself even more than usual. At the studio one day he told me the story about approaching Faulkner on Royal Street and congratulating him on winning the Nobel Prize. I'd always loved that one, but an hour later he was telling it again.

Faulkner's wearing a seersucker top and khaki pants, and John's wearing a khaki top and seersucker pants, and as John turns to walk away Faulkner says, "We look to be about the same size. Why don't we switch jackets?"

John and I laughed when he finished. But it scared me.

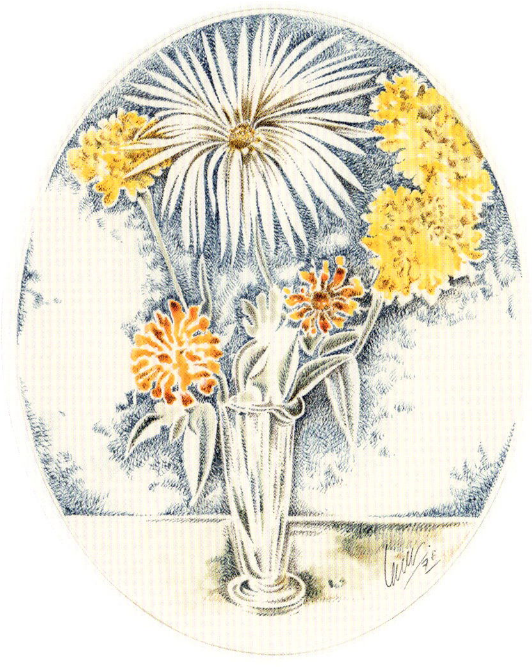

Not long after, he fell asleep while we were talking about Hazel
Guggenheim McKinley. According to John, she had an insatiable appetite
for young men, and on more than one occasion he'd rebuffed her attempts
to seduce him. She was taking yet one more shot when John nodded off—
not in the story but in front of me, and right when he should've been most
awake. Twenty minutes passed before his eyes reopened. He seemed sur-
prised to find me still sitting there. "Where were we?" he asked, shuffling
over to his easel.

I wasn't sure if he was talking to me or to his work in progress. "Hazel,"
I said.

"Oh, right." He laughed and picked up the story where he'd left off.

His step also had grown increasingly unsteady, so much so that I
began to walk behind him in case he fell. Heading back to the studio from
Barcia's, I surrendered the sidewalk and kept to the grass, my arms out for
when it happened.

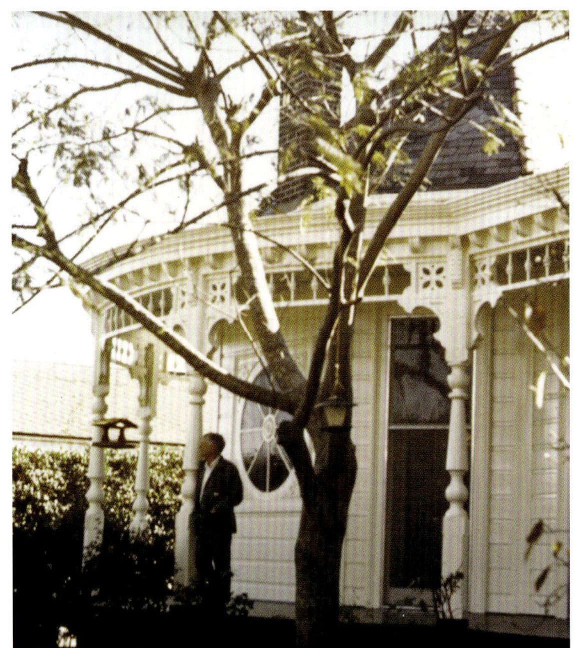

We reached the gate to the studio. He paused and looked down at the bottom of the slender bars. Algae grew on the black iron, a green so bright and pure it burned like Day-Glo. "Lovely," he said.

"What? The fence?"

"No, the green. Have you ever seen a lovelier green?"

Up ahead the cypress trees were shedding their needles. He turned and looked past a wall of vegetation at the large Victorian house that had been his home for nearly forty years [FIGURE 3.12]. No longer sure that such a demanding place made sense, John and Dottie sold it in 1994 and moved to a condo in the Carol, a tall modern building on St. Charles Avenue. The condo required little maintenance, and from the kitchen window they now could watch Carnival parades pass by, but for John having to give up the house remained a painful loss.

It was where he and Dottie raised their sons, Jonathan and David. He'd kept up the yard here, and he knew "every plant and blade of grass," he said, gazing past the fence. "I'm still not right with it. This is . . . Oh, God, what did we do?"

We stood without speaking. Then he pivoted and headed back to the studio, his head down. When we arrived at the gate, he spent another long moment admiring the algae. "Whatever you do, don't get old," he said, then moved inside.

HOW STRANGE, I THINK NOW, all these years later, but despite the many things we talked about I never asked him what he thought about my letter, the first one in which I asked to interview him. He had Dottie reply. "What was a good time for the two of you to get together?" she asked on the phone.

I remember changing the batteries in my recorder. I remember ironing my favorite shirt. Dottie answered the door. Then John came walking toward me from down the hall. "Hello, young man," he said and brought his eyes up to mine. "I understand you have some questions for me."

Sometimes it all feels like a dream, and I wonder if it really happened—if John really happened. He felt the same way about seeing *Guernica*. He wondered if he imagined it. But there he was at the museum that day, opening the door, stepping toward the painting at the foot of the stairs.

HE WOULD OFTEN CALL ME from the retirement home in Milwaukee where he and Dottie were living. It offered the best of care, and Sheboygan was close by, and Dottie's younger sister, Judy, lived in Highland Park, Illinois, a little more than an hour away. John was ninety-two years old. When I asked how he was doing, he would say, "Not good. I'm falling apart. Nothing works anymore."

He hadn't been able to paint but he had been drawing. "I can't wait to see the new work," I told him.

"I have to ask you this," he said. "Do you think you could come get me? And take me home? I can't take it anymore."

"John . . . ? Home to New Orleans? I don't think so, John. They wouldn't let me. I mean . . . no, John, forgive me."

"Do you remember what we talked about?"

I knew he meant the studio and dying in front of his easel. "I do, but John . . . John, I can't."

"Just come," he said.

I remember little of the rest—the end, whenever it came, the time on the clock, the date on the calendar. It was like sleeping through a storm and waking up in the morning to find the old oak down in the yard.

David gave me a key to the studio, and on occasion I return to show the art to collectors. I also go there when I need to feel John again, and the paintings on the walls at home aren't enough.

"She was old, so old to me," he said. "There was an event at the Arts and Crafts Club, I forget what exactly, but it called for formal evening attire. Alberta showed up in a nightgown. A nightgown instead of an evening gown. I can laugh now because I'm old and tired myself, but I didn't then. And I didn't say anything. No, we cared too much for her happiness for that."

You can see the big front room where he painted. It's exactly as it used to be, the old metal desk with his brushes and tools and little mounds of paint, light from the windows falling across the drips on the floor [FIGURE 3.13]. You can put the stereo on and listen to the music he liked. You can even pull a painting from the racks and run your fingertips over its surface. But you can't have John back, and that's why I'm never able to stay long. □

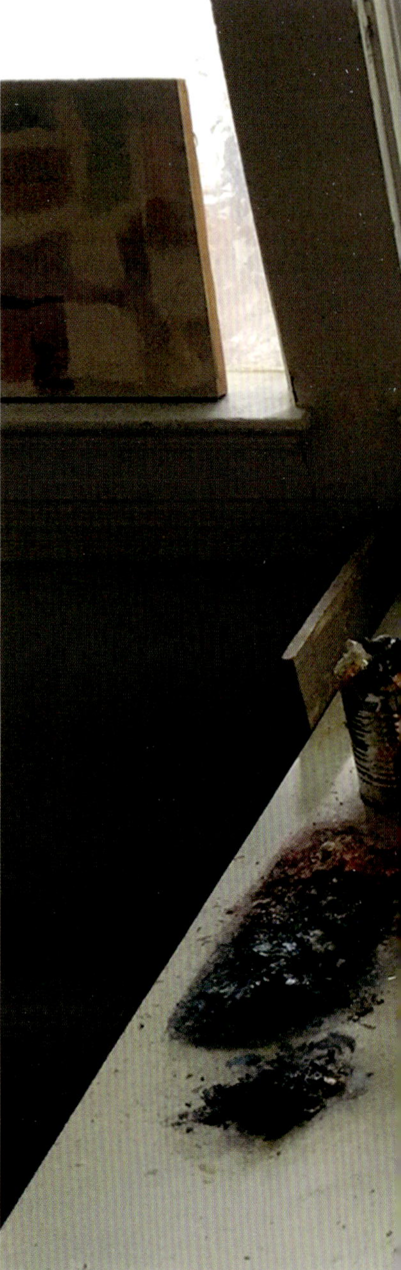

[FIGURE 3.13]
Laurel Street studio, 2019, photograph by John Ed Bradley, *courtesy of John Ed Bradley*

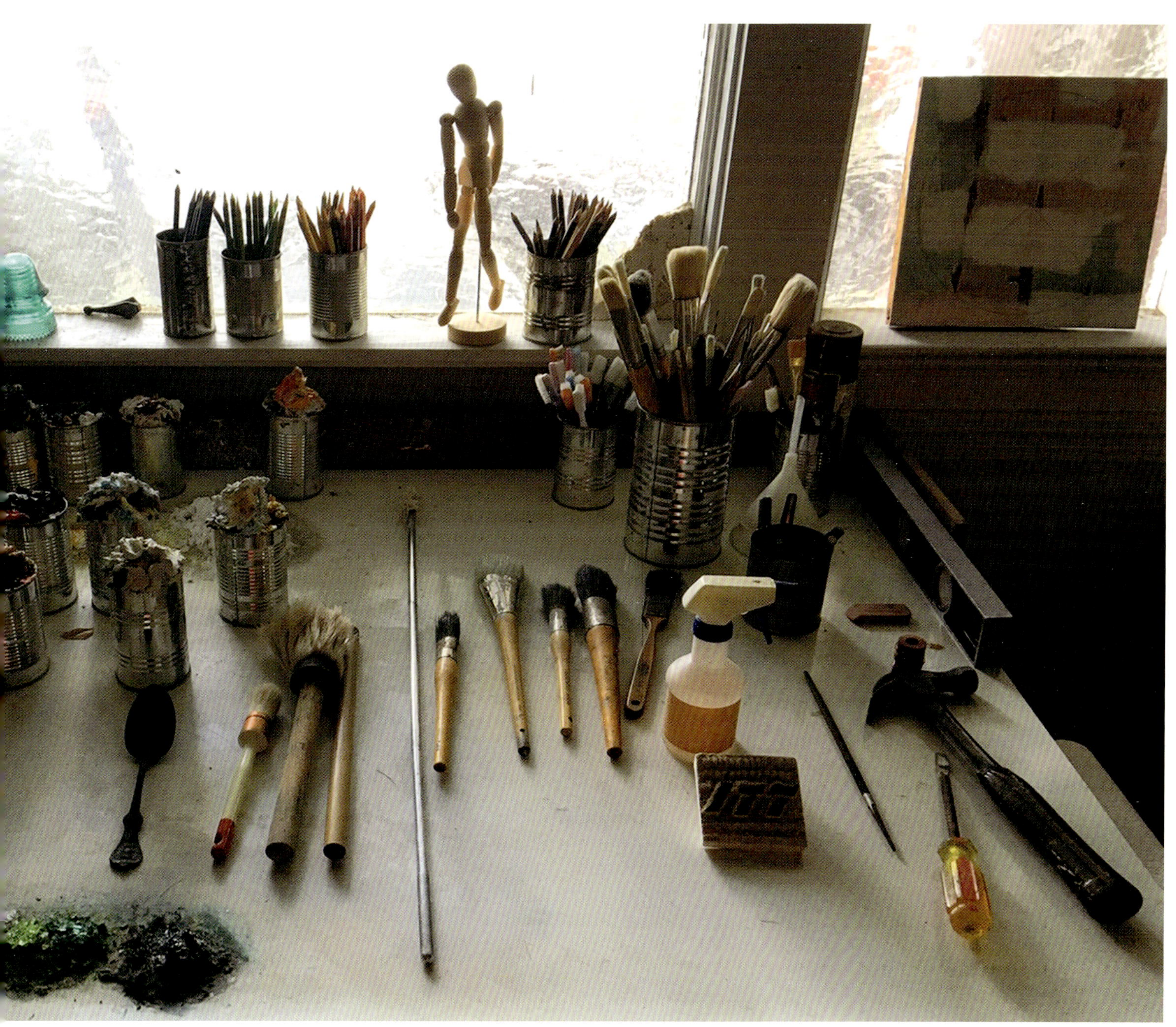

PLATES

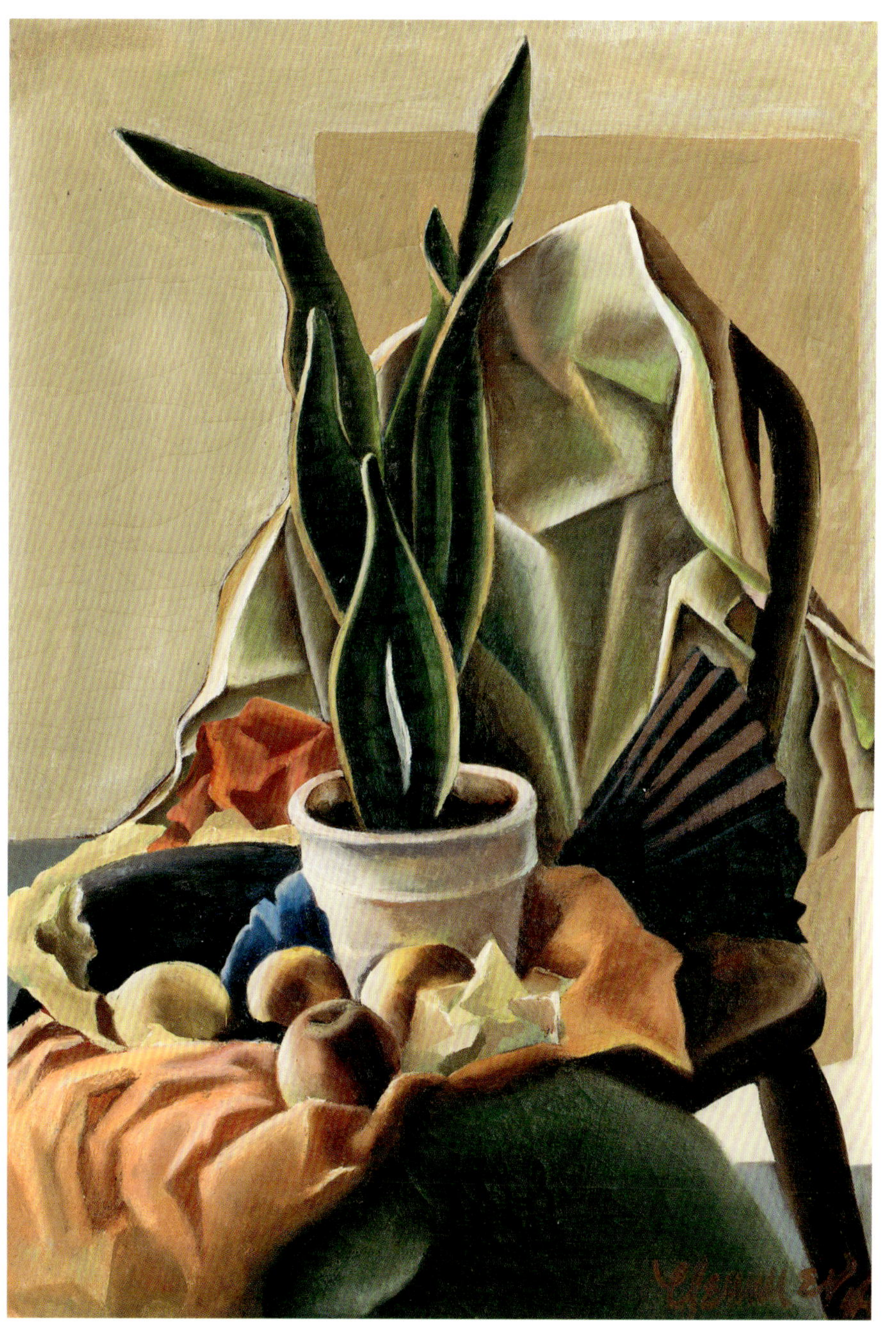

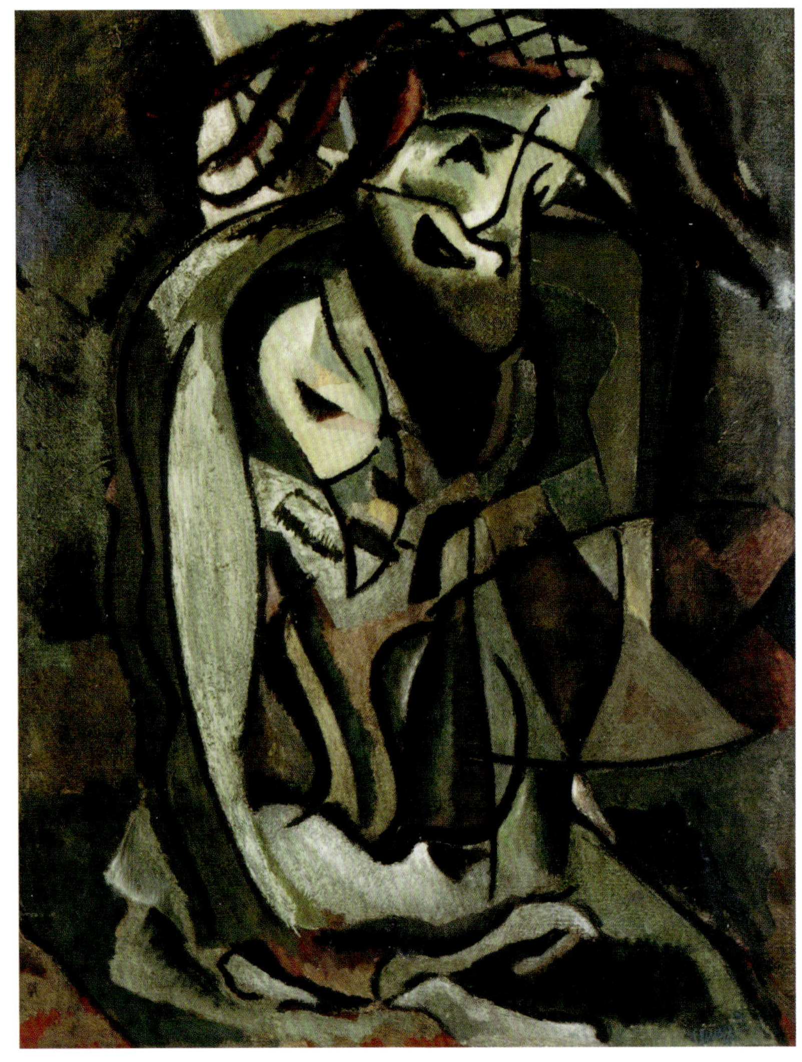

How Men Their Brothers Maim, 1942, oil on canvas, 35 × 26 in.,
courtesy of Edwin and Donna Lupberger

94

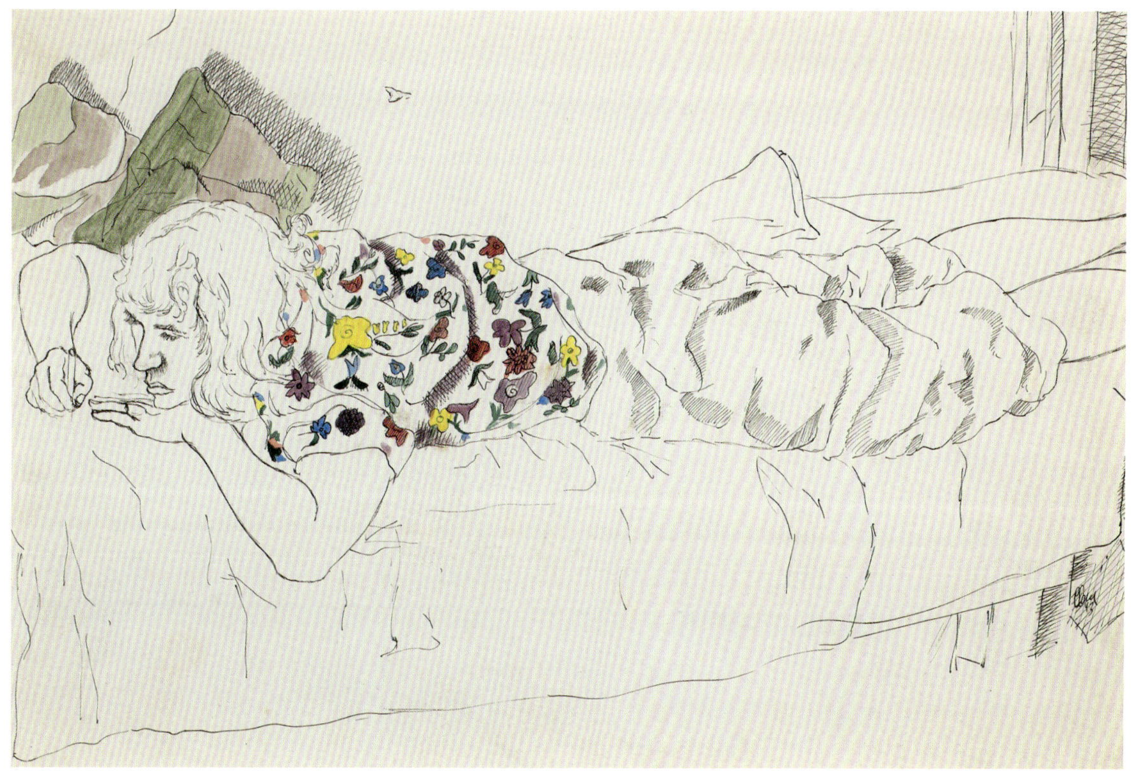

[PLATE 3]
Writing (Marjorie in Floral Shirt), 1943, pencil on paper, 10 × 14 in.,
courtesy of David Clemmer, Santa Fe, NM

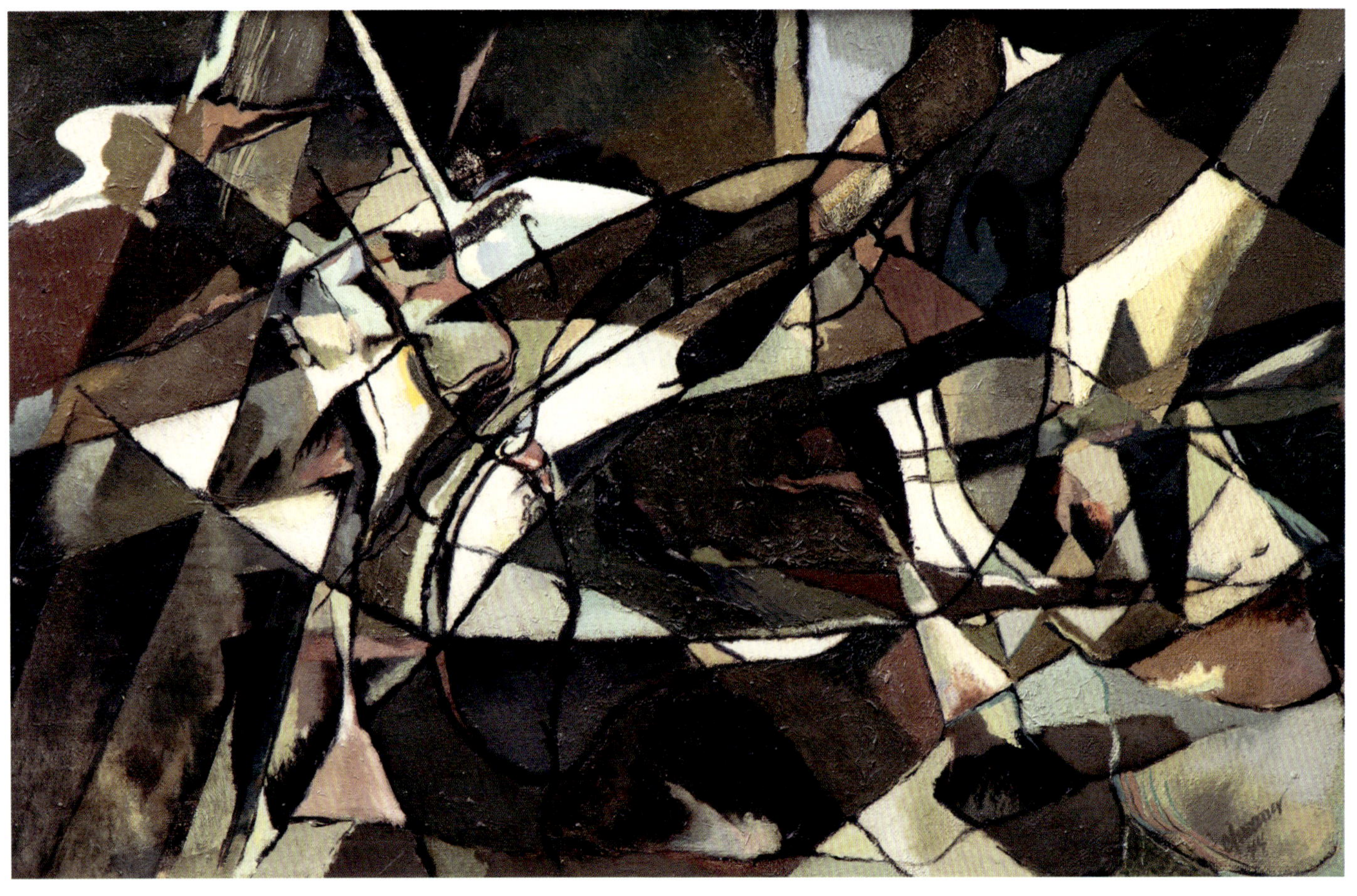

[PLATE 4]
See Ungeheuer (Sea Monster), 1944, oil on panel, 24 × 36 in., *courtesy of Jacqueline Bishop and Herbert Halpern*

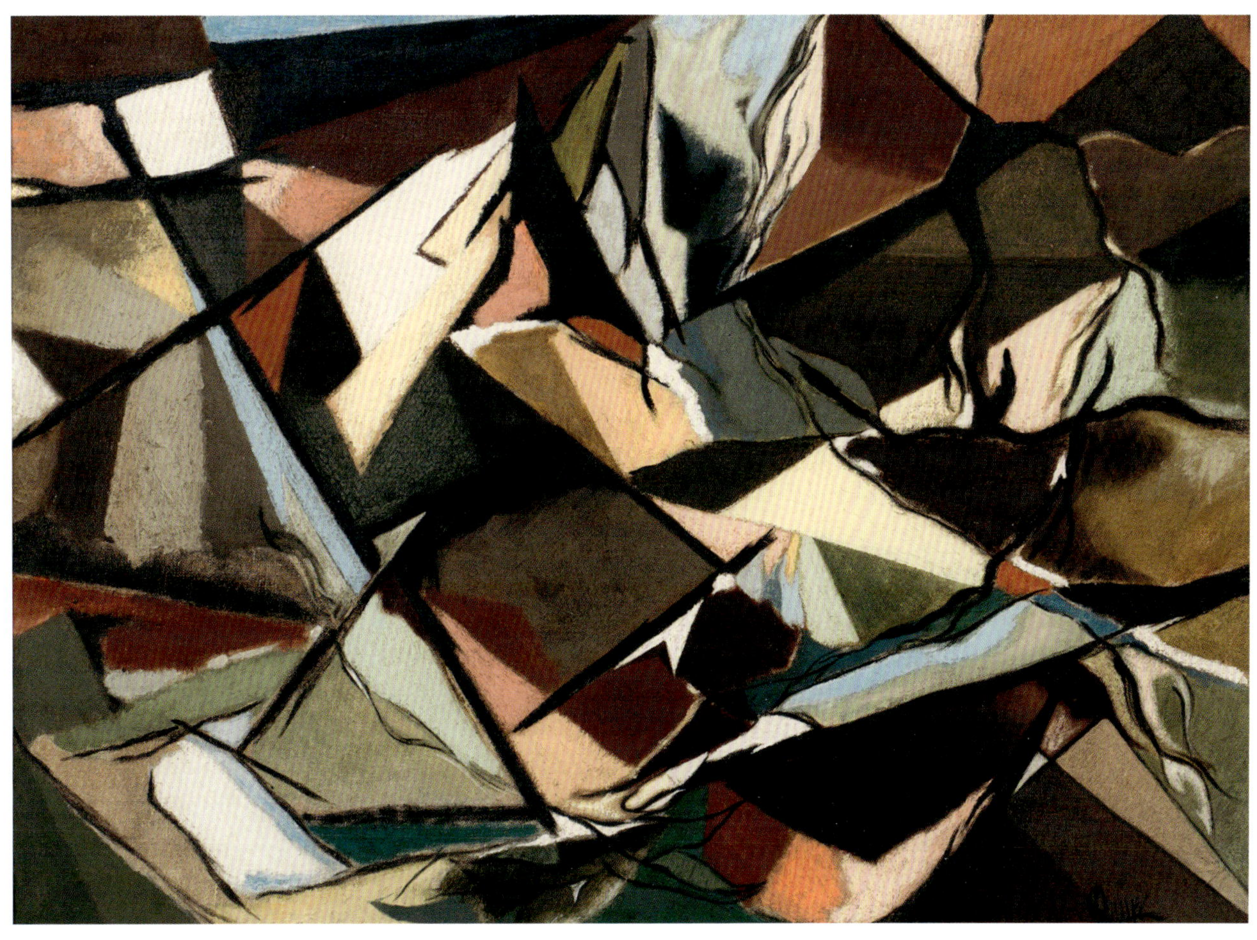

[PLATE 5]

Coup d'Oeil, between 1945 and 1949, oil on canvas, 18 × 24 in.,
courtesy of Don Fuson

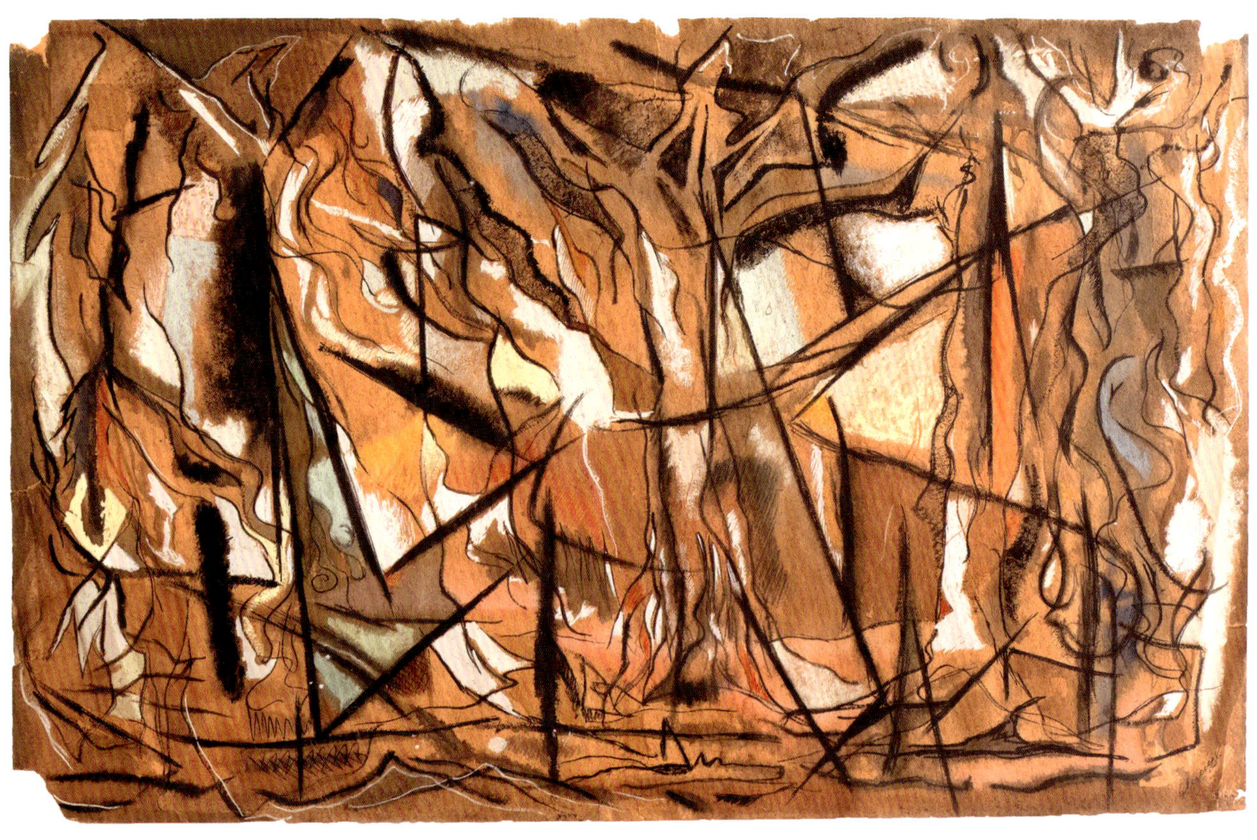

Swamp Fire, 1947, watercolor and gouache on paper, 18 × 24 in.,
collection of Ogden Museum of Southern Art, gift of Allison Kendrick

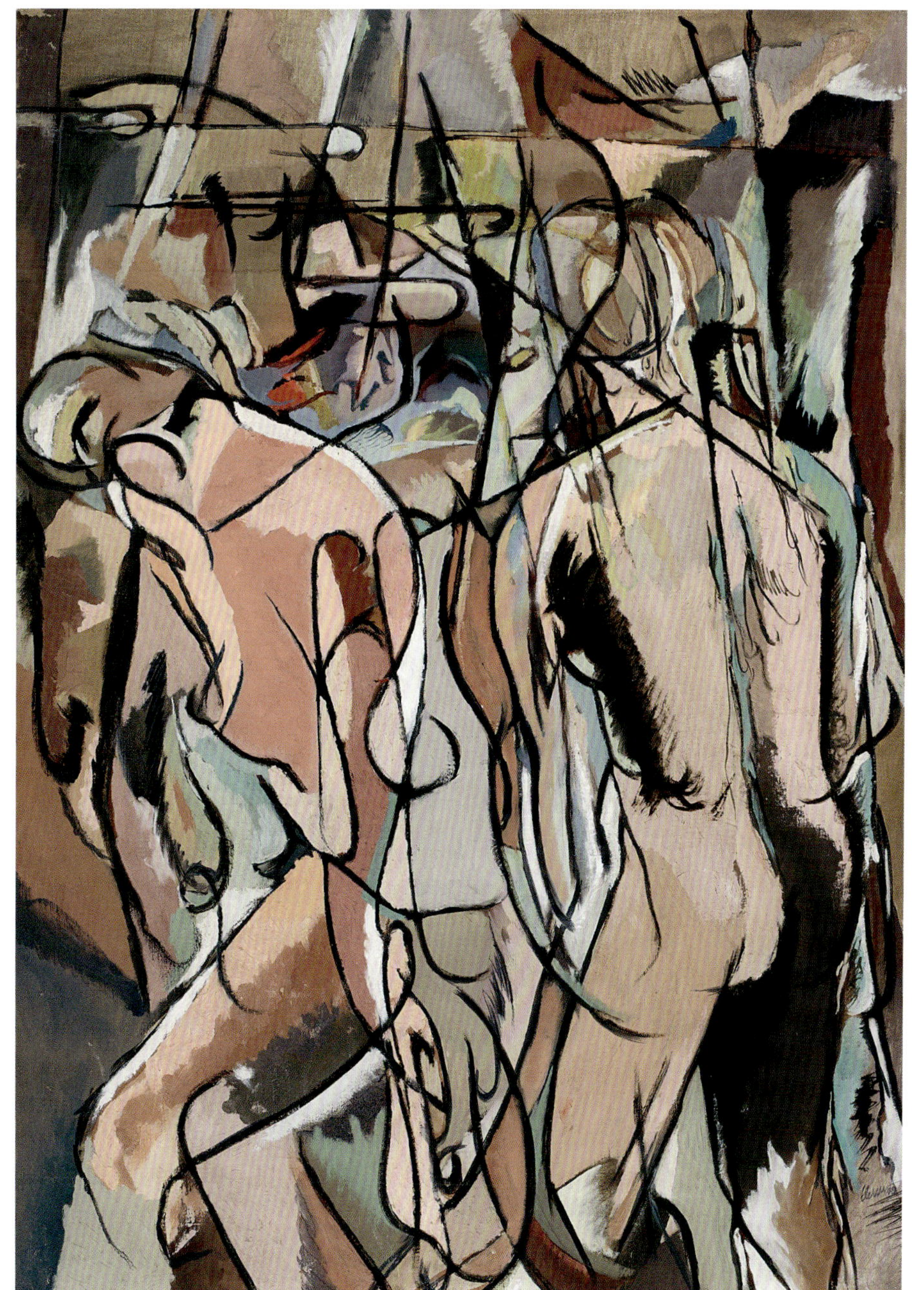

[PLATE 7]
Two Nudes in a Landscape, 1949, oil on
canvas, 50 × 34 in., *courtesy of Don Fuson*

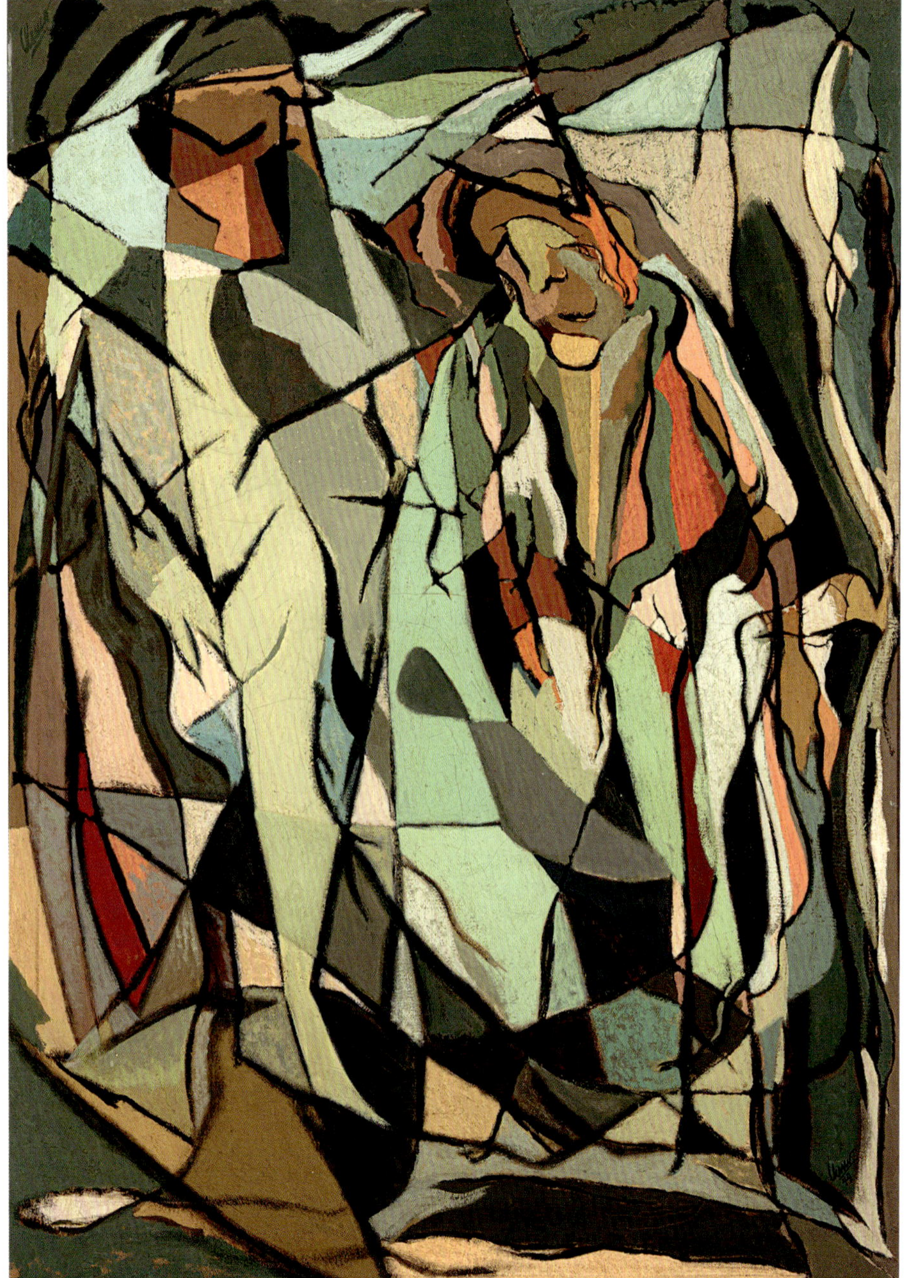

[PLATE 8]

Two Figures—Macbeth, 1949, oil on canvas,
59 ¾ × 40 ¾ in., *New Orleans Museum of
Art, gift of David J. Clemmer, 97.822*

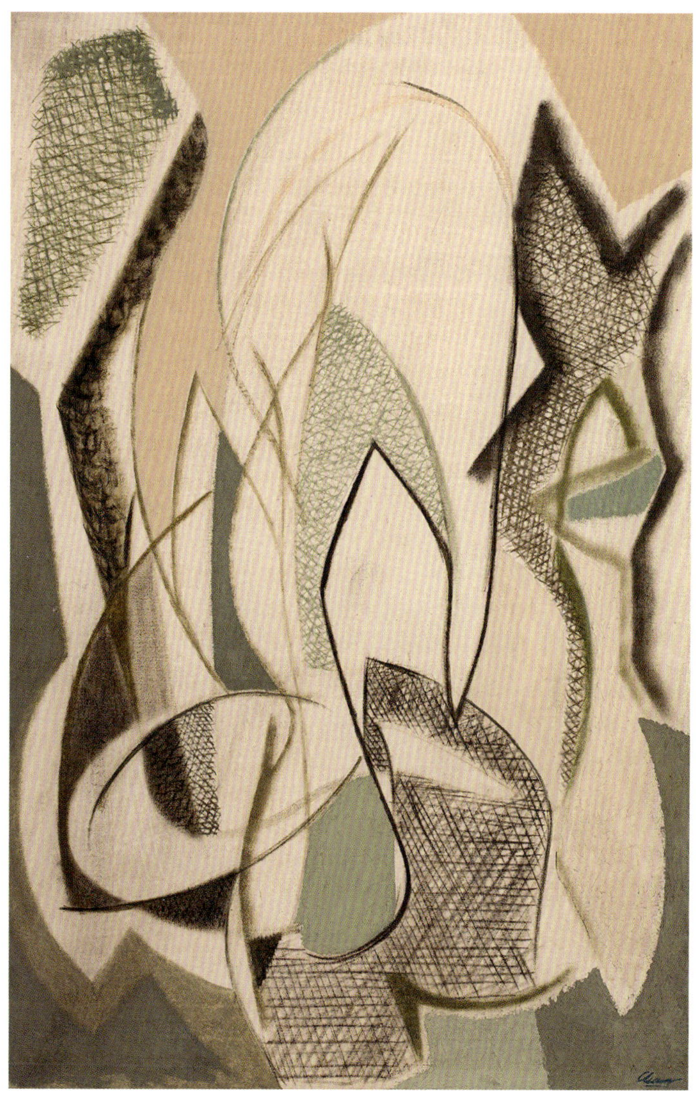

[PLATE 9]
Abstraction, ca. 1949, oil on canvas,
35 × 22 in., *The Historic New Orleans
Collection*, 1988.105

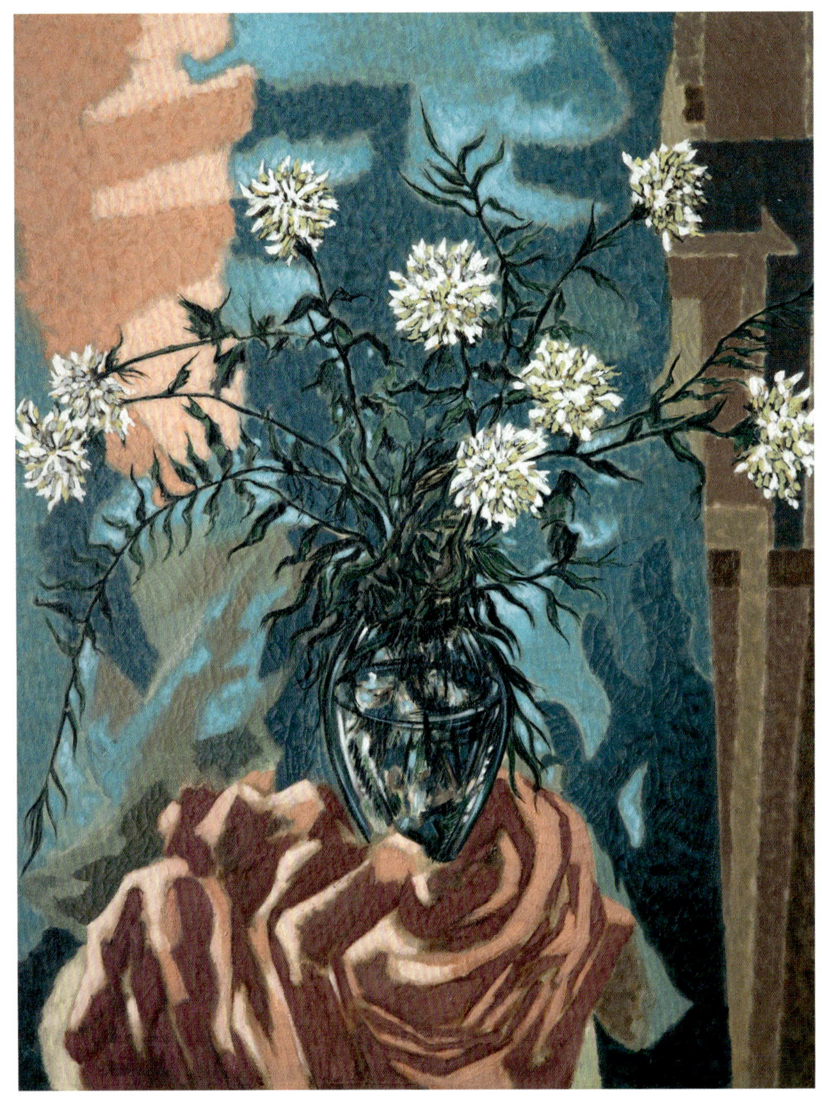

[PLATE 10]

Floral II, 1949, oil on canvas, 35 × 26 in., *courtesy of Mathile and Steven Abramson*

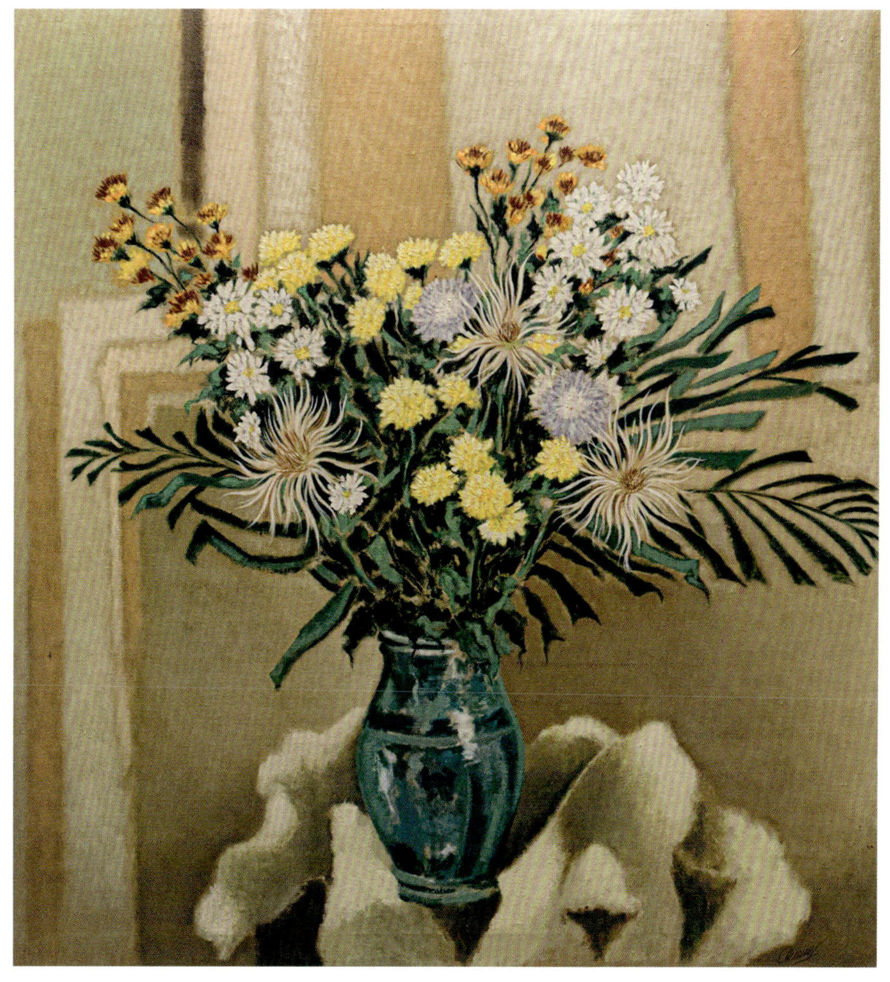

Blue Vase, 1955, oil on canvas, 42 × 37 in. (framed), *New Orleans Museum of Art, gift of Judith and Robert Stein, 96.239*

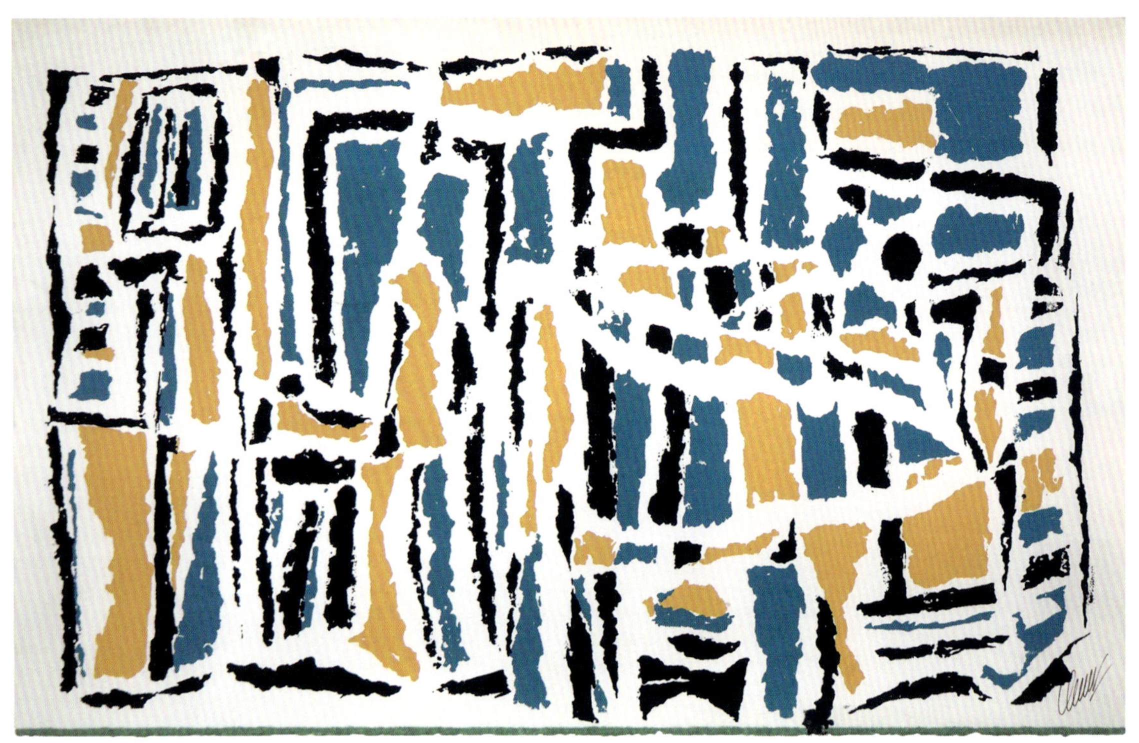

[PLATE 12]

Maze, late 1950s, silkscreen print on deckled paper, 13 × 20 in.,
courtesy of 3618 Studio, LLC, New Orleans, LA

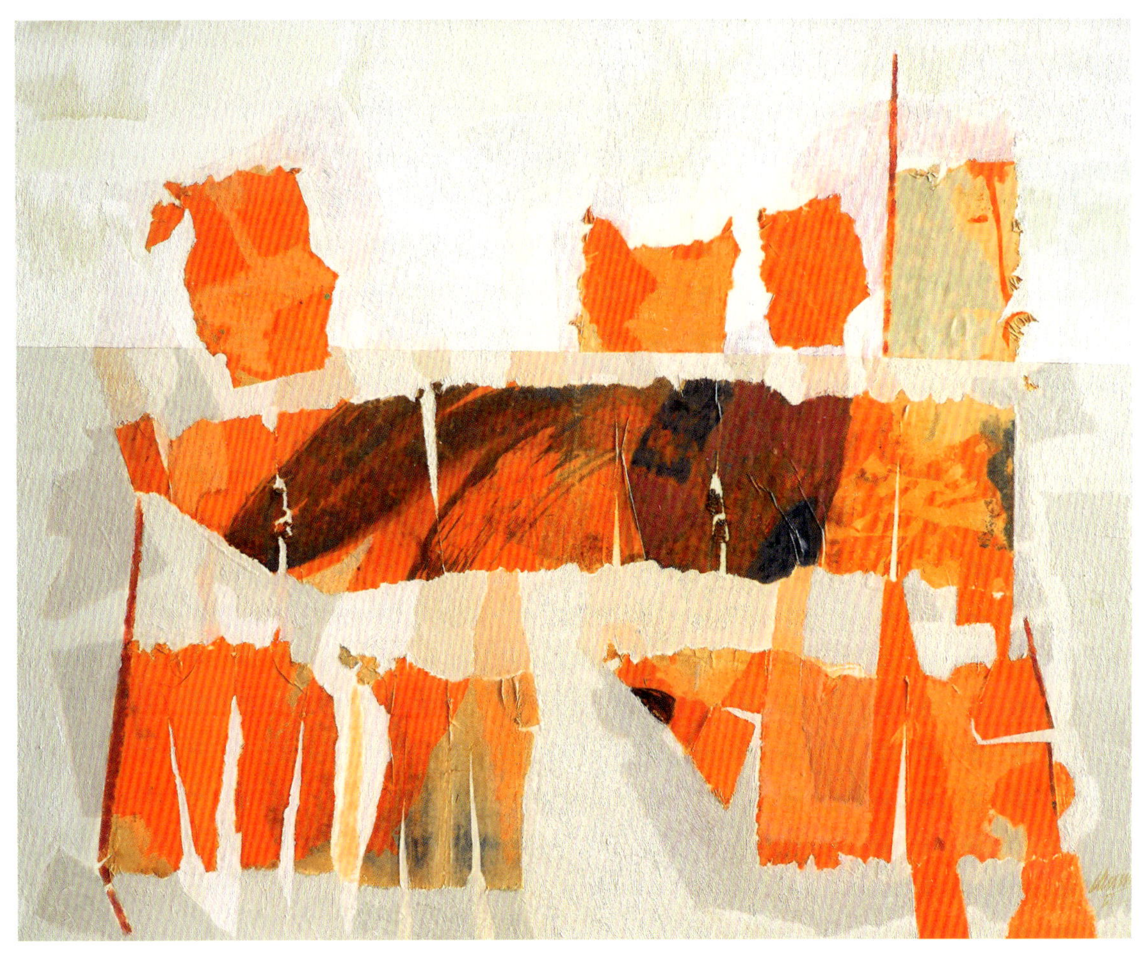

Collage I—Red, Orange, 1962, oil and collage on panel, 20 × 24 in.,
courtesy of David Clemmer, Santa Fe, NM

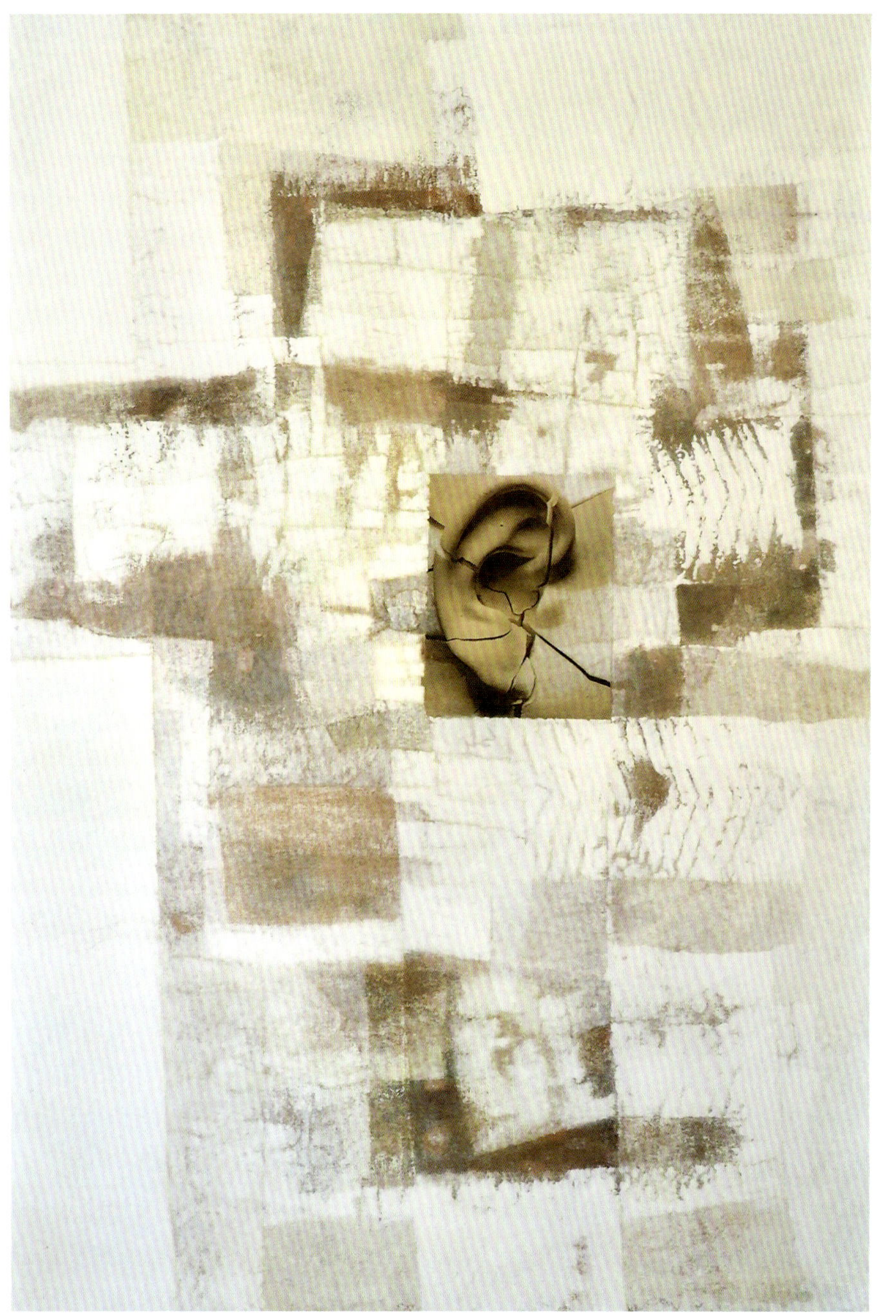

[PLATE 14]
Almedia, 1962, oil and collage on panel,
72 × 48 in., *courtesy of David Clemmer,
Santa Fe, NM*

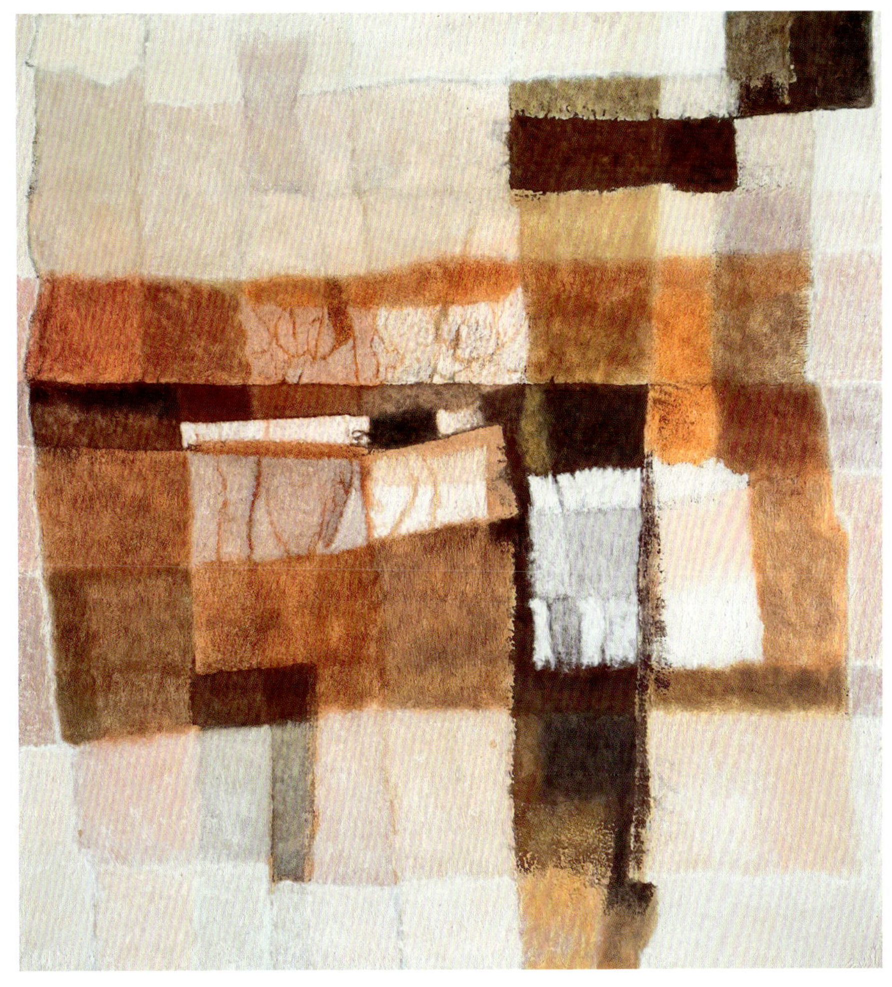

Siloé, 1964, oil on panel, 47 ⅝ × 42 in., *courtesy of David Clemmer, Santa Fe, NM*

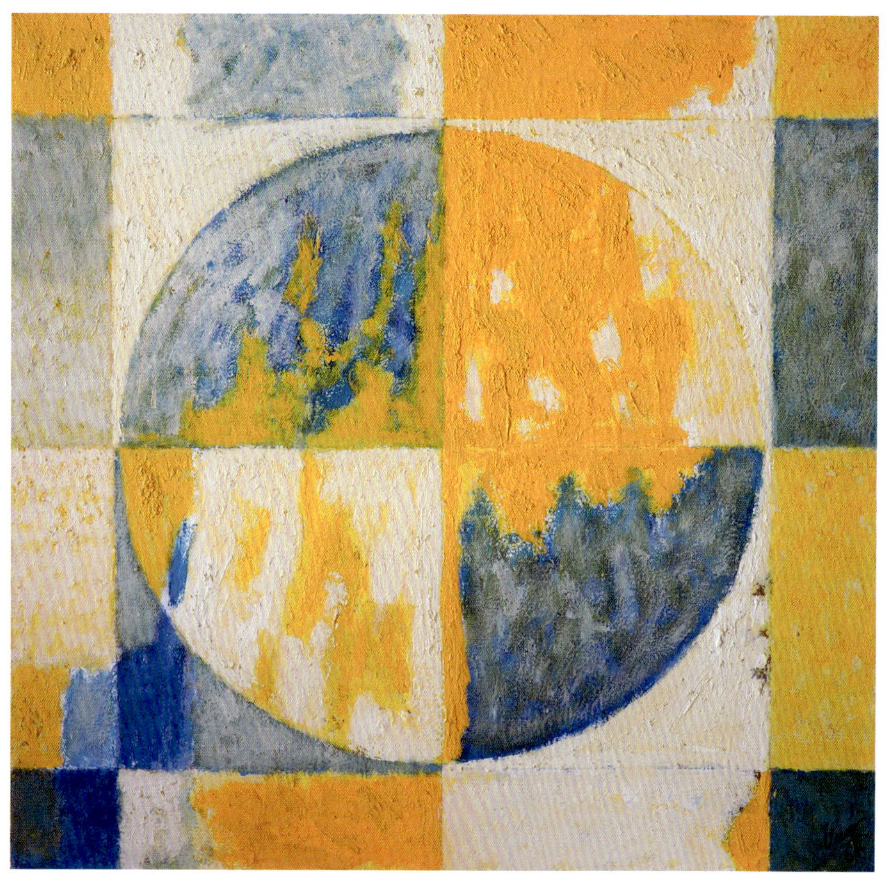

Summery—Season II, 1964, oil on panel, 20 × 20 in., *courtesy of David Clemmer, Santa Fe, NM*

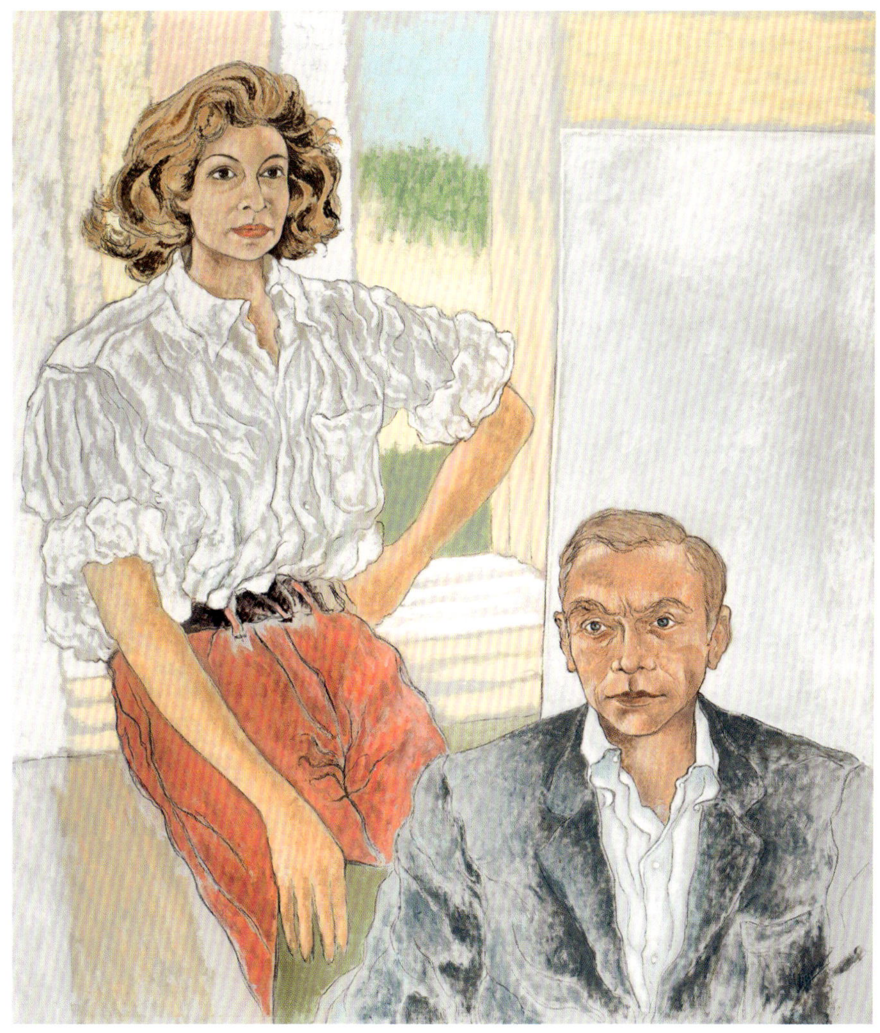

[PLATE 17]
Portrait of Lin Emery and Shirley Braselman, 1967–1968, oil on
canvas, 60 × 50 in., *courtesy of Brooks Emery Braselman*

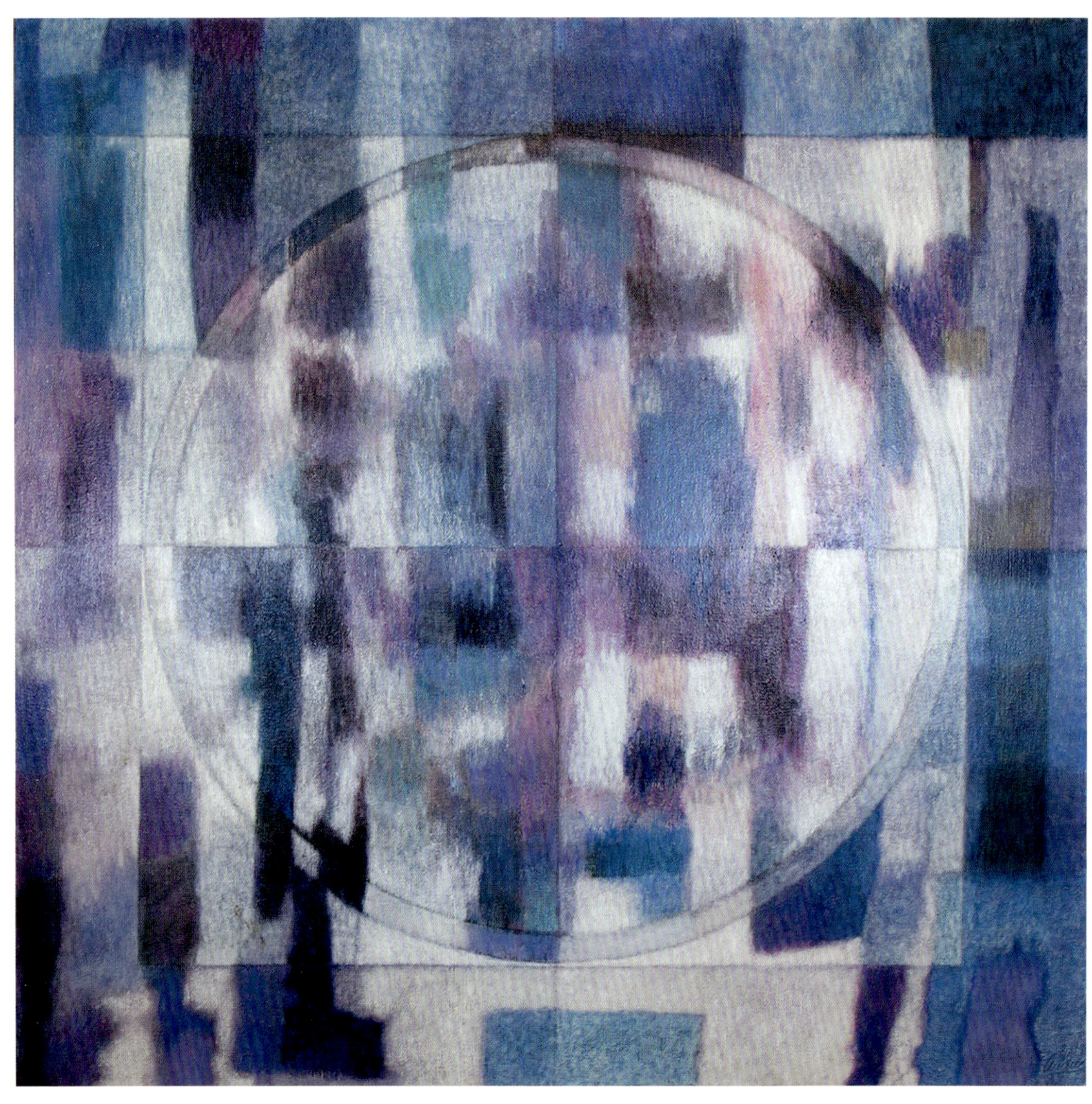

[PLATE 18]

Topographia II—Atitlan, 1969, oil and acrylic polymer on linen,
48 × 48 in., *collection of Newcomb Art Museum of Tulane University*

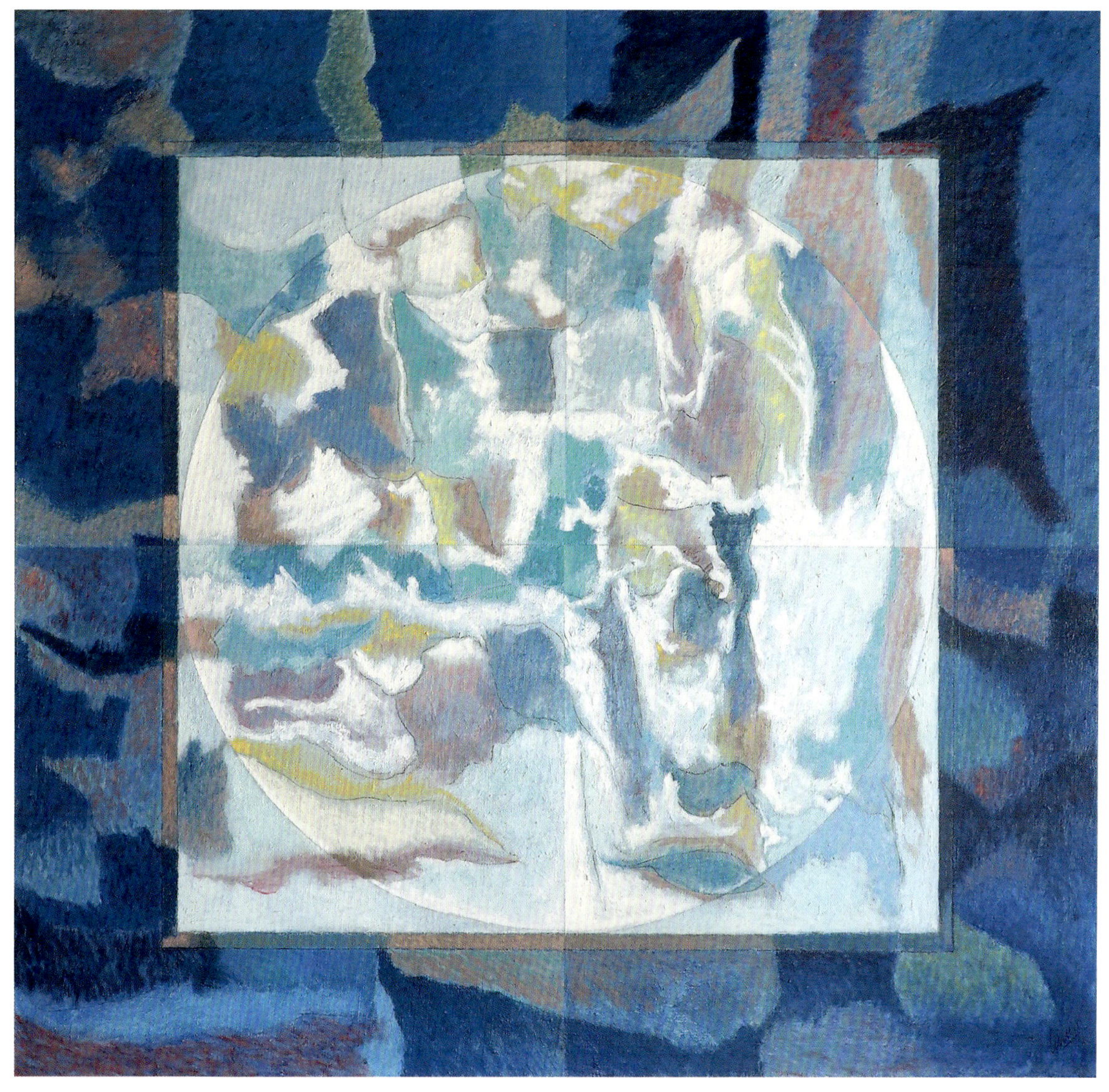

Topographia VI—Luna, 1969, polymer and oil on canvas, 48 × 48 in.,
courtesy of David Clemmer, Santa Fe, NM

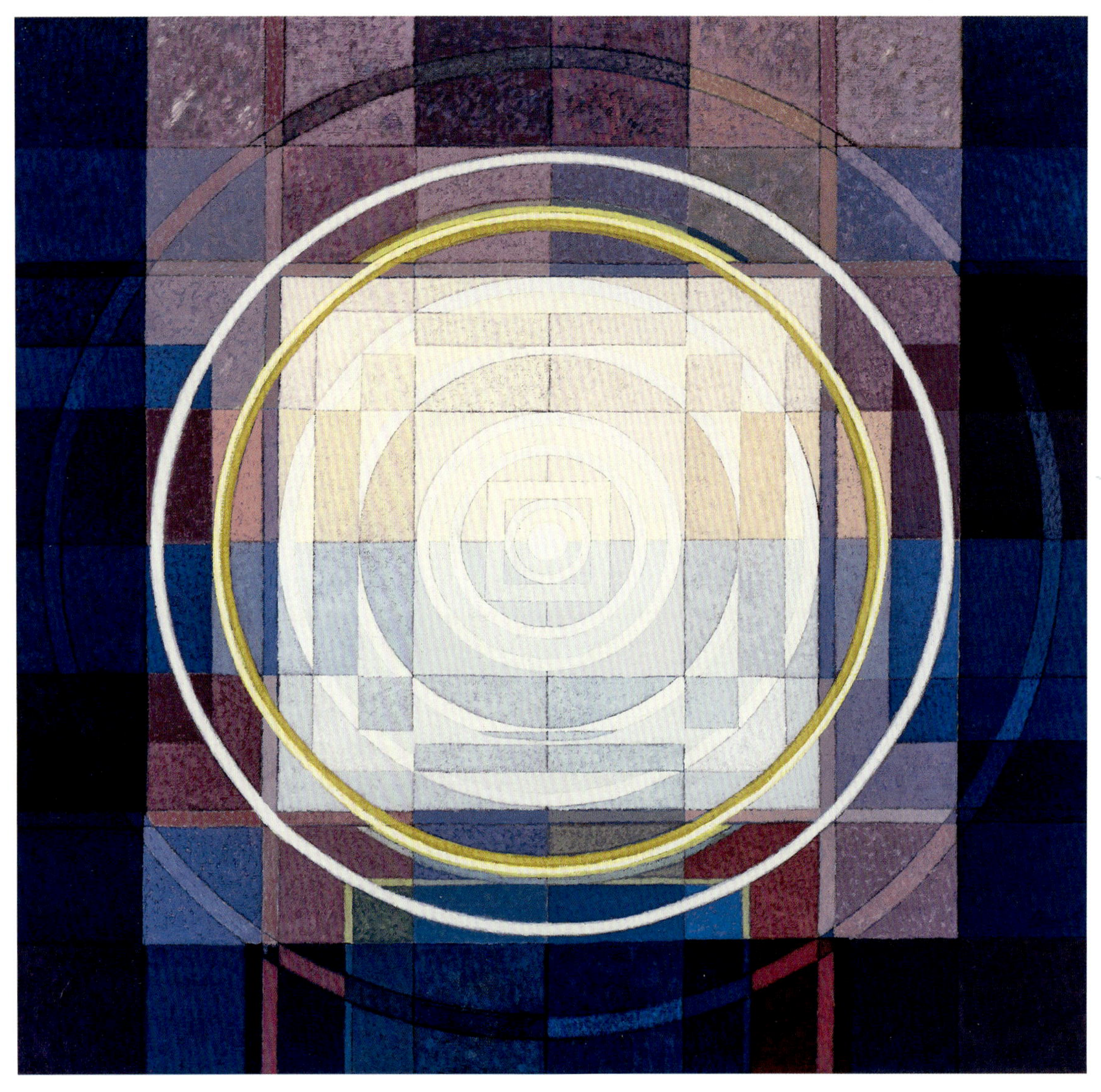

[PLATE 20]
Topographia IV—Cosmas II, 1970, oil on canvas, 48 × 48 in.,
New Orleans Museum of Art, gift of Jonathan C. Clemmer, 97.823

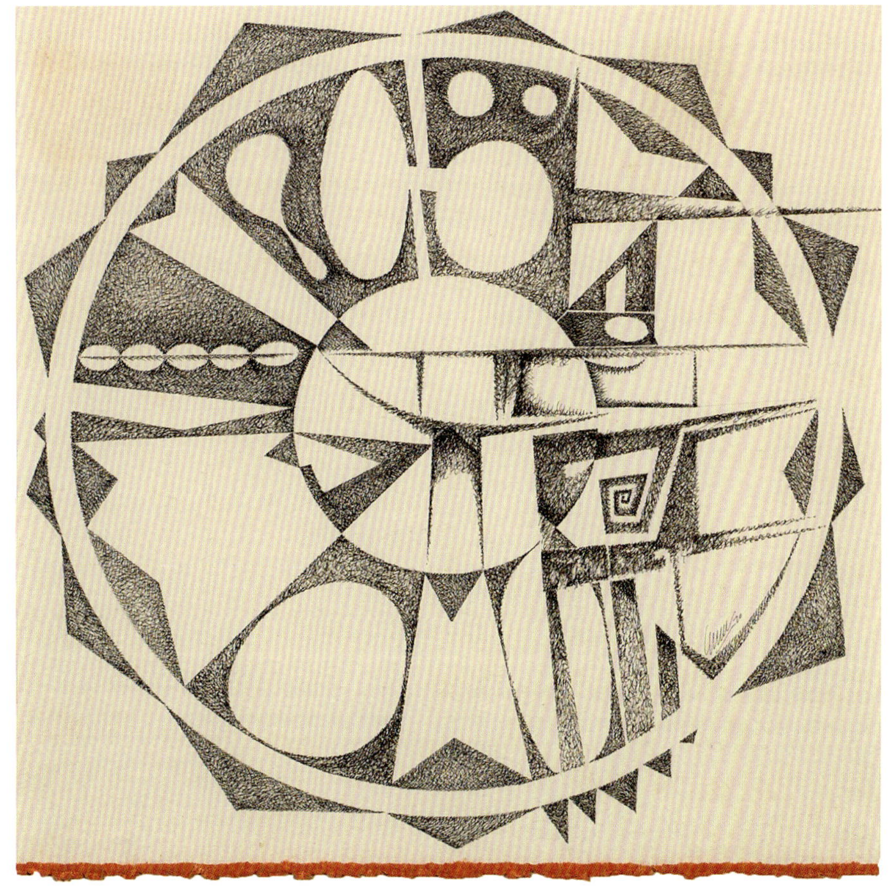

[PLATE 21]
Drawing—Shield, 1970, ink on deckled Strathmore paper, 10 × 10 in.,
courtesy of David Clemmer, Santa Fe, NM

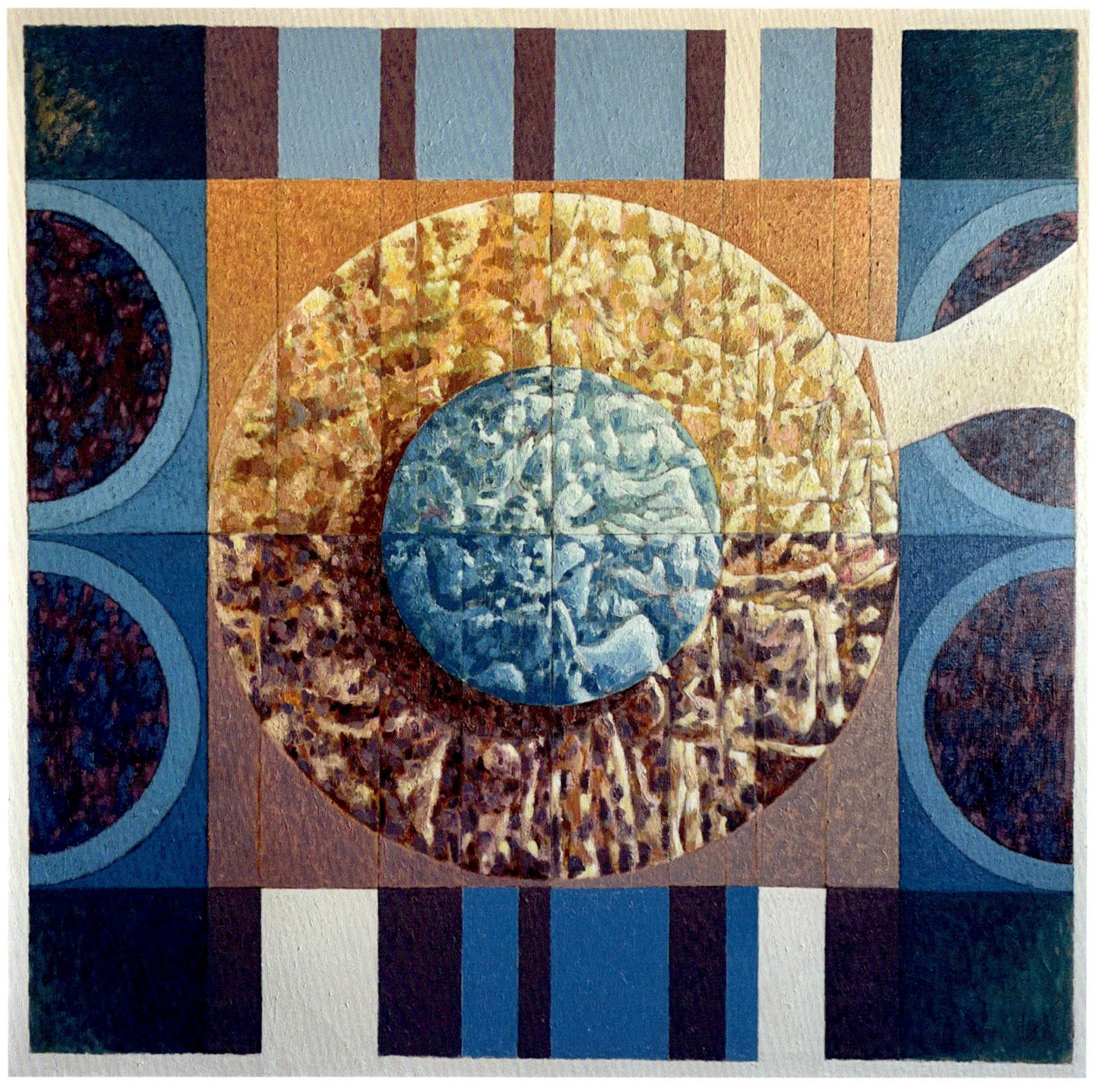

[PLATE 22]

Topographia VIII—Azteca, 1970–1971, acrylic polymer and oil on canvas, 48 × 48 in., *courtesy of 3618 Studio, LLC, New Orleans, LA*

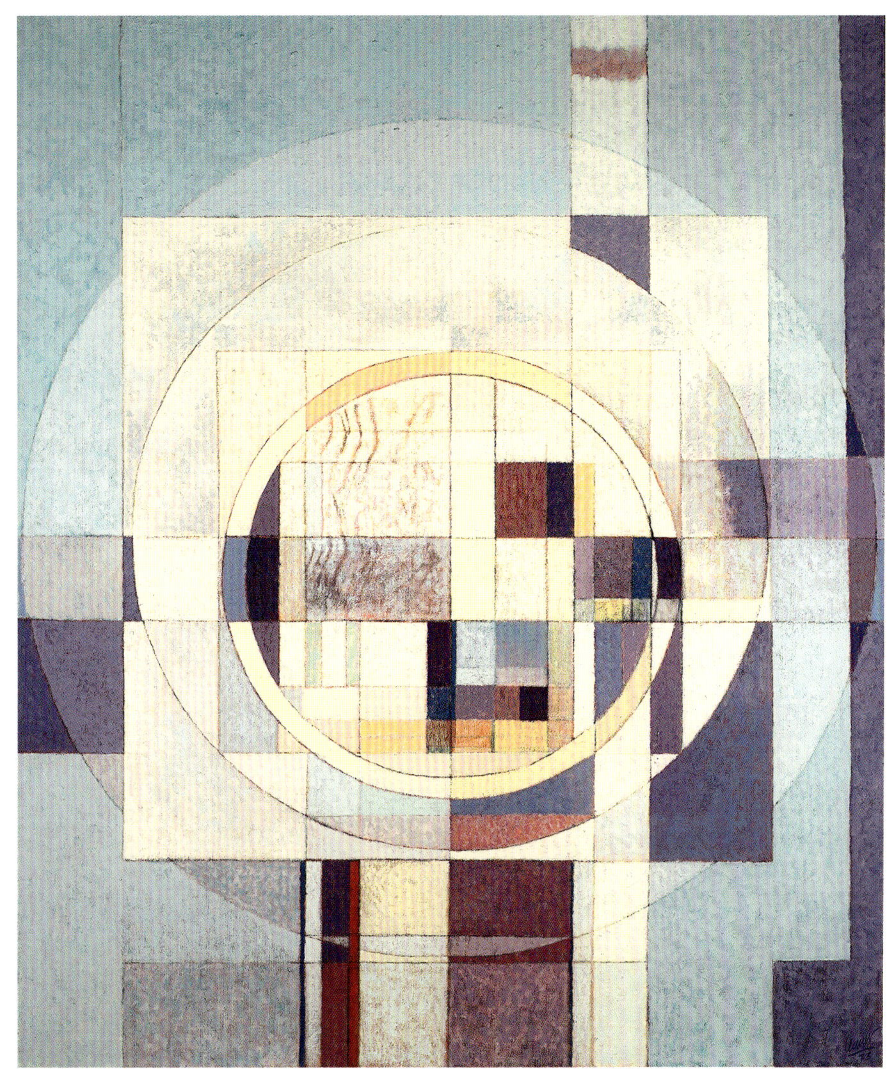

Topographia V—Capricorn, 1973, oil on canvas, 60 × 48 in., *courtesy of Jonathan Clemmer and Michael Barnes, Royal Oak, MI*

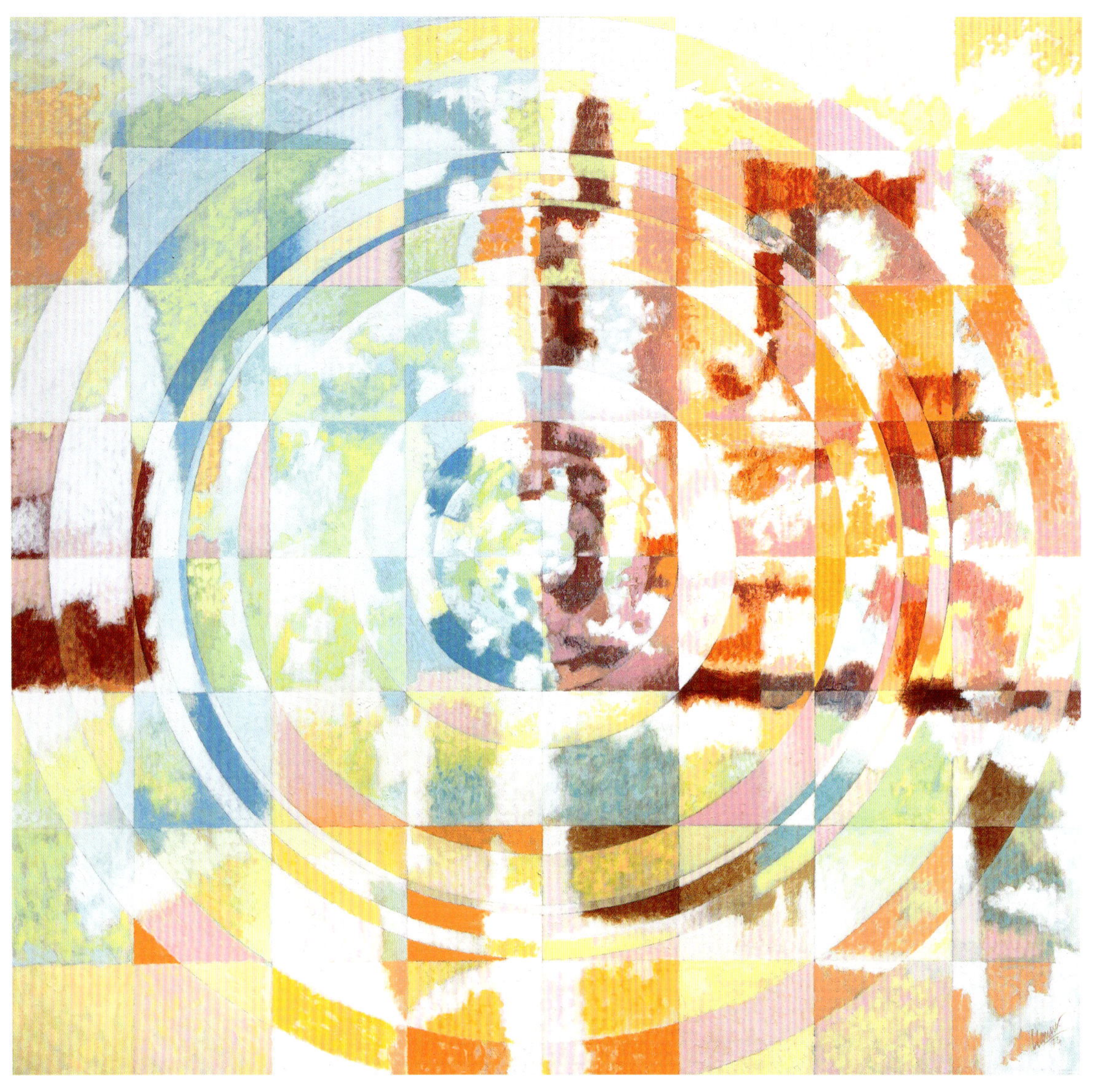

Circles—Homage to JMWT [James Mallord William Turner], 1973, oil
on Masonite, 48 × 48 in., *courtesy of Kimberly and John Ed Bradley*

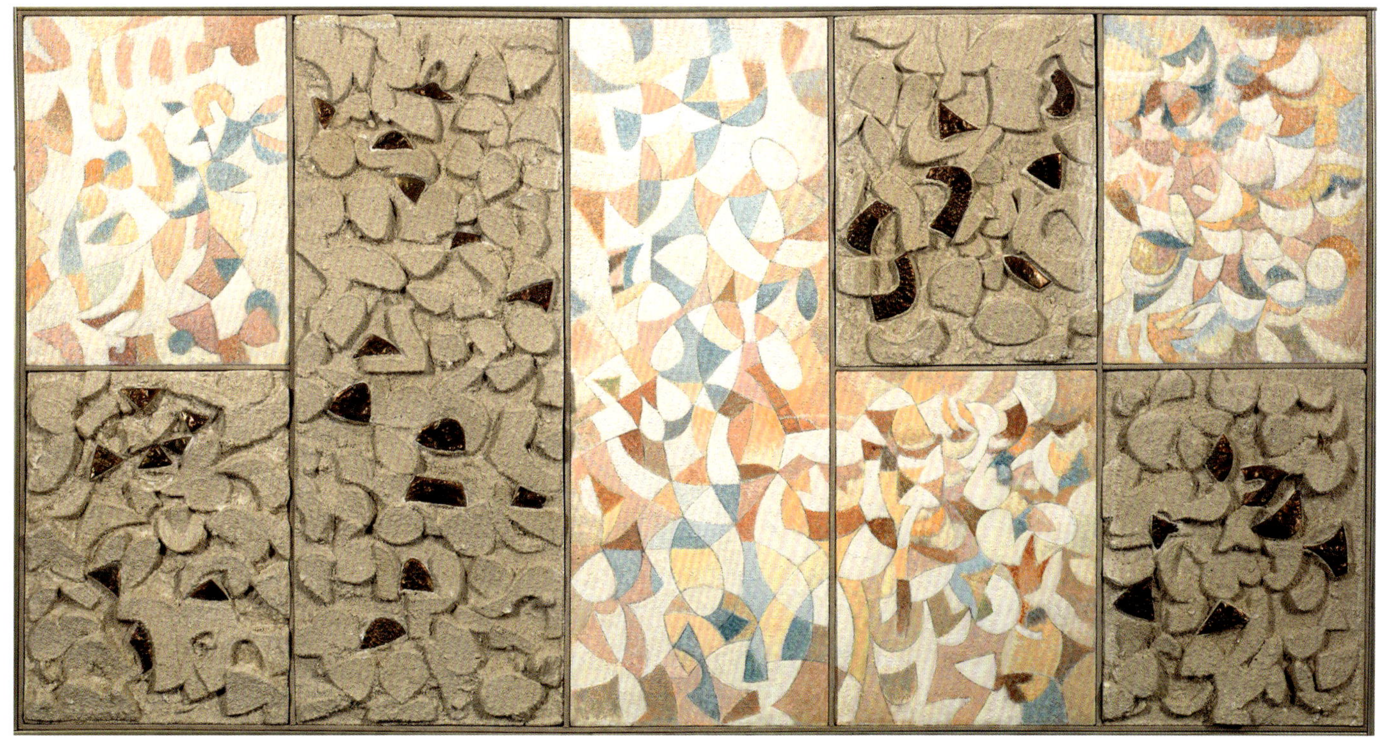

Painting—Sandcasting (Ten-Piece), 1975, oil on canvas with bronze and Portland cement, 30 ¼ × 55 ¾ in., *The Historic New Orleans Collection*, 2020.0015.1.6

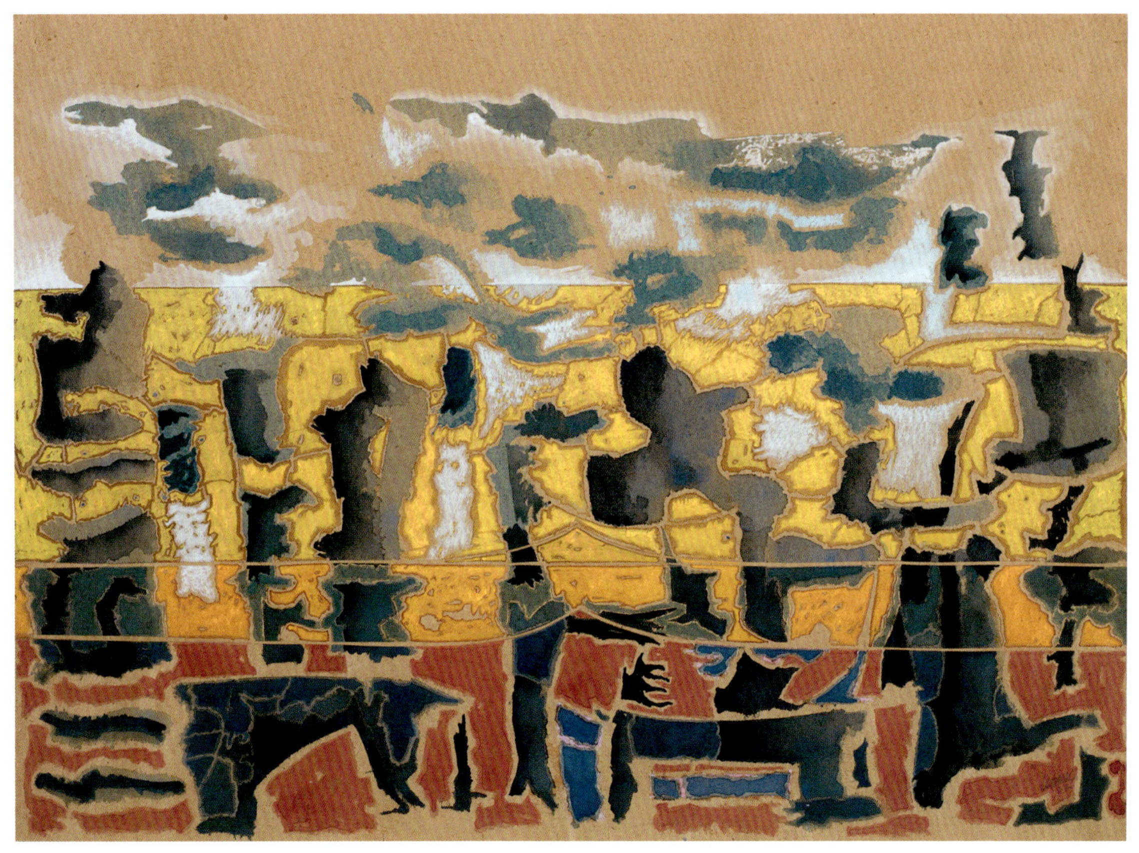

Landscape, 1977, watercolor, gouache, and collage on oatmeal paper,
18 × 24 in., *courtesy of David Clemmer, Santa Fe, NM*

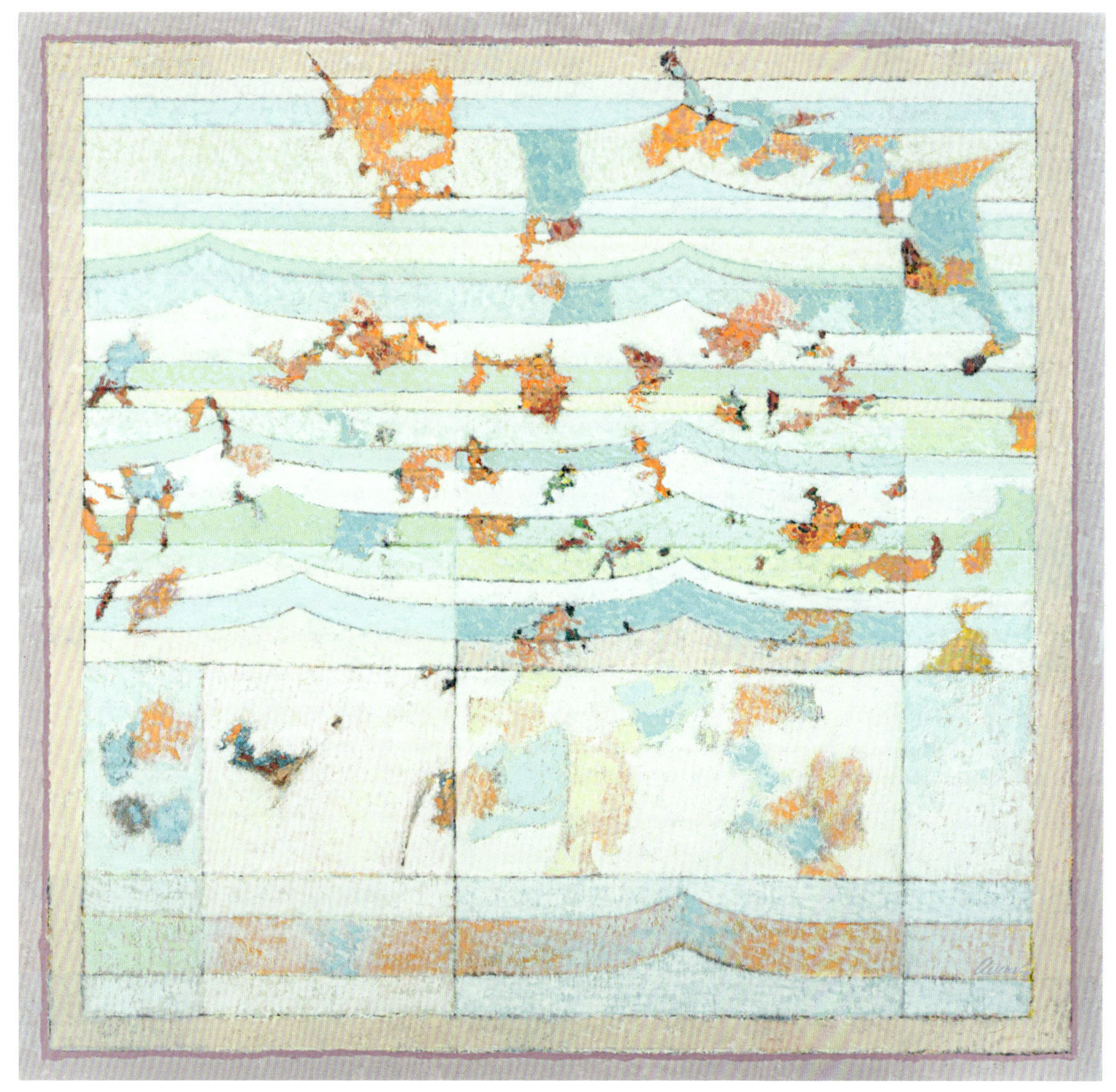

[PLATE 27]
Portal—Itea, 1978, oil on canvas, 30 × 30 in., *New Orleans Museum of Art, The Muriel Bultman Francis Collection, 86.171*

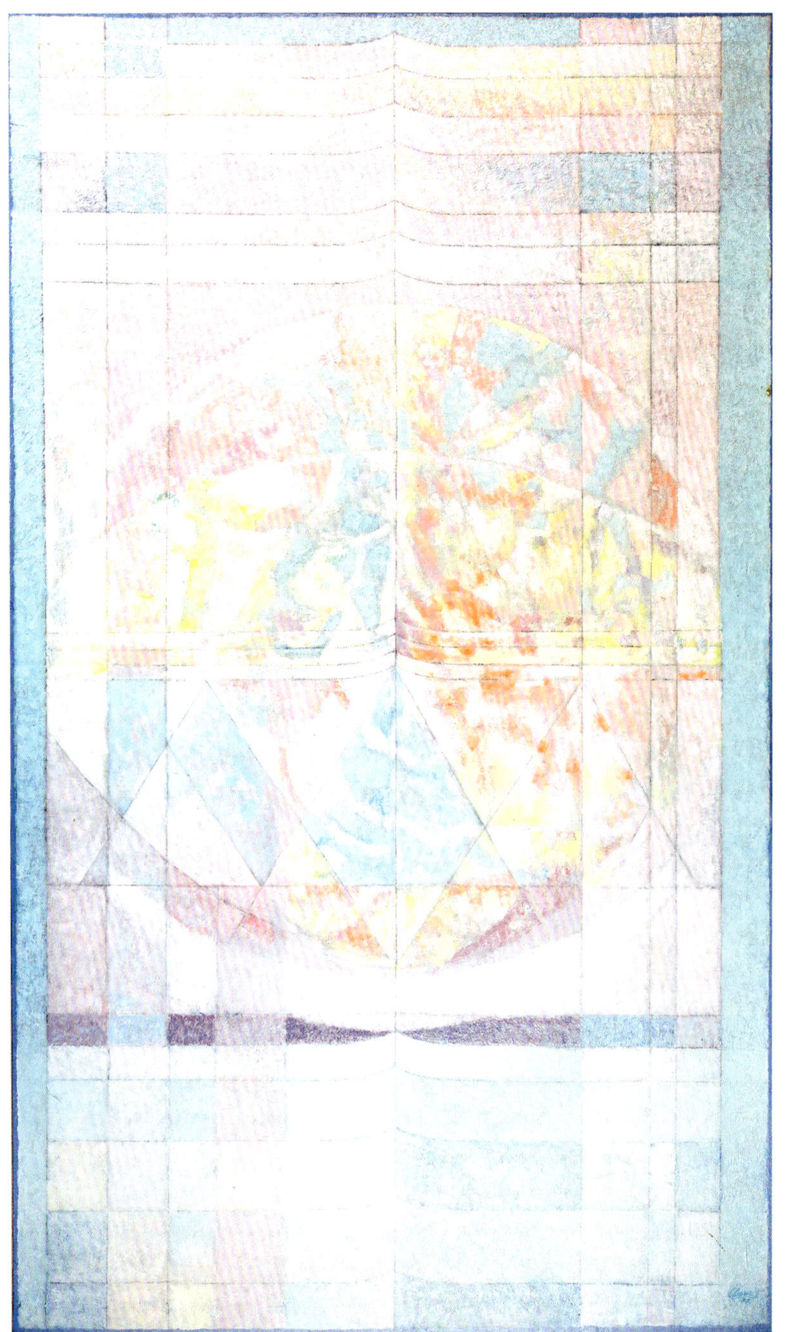

[PLATE 28]

Portal II, 1978, oil crayon on canvas, 76 × 44 in.,
courtesy of Martha and Rick Barnett

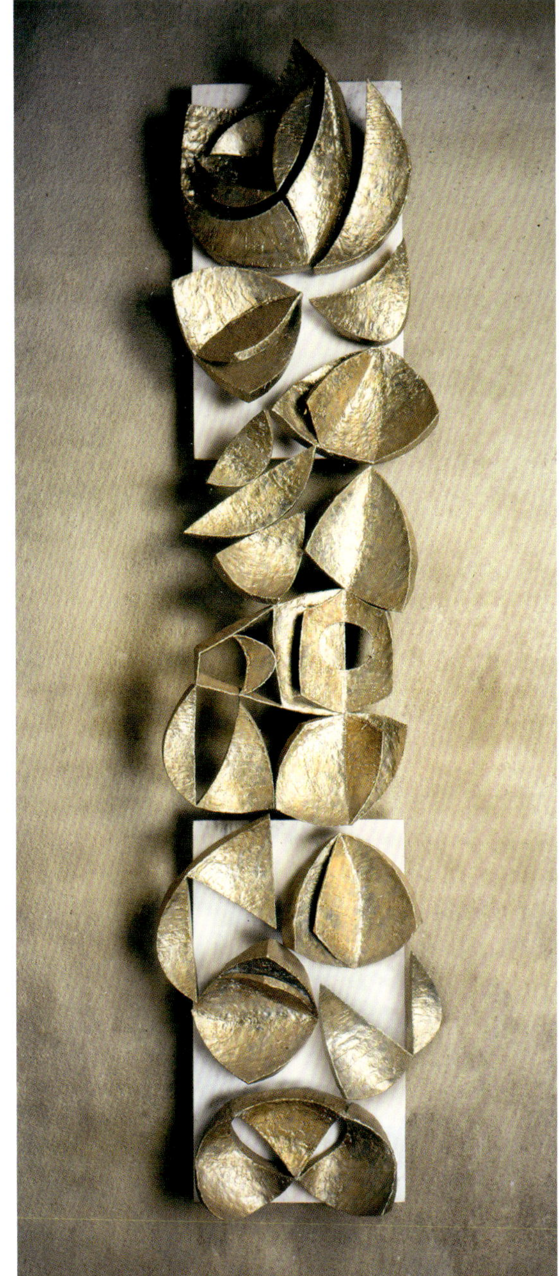

[PLATE 29]
Sculpture, 1986, bronze and nickel silver
on Monel, 120 × 30 × 15 in., *courtesy of Martha
and Rick Barnett, image courtesy New Orleans
Museum of Art, photograph by Judy Cooper*

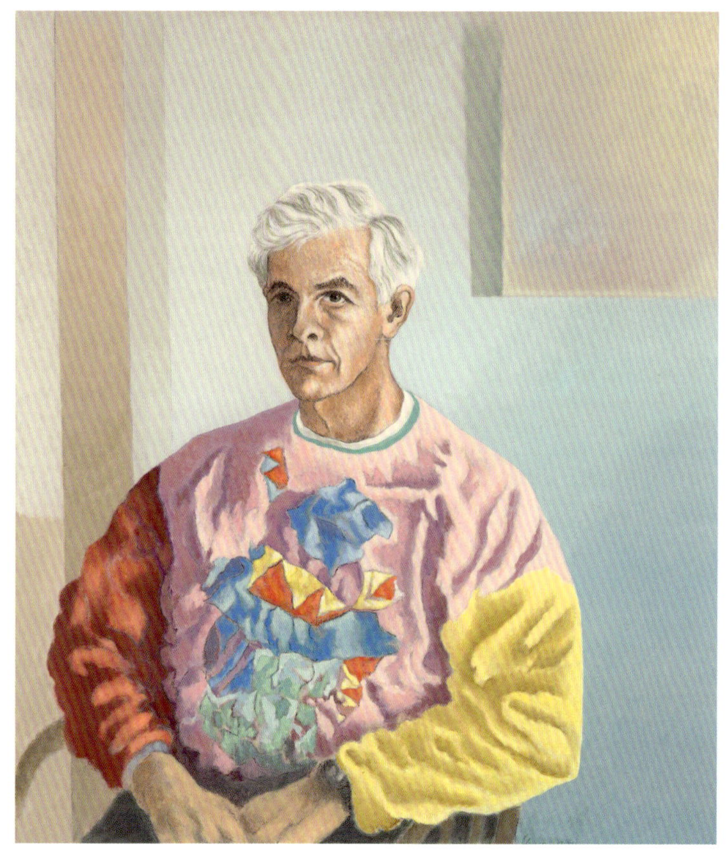

Portrait of Richard Charles, 1991, oil on canvas, 36 × 30 in., *The Historic New Orleans Collection, gift of Valerie Charles Beaudette, 2020.0226*

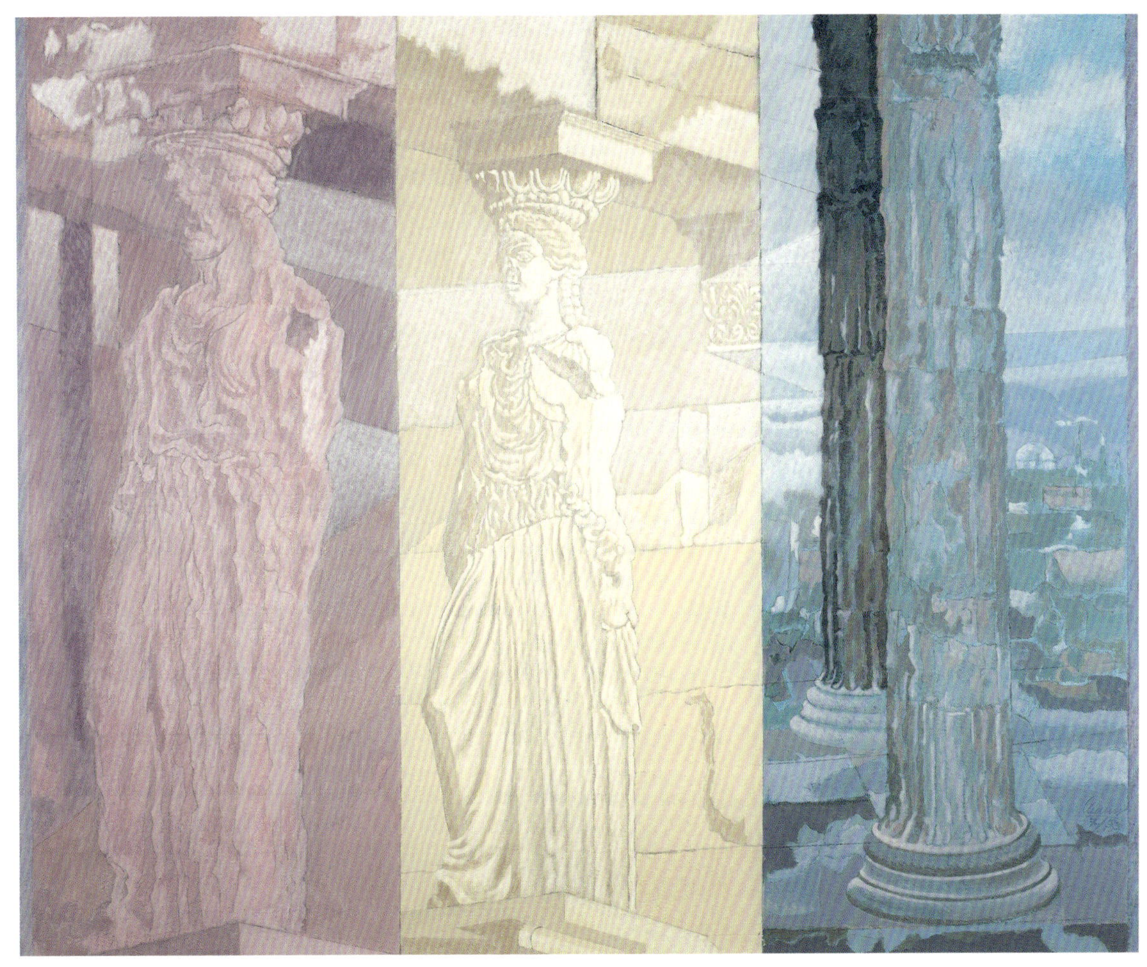

[PLATE 31]

From the Erectheum, 1993, mixed media on canvas, 48 × 56 in.,
courtesy of 3618 Studio, LLC, New Orleans, LA

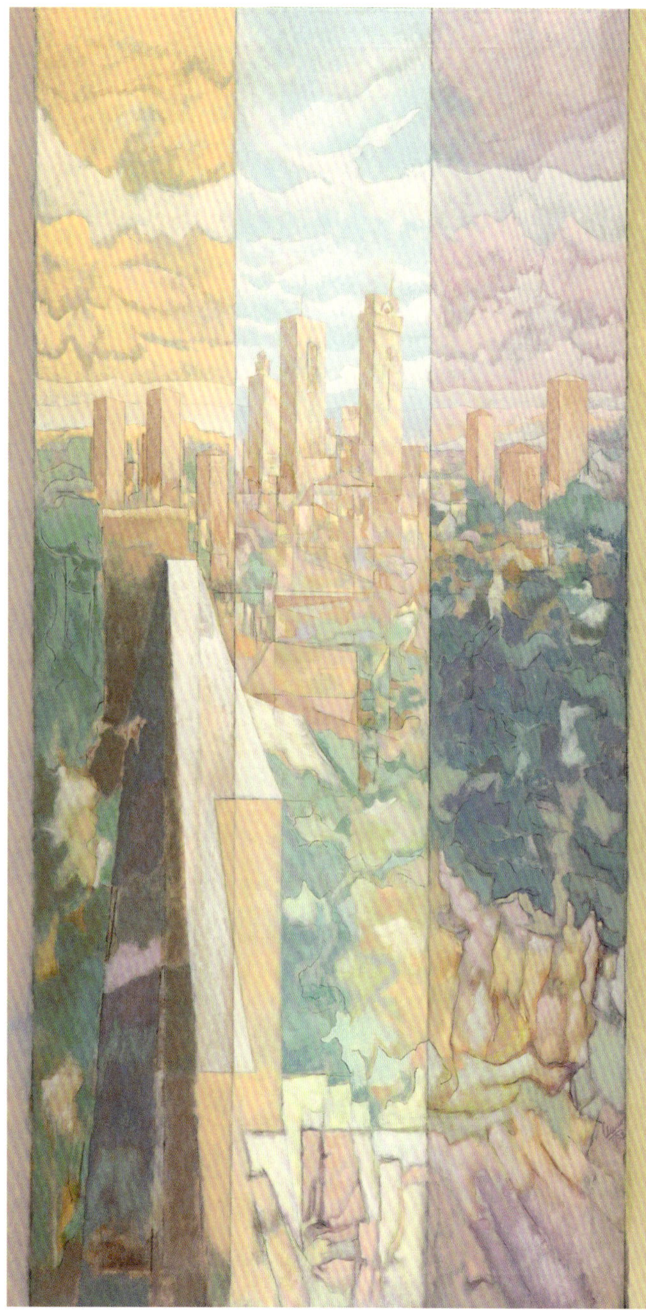

[PLATE 32]
San G. II, 1993, oil on canvas, 72 × 36 in.,
*The Historic New Orleans Collection, gift
of Susan Brill and Michael S. Hershfield,
2018.0025*

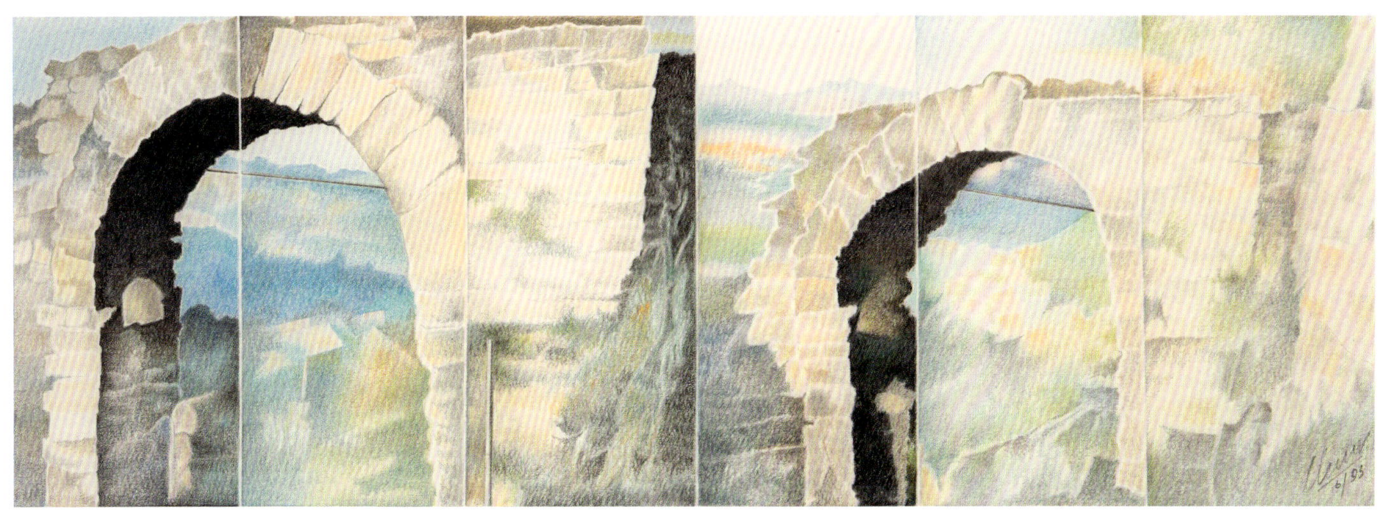

[PLATE 33]
Porta Libera—Todi, 1993, colored pencil on Bristol board, 17 × 25 in.,
courtesy of Dr. Joseph J. Roniger and Mary Sue Roniger

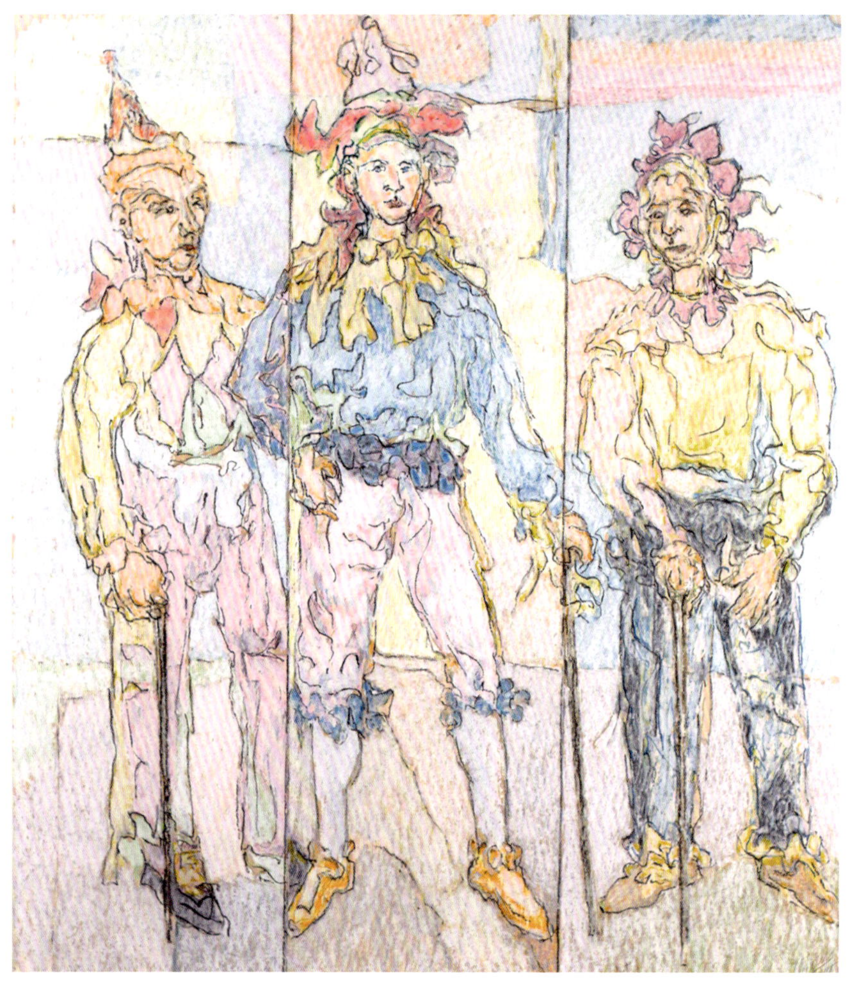

Trilogy V, San Marco, 1994, oil crayon on Strathmore paper, 30 × 26 in.,
courtesy of Martha and Rick Barnett

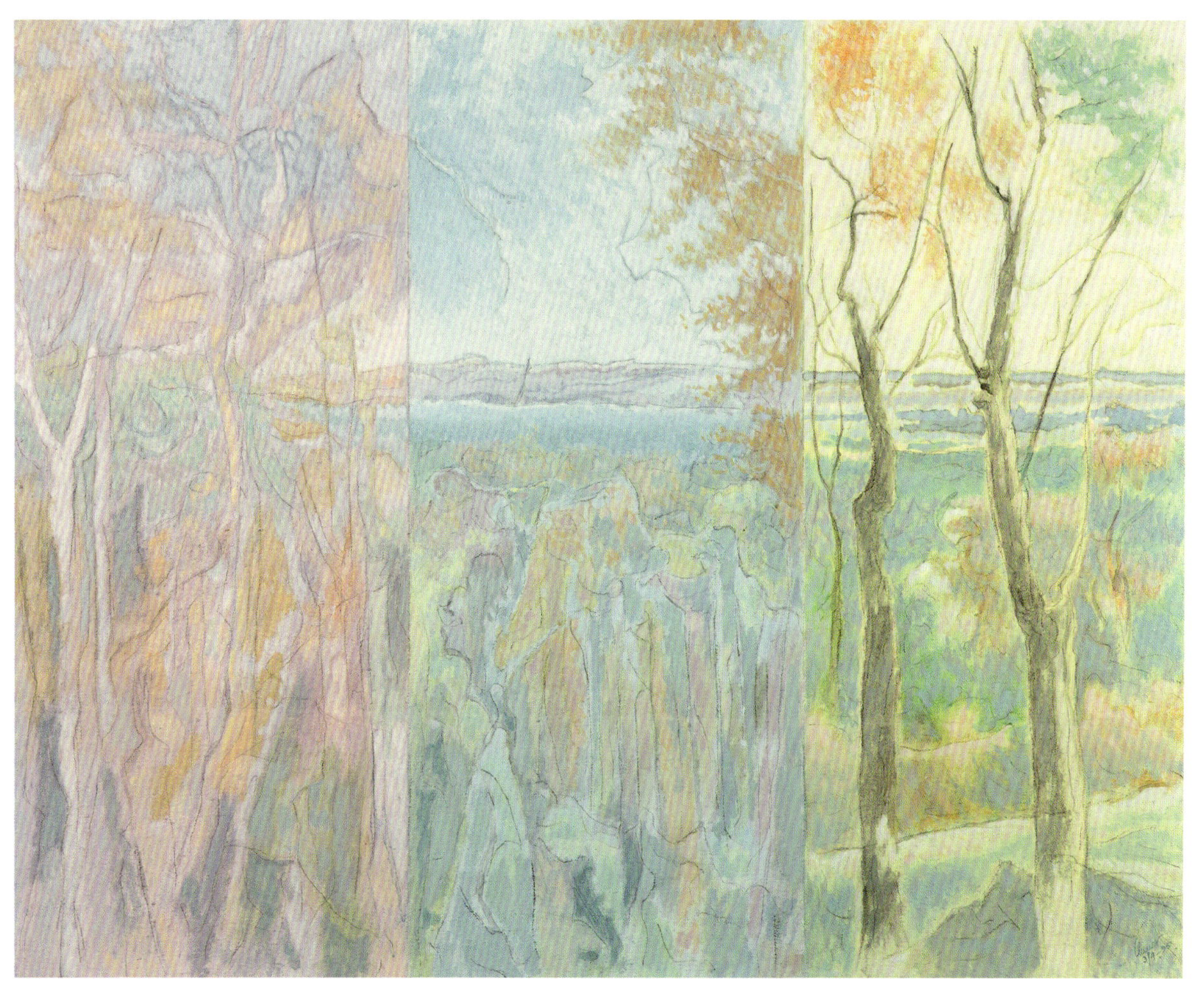

From the Country House IX, 1995, oil on Masonite, 40 × 48 in.,
The Historic New Orleans Collection, gift of Lois Charles, 2019.0434

127

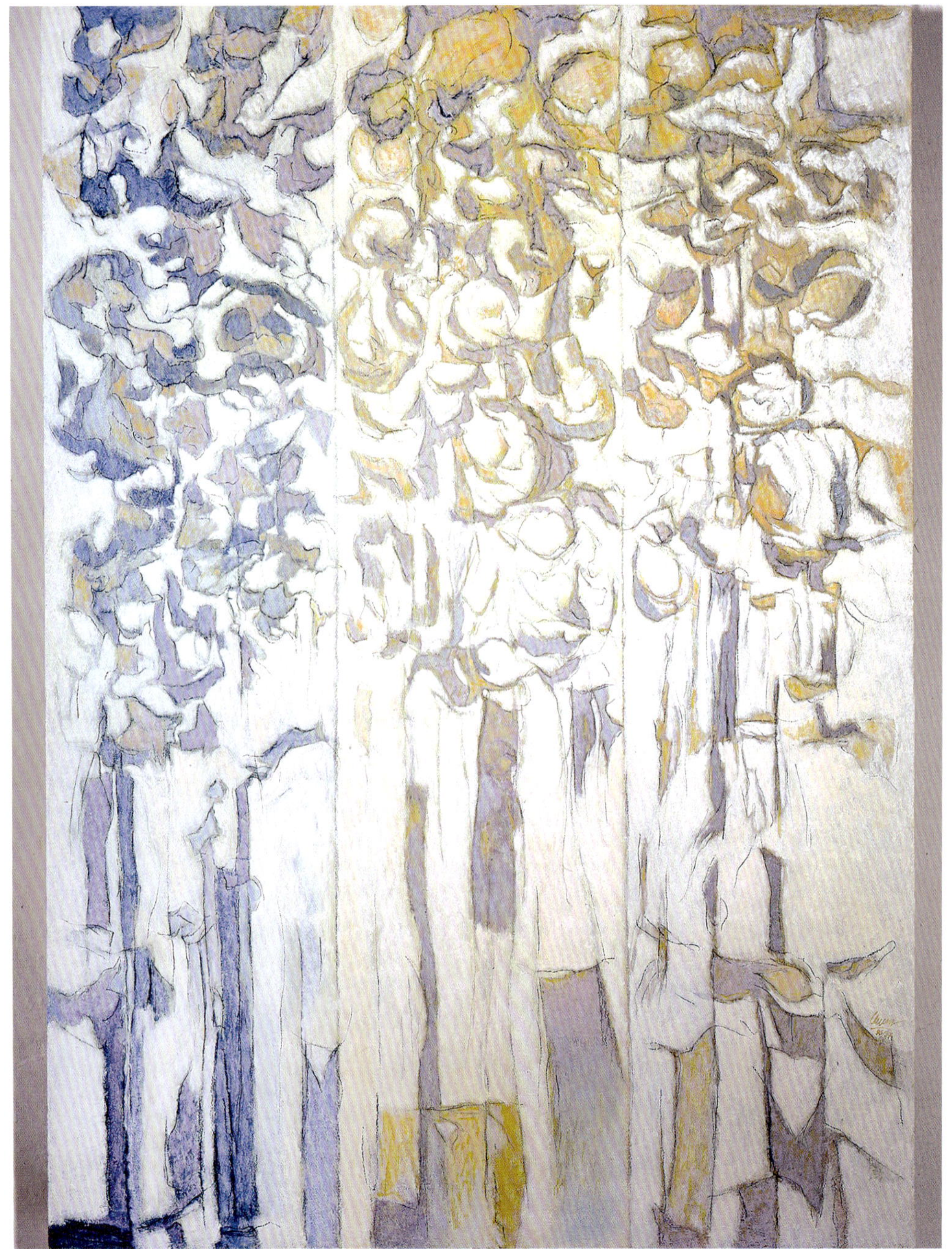

Triunity II, 1997, mixed media on canvas, 70 × 48 in., *courtesy of Kimberly and John Ed Bradley*

128

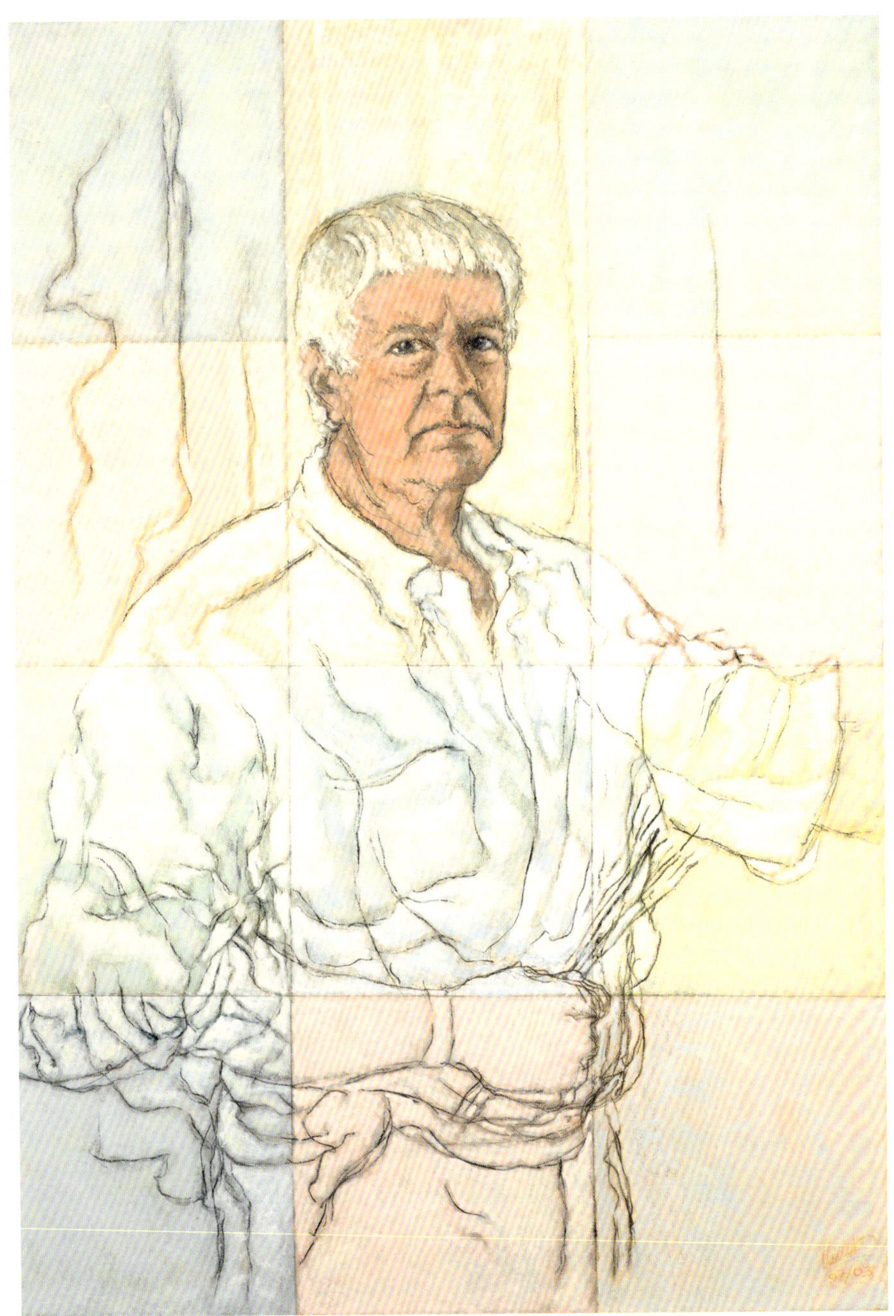

[PLATE 37]
Self-Portrait, 2003, oil on canvas, 36 × 24 in.,
courtesy of 3618 Studio, LLC, New Orleans, LA

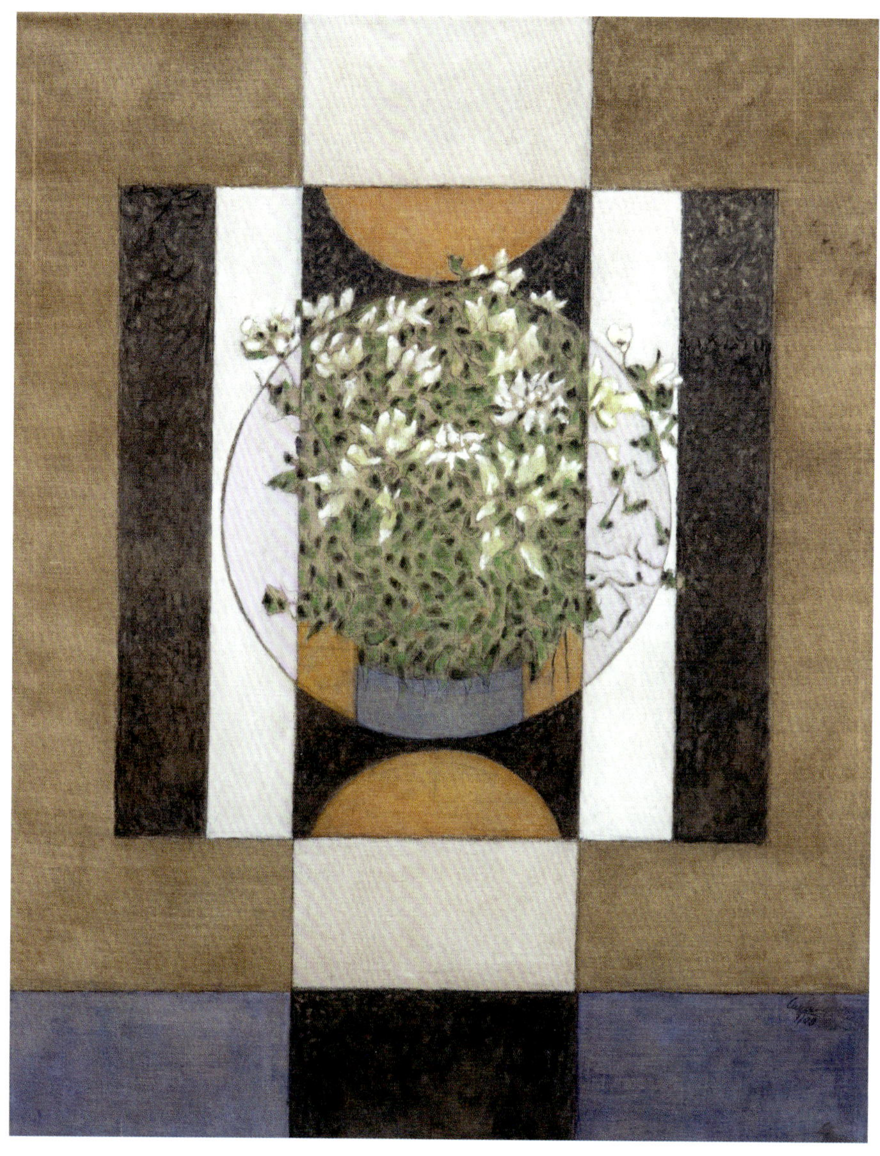

Floral Circle, 2008, oil on canvas, 48 × 36 in., *courtesy of Kimberly and John Ed Bradley*

130

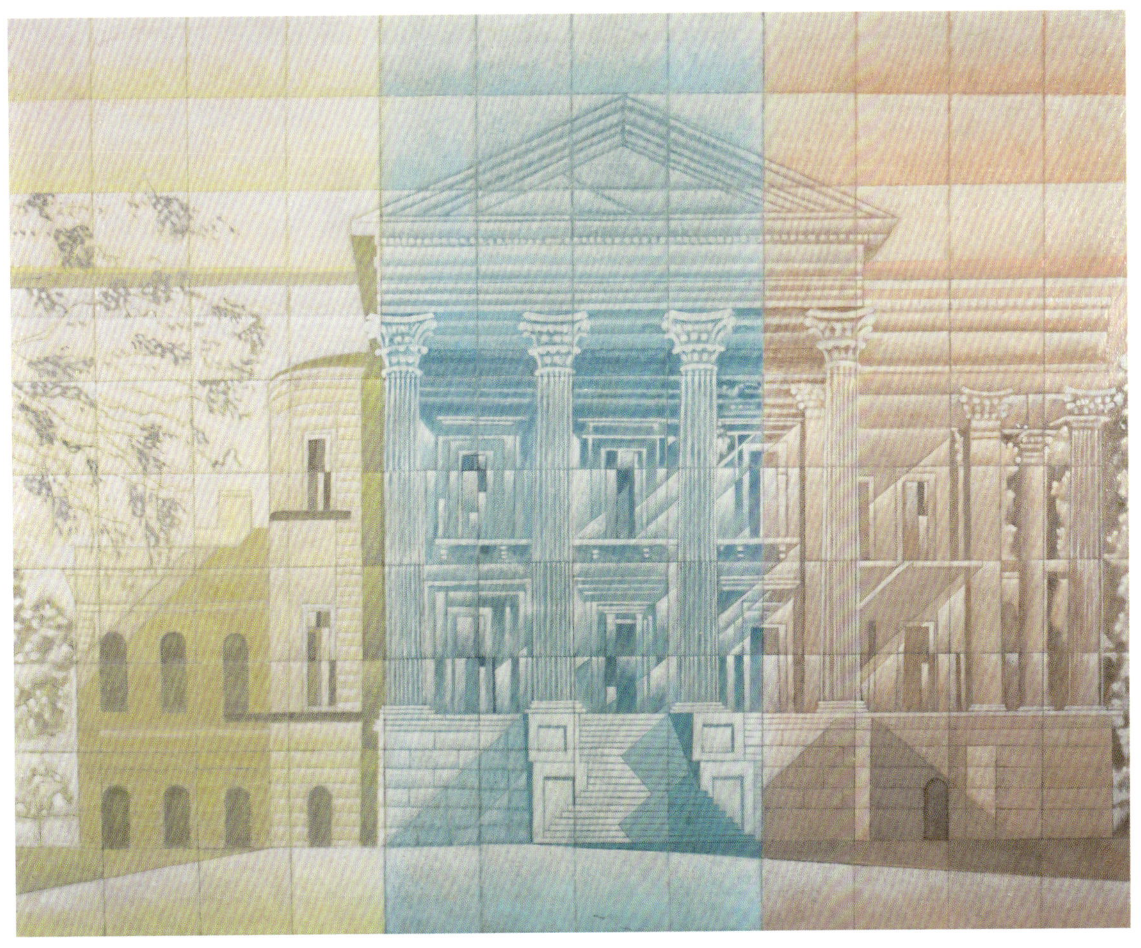

Belle Grove II, 2007, oil on canvas, 50 × 60 in., *The Historic New Orleans Collection, gift of Susan Brill and Michael S. Hershfield,* 2016.0400.1

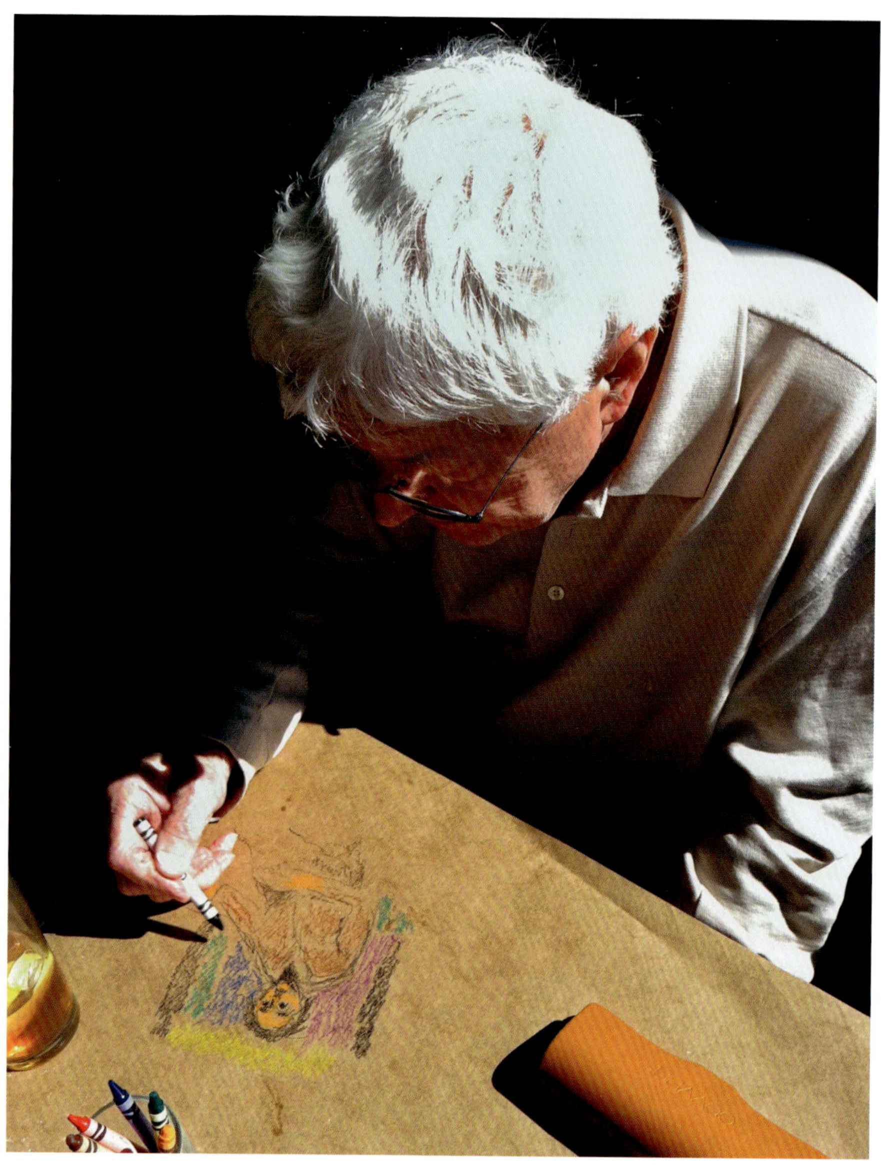

John Clemmer drawing a portrait of Albert Einstein, Oshkosh, Wisconsin, 2011, photograph by David Clemmer, *courtesy of 3618 Studio, LLC, New Orleans, LA*

1921 Born on July 22, 1921, near Donaldsonville, Louisiana, the first child of John Franklin Clemmer Sr. (b. 1874) and Marie Landry Clemmer (b. 1884).

1928 Leaves the Louisiana countryside for New Orleans with the Clemmer family, moving into a rented house in the Irish Channel neighborhood.

1937 Marie Clemmer dies on November 26 from injuries suffered in a gas explosion at the family home on Magazine Street.

1939 Graduates from Fortier High School. Begins studies at the New Orleans Art School, continuing until 1942. Early works on canvas and paper executed through the 1940s are primarily figurative but evidence cubist-influenced abstraction.

1941 John Franklin Clemmer Sr. dies from heart disease on May 10. John Clemmer marries Marjorie Fischer on June 14.

1942 A daughter, Trina Marie Clemmer, is born on September 19.

1944 Inducted into the US Army, January 27.

1945 A son, Erik Patrick Clemmer, is born on March 17.

Awarded first prize in the annual exhibition of the Arts and Crafts Club of New Orleans—his first recognition as a professional artist.

1946 Honorably discharged from the US Army Air Forces with the rank of corporal on January 19. Returns to New Orleans and assumes the jobs of executive secretary of the Arts and Crafts Club of New Orleans and director of the New Orleans Art School.

1947 Dorothy (Dottie) Iker and her first husband arrive in New Orleans and enroll in night drawing classes at the New Orleans Art School, with John Clemmer as instructor.

Divorce from Marjorie Fischer is finalized in June. Marries Litza Scoville on October 7.

1948 Solo exhibition at Arts and Crafts Club of New Orleans.

Executes first public commission, a mural for the International Trade Mart, New Orleans.

1949 Solo exhibition at Arts and Crafts Club of New Orleans.

1951 Accepts position as instructor of drawing, painting, and basic design in the Tulane School of Architecture, and as instructor in art fundamentals in the University College. Paints primarily in a figurative mode with emphasis on nudes and still lifes.

1953 Divorce from Litza Scoville is finalized in March.

Converts to Judaism on December 11 and marries Dottie Iker on December 19.

Maintains studio on Conti Street in the French Quarter.

1955 Purchases a home on Foucher Street on the Uptown edge of the Irish Channel. Moves his studio from the French Quarter to a small building on the Foucher Street property.

Spends summer vacation at the Iker family cottage in Sheboygan, Wisconsin.

Solo exhibition at the 331 Gallery, New Orleans.

1956 First trip to Europe, visiting Turkey, Greece, Italy, and Great Britain.

Solo exhibition at the Tulane School of Architecture.

1957 A son, Jonathan Charles Clemmer, is born on September 27.

1958 Paints first Wisconsin landscape, *Franklin, WI*, and begins to experiment with collage.

1959 Promoted to assistant professor at Tulane School of Architecture.

A son, David John Clemmer, is born on October 2.

1960 Solo exhibition at the Tulane School of Architecture.

Solo exhibition at the Orleans Gallery, New Orleans.

Begins working in the sand sculpture medium.

1962 Awarded travel grant from the Tulane School of Architecture, to visit schools of architecture in Colombia. Begins major series of abstract paintings and collages, most on panel, and many utilizing a paint roller, based on South American experience. This series continues through 1970.

Solo exhibition at Orleans Gallery, New Orleans.

1966 Promoted to associate professor, Tulane School of Architecture.

Travels to Guatemala and Yucatán Peninsula during summer recess.

1967 Receives study grant from Tulane School of Architecture to attend a summer seminar, Form and Color, at Massachusetts Institute of Technology, with instructors György Kepes, Richard Filipowski, and Robert Preusser.

1968 Travels to Greece, Italy, and Switzerland during summer recess.

Solo exhibition at Clemmer residence on Foucher Street.

Begins *Topographia* series of large abstractions with strong geometric elements, continuing until 1973.

1969 Rents a studio on Magazine Street near Louisiana Avenue for producing large-scale sculptural projects, sharing the space with plexiglass artist Jamie Allen through 1975. Begins working on several sculptural fountain commissions.

1970 Begins working with oxyacetylene welding and investigating a variety of sculptural media, including bronze, Lucite (in collaboration with Jamie Allen), and wood, often in combination with sand sculpture.

Solo exhibition at Clemmer residence on Foucher Street.

1971 Solo exhibition at Clemmer residence on Foucher Street.

Undertakes first in a series of sculptural commissions on Jewish religious themes.

1972 Solo exhibition at Louisiana State University, Alexandria, Louisiana.

Solo exhibition at Jewish Community Center, New Orleans.

1973 Takes sabbatical from Tulane School of Architecture. During summer the Clemmer family travels to Europe, visiting Greece, Italy, Spain, Portugal, England, and Scotland.

Abstract paintings during the 1970s reflect European and Central American travels.

1974 Promoted to full professor, Tulane School of Architecture.

Solo exhibition at Clemmer residence on Foucher Street.

1975 Purchases and remodels double shotgun house on Laurel Street adjacent to Foucher Street property to serve as a combined painting and sculpture studio.

1977 Begins *Portal* series of paintings, continuing to 1979.

1978 Appointed chairman, Department of Art, Newcomb College, Tulane University.

Discovers papel de amate while on a family trip to Mexico. Begins a series of paintings utilizing this medium, continuing into 1980s.

Solo exhibition at Clemmer residence on Foucher Street.

1981 First recipient of Maxine and Ford Graham Chair in Fine Art, Tulane University. Takes sabbatical leave, traveling to Italy. Builds a studio in Sheboygan, Wisconsin, on property adjacent to the family's summer cottage.

1986 Retires from Tulane University. Elected professor emeritus of art, Newcomb College.

1988 Solo exhibition at Carmen Llewellyn Gallery, New Orleans.

1989 Dottie retires from Tulane Medical School.

Travels in the Soviet Union and Sweden. Thereafter, travels to Europe at one- to two-year intervals, most frequently to Italy and Greece. Begins spending summer and fall months in Sheboygan, Wisconsin.

<table>
<tr><td valign="top">1991</td><td>Begins continuing series of landscape drawings and painting of Greece, Italy, and Wisconsin, most divided into three vertical registers. First use of color pencil for drawings.</td></tr>
</table>

1991 Begins continuing series of landscape drawings and painting of Greece, Italy, and Wisconsin, most divided into three vertical registers. First use of color pencil for drawings.

1993 Solo exhibition at president's residence, Tulane University.

Solo exhibition at Academy Gallery, New Orleans.

1994 Begins *Triunity* series of large abstractions and related *Trilogy* series of oil crayon on paper.

John and Dottie sell their Foucher Street property and move to a condominium on St. Charles Avenue at the edge of the Garden District. John retains his Laurel Street studio. They continue to travel regularly with trips to Greece, Italy, France, the Middle East, the United Kingdom, and Scandinavia.

1995 Begins the continuing series of *Country House* landscapes named after a resort in Door County, Wisconsin.

1999 Career retrospective exhibition, *John Clemmer: Exploring the Medium, 1940–1999*, is presented at the New Orleans Museum of Art.

Solo exhibition at the Academy Gallery, New Orleans.

2000 *John Clemmer: Exploring the Medium, 1940–1999* travels to venues in Alexandria and Shreveport, Louisiana.

2005 John and Dottie are in Wisconsin when Hurricane Katrina strikes, devastating much of the Gulf Coast region and flooding the city of New Orleans. They remain in Wisconsin until February 2006.

2010 Receives the Louisiana Artist Recognition Award, presented by the New Orleans Museum of Art's Delgado Society.

2012 *John Clemmer: New and Selected Work* opens at the Louisiana Art and Science Museum, Baton Rouge.

2013 John and Dottie sell their condominium in New Orleans and move to Wisconsin to become full-time residents.

Over the summer John completes his final body of work—a series of over thirty watercolors and pastels on variously colored construction paper.

2014 Solo exhibition at LeMieux Galleries, New Orleans.

Suffers stroke on March 26 at home in Milwaukee. Dies from complications on the morning of April 11, aged ninety-two.

2021 The Historic New Orleans Collection presents an exhibition, *John Clemmer: His Legacy in Art*, to celebrate the centennial of his birth.

Chronology text 1921–1999 courtesy New Orleans Museum of Art.

EXHIBITION CHECKLIST

CLEMMER'S CIRCLE

Pottery Bowl with Birds
1901; glazed pottery
by Sarah Henderson (1871–1944), decorator
by Joseph Fortuné Meyer (1848–1931), potter
4 ¾ × 10 ¾ in.
courtesy of Don Fuson

Farmhouse with Windmill
1906; watercolor on gouache on paper
by Julius Woeltz (1911–1956), painter
10 ¾ × 8 ⅛ in.
The Historic New Orleans Collection, gift of John F.
Clemmer, 1991.116.23

Garden Pavilion
between 1908 and 1918; watercolor on board
by Arthur Henry Feitel (1891–1982), painter
19 × 24 ⅞ in.
The Historic New Orleans Collection, 1984.74.81

San Gimignano
1912; watercolor and pencil
by Richard Koch (1889–1971), painter
12 ⅝ × 9 ⅝ in.
The Historic New Orleans Collection, bequest of Richard Koch, 1971.31

Emma
1924; plaster with paint
by Collette Pope Heldner (1902–1990), sculptor
20 × 9 × 8 ½ in.
courtesy of Don Fuson

Portrait of Francis Gains
between 1928 and 1935; oil on canvas
by Josephine Marien Crawford (1878–1952), painter
24 ¾ × 20 in.
The Historic New Orleans Collection, bequest of Charles C. Crawford,
1978.23.12

Head of a Girl
1930s; terra cotta
by Nell Pomeroy O'Brien (1897–1966), sculptor
10 ¼ × 6 × 8 in.
courtesy of Don Fuson

Duluth: Canal, Boats and Bridge
1930s; oil on Masonite
by Knute Heldner (1877–1952), painter
23 ⅞ × 30 in.
The Historic New Orleans Collection, gift of Laura Simon Nelson,
2012.0411.8

Still Life of Daisies in a Green Vase
between 1930 and 1948; oil on canvas affixed to Masonite
by Alberta Kinsey (1875–1952), painter
18 × 22 ½ in.
The Historic New Orleans Collection, 2019.0173

Foliage
between 1931 and 1951; watercolor on paper
by Hazel Guggenheim McKinley (1903–1995), painter
11 ¾ × 17 ½ in.
The Historic New Orleans Collection, gift of John F. Clemmer,
1991.116.47

Ceramic Horse with Two Nude Women
between 1932 and 1945; glazed pottery
by Rudolf Staffel (1911–2002), ceramicist
13 × 5 × 11 in.
The Historic New Orleans Collection, gift of Mr. and Mrs. Albert Louis
Lieutaud, 1961.83

Houses and Cemetery
between 1933 and 1939; watercolor on paper
by Clayre Barr (1913–1980), painter
22 × 27 ¾ in.
The Historic New Orleans Collection, gift of Albert Louis Lieutaud,
1968.12.2

Sugar Cane Cutter
ca. 1935; plaster
by Albert Rieker (1886–1959), sculptor
20 ½ × 10 × 2 in.
The Historic New Orleans Collection, 1981.348.2

French Quarter, New Orleans
ca. 1935; pastel on paper
by Will Henry Stevens (1881–1949), pastelist
30 ¼ × 26 ½ in.
The Historic New Orleans Collection, 2020.0283.2

Louisiana Railroad Crossing
ca. 1935; oil on canvas board
by Roger C. Holt (1905–1979), painter
17 ⅞ × 23 ¾ in.
The Historic New Orleans Collection, 1999.7

Louisiana Bayou
1936; watercolor on paper
by Charles Gresham (1913–1979), painter
11 ¼ × 15 ¹⁄₁₆ in.
The Historic New Orleans Collection, 2015.0464.15

Oyster Docks, Gulfport, Mississippi
1937 or 1938; oil on canvas
by Jane Smith Ninas (1913–2005), painter
24 ¾ × 29 ¾ in.
*The Historic New Orleans Collection, gift of Jane S. N. E. Sargeant,
1990.121.1*

Belle Grove Rear View
1938; watercolor and gouache on paper
by Boyd Cruise (1909–1988), painter
15 × 21 in.
The Historic New Orleans Collection, bequest of Richard Koch, 1971.68

John Edmond "Jack" Sparling
1938; bronze, wood, paint
by Angela Gregory (1903–1990), sculptor
15 × 8 ¼ × 6 ¾ in.
*The Historic New Orleans Collection, gift of the Estate of Angela
Gregory, 2006.0156.3*

The Concert
ca. 1940; oil on canvas
by Marion Souchon (1871–1954), painter
26 ¾ × 35 ¾ in.
The Historic New Orleans Collection, gift of Elizabeth Darling, 1979.1

Portrait Relief of Albert Rieker
ca. 1940; bronze
by Alexander Calder (1898–1976), sculptor
5 ¼ × 5 ¼ × ⅜ in.
*The Historic New Orleans Collection, gift of George E. Jordan in
memory of Juanita Elfert, 1996.42.1*

Two Black Women
ca. 1940; oil on canvas
by Weeks Hall (1894–1958), painter
24 × 19 ¾ in.
The Historic New Orleans Collection, 1986.94

Weeks Hall
ca. 1940; oil on canvas board
by Olive Leonhardt (1895–1963), painter
15 × 18 in.
*The Historic New Orleans Collection, gift of Marie Louise Stauffer
Posey, 1986.192.1*

Corner of St. Peter and Chartres Streets
ca. 1940; oil on canvas board
by Clarence Millet (1897–1959), painter
15 × 18 in.
*The Historic New Orleans Collection, gift of Laura Simon Nelson,
2017.0111*

After the Parade
between 1940 and 1955; linocut
by Tilden Landry (1911–1968), artist
17 × 11 ¼ in.
The Historic New Orleans Collection, 2019.0440

Audubon Park
1942; pencil on paper
by John W. Lawrence (1923–1971), draftsman
10 ⅞ × 6 ⅜ in. (sight)
courtesy of Priscilla and John H. Lawrence

Portrait of Alberta Kinsey
1942 or 1943; oil on paper
by James Lamantia (1923–2011), painter
20 ⅞ × 14 ⅞ in.
The Historic New Orleans Collection, 1993.108.7

The Night Life-Drawing Class at the Arts and Crafts Club
between 1942 and 1945; oil on board
by David Sinclair Nixon (1904–1967), painter
20 × 24 in.
*The Historic New Orleans Collection, gift of Evelyn Gladney
Witherspoon, 1983.129*

Dauphine Street
1943; watercolor on paper
by Charles Henry Reinike (1906–1983), painter
16 × 22 ¾ in.
*The Historic New Orleans Collection, gift of Mrs. P. Roussell Norman,
1980.47.13*

Boredom
1944; lithograph
by Caroline Durieux (1896–1989), lithographer
24 × 19 ¾ in.
The Historic New Orleans Collection, 1975.41

The Emporium
1946; tempera and oil on canvas
by John McCrady (1911–1968), painter
26 × 37 ½ in.
The Historic New Orleans Collection, 1975.129

Elegy for a Leaning Column
1947; gelatin silver print
by Clarence John Laughlin (1905–1985), photographer
9 ¼ × 7 ¾ in.
courtesy of David Clemmer, Santa Fe, NM

After the Accident
between 1947 and 1949; watercolor and gouache on Masonite
by Charles Whitfield Richards (1906–1992), painter
16 ⅛ × 20 ⅛ in.
*The Historic New Orleans Collection, from the Richard Lebherz
Collection, 2004.0053*

Scene with Palm Trees
between 1947 and 1951; watercolor and ink on paper
by Alice Frances Goodall (1866–1951), painter
22 × 29 ½ in.
*The Historic New Orleans Collection, gift of John F. Clemmer,
1991.116.46*

Untitled
between 1947 and 1957; oil on canvas
by Pat Trivigno (1922–2013), painter
62 × 29 ¾ in.
*collection of Newcomb Art Museum of Tulane University, gift of Dr.
and Mrs. Sidney Lassen, 1987.1*

The White Vase
1949; oil on canvas board
by Elizabeth Heintzen Laughlin (1914–2014), painter
32 × 16 in.
*The Historic New Orleans Collection, gift of Elizabeth Heintzen
Laughlin, 1995.73*

Sketches of Trees and Palmettoes
April 1950; ink and ink wash on paper
by Joseph Donaldson Jr. (1914–1997), painter
14 × 11 in.
*The Historic New Orleans Collection, gift of John F. Clemmer,
1991.116.22*

Dock Scene #1
1950; gouache and watercolor on paper
by Paul Ninas (1903–1964), painter
19 × 25 ⅜ in.
The Historic New Orleans Collection, 1998.103

Rebirth
between 1950 and 1955; oil on canvas
by Daniel Webster Whitney (1896–1965), painter
30 × 24 in.
*The Historic New Orleans Collection, gift of Mrs. Daniel Whitney,
1984.231.2*

Angel
between 1950 and 1961; plaster
by Lin Emery (1926–2021), sculptor
34 × 15 × 15 in.
*The Historic New Orleans Collection, the L. Kemper and Leila Moore
Williams Founders Collection, 1961.79.1*

Children Playing
1950s; oil on Masonite
by Leonard Flettrich (1916–1970), painter
29 × 35 in.
*The Historic New Orleans Collection, gift of Laura Simon Nelson,
1997.120.7*

Abstract House
1950s; watercolor and india ink
by Johnny Donnels (1924–2009), painter
14 ¹¹⁄₁₆ × 20 ⅝ in.
The Historic New Orleans Collection, 2007.0388.13

Crucifixion
1947; oil on Masonite
by Xavier Gonzalez (1898–1993), painter
48 × 38 in. (framed)
New Orleans Museum of Art, Museum purchase, 50.3

Tower
1951; oil on Masonite
by George Dunbar (b. 1927), painter
23 ¼ × 19 ¾ in.
The Historic New Orleans Collection, 1988.104

Untitled (Urban Scene)
1952; acrylic on board
by Marilyn Conrad (b. 1923), painter
11 ½ × 15 in.
The Historic New Orleans Collection, 2012.0164.1

New Orleans Banana Wagon
1953; color woodcut on rice paper
by James Louis Steg (1922–2001), printmaker
19 ¾ × 25 in.
The Historic New Orleans Collection, 1990.74.1

Nodule Vase
between 1953 and 1960; glazed stoneware
by Evelyn Gladney Witherspoon (1901–1998), potter
13 × 6 ½ × 2 ¾ in.
*The Historic New Orleans Collection, the L. Kemper and Leila Moore
Williams Founders Collection, 1960.78*

The Bottle Man
between 1954 and 1964; gouache on illustration board
by Robert Helmer (1922–1990), painter
15 ¼ × 10 ⅛ in.
*The Historic New Orleans Collection, gift of John F. Clemmer,
1991.116.19*

Madonna and Child, #18
1956; oil on canvas
by Ida Kohlmeyer (1912–1997), painter
60 × 36 in.
*The Historic New Orleans Collection, gift of The Ida and Hugh
Kohlmeyer Charitable Foundation, 1999.22.10*

Tall Vessel
1956; stoneware
by Katherine Choy (1927–1958), ceramicist
37 × 6 ½ in.
*New Orleans Museum of Art, gift of Mr. and Mrs. John Clemmer,
94.209*

Prytania
1957; oil on board
by Fritz Bultman (1919–1985), painter
24 × 20 in.
collection of Michael Wilkinson

King Oliver's Jazz Band at Milneburg
giclée print of original 1958 oil painting
by Challis Walker Calandria (1912–2000), painter of original
23 × 27 in.
courtesy of Andrés Calandria and Antoinette Calandria

Fauna
giclée print of original 1969 acrylic painting
by Juan José Calandria (1902–1980), painter of original
21 × 38 in.
courtesy of Andrés Calandria and Antoinette Calandria

Gov. John McKeithen of La.
March 1966; oil on canvas
by Hal Carney (1929–1985), painter
20 × 16 in.
*The Historic New Orleans Collection, gift of Diane Laizer Carney,
1998.79*

Three Heads
1969; color lithograph
by Abraham Rattner (1895–1978), lithographer
28 ¾ × 35 in.
The Historic New Orleans Collection, 1998.56.3

Mini
1970; oil on Masonite
by Mildred Rittenberg Wohl (1906–1977), painter
10 × 8 in.
The Historic New Orleans Collection, 2019.0231

Ashton Phelps Sr. as Rex
1970; enamel and aluminum
by Helen Trivigno (1920–1985), artist
61 × 26 in.
courtesy of Ashton Phelps Jr.

Jonah and the Whale Liberation
between 1971 and 1973; color collagraph on wove paper
by John Scott (1940–2007), printmaker
38 ¹³⁄₁₆ x 26 ¾ in.
The Historic New Orleans Collection, 2020.0103

Marsh Scene
1974; oil on canvas
by Newton Reeve Howard (1912–1984), painter
14 ½ × 29 ½ in.
*The Historic New Orleans Collection, gift of Evelyn Gladney
Witherspoon, 1988.178*

Charro with Cape Over Shoulder
1977; bronze and wood
by Enrique Alférez (1903–1999), sculptor
15 ½ × 5 ⅞ × 4 ⅛ in.
The Historic New Orleans Collection, 1981.215

722 Toulouse Street
1978; xerograph with ink additions
by Arthur Q. Davis (1920–2011), delineator
11 × 17 in.
The Historic New Orleans Collection, 1978.223.28

Conglomerate #2
1978; mixed media with gold leaf and silver leaf
by Shearly Grode (1925–2003), painter
16 ½ × 24 ¾ in.
The Historic New Orleans Collection, gift of John Clemmer, 2009.0171

Trinity Episcopal / 1329 Jackson Ave.
between 1978 and 1997; graphite and pastel on paper
by Nathaniel C. Curtis (1917–1997), draftsman
11 ¼ × 17 ¾ in.
The Historic New Orleans Collection, gift of Mrs. Nathaniel C.
Curtis, Jr., 2003.0176.44

Shadows
1979; two-color intaglio on paper
by Dorothy Furlong-Gardner (b. 1928), etcher
15 × 18 ⅝ in.
The Historic New Orleans Collection, gift of Dorothy Furlong-Gardner,
1997.131.1

Kerry Corrona
1980s; oil on canvas board
by Margaret Witherspoon (1914–2005), painter
9 ¾ × 7 ⅝ in.
The Historic New Orleans Collection, gift of Nancy A. Hogarth,
2015.0121

The Poet
1981; oil on canvas
by Jack Hastings (1925–2013), painter
25 ½ × 23 ⅝ in.
The Historic New Orleans Collection, 1997.131.3

Alligator Egg
1983; ceramic and mixed media
by George Febres (1943–1996), artist
6 ½ × 9 × 6 in.
courtesy of Jacqueline Bishop and Herbert Halpern

Study for Hurricane in Pensacola
1985; bronze and plaster
by Eugenie "Ersy" Schwartz (1951–2015), sculptor
5 ½ × 2 ⁷⁄₁₆ × 1 ¹³⁄₁₆ in.
The Historic New Orleans Collection, gift of Grover E. Mouton III,
1992.36 a,b

Goodbye Dad
1989; mixed media with photographic print
by Jan Gilbert (b. 1953), artist
29 ½ × 24 ½ × 1 ¾ in.
The Historic New Orleans Collection, acquisition made possible by an
anonymous donor, 2019.0447.1

Expanding Circles
ca. 1990; paint on metal and wood
by George Rickey (1907–2002), sculptor
8 × 3 ½ in.
collection of Newcomb Art Museum of Tulane University, bequest of
Professor Alfred Moir, 2011.14

Maquette
between 1990 and 1996; wood, paint
by Ida Kohlmeyer (1912–1997), sculptor
11 ⅝ × 7 ¹¹⁄₁₆ × 12 ⅝ in.
The Historic New Orleans Collection, bequest of the Estate of Ida
Kohlmeyer, 1999.23.8

Metamorphosis
1991; polyester resin
by Arthur Kern (b. 1931), sculptor
68 ½ × 14 × 16 ½ in.
courtesy of Jacqueline Bishop and Herbert Halpern

Landscape
December 15, 1993; acrylic on canvas
by Mary Basso McCrady (1911–1994), painter
24 × 30 in.
courtesy of Mr. and Mrs. Matthew J. Martinez

Inga Tree
1994; oil on linen
by Jacqueline Bishop (b. 1955), painter
24 × 20 in.
courtesy of Jacqueline Bishop and Herbert Halpern

Self-Portrait in White Overalls
2003; oil on canvas
by Jean Seidenberg (b. 1930), painter
27 × 26 in.
collection of Michael Wilkinson

Sardines
2003; oil on canvas
by Simon Gunning (b. 1956), painter
17 ⅞ × 24 in.
The Historic New Orleans Collection, gift of John and Dorothy
Clemmer, 2013.0156.1

Power Plants on the Westbank
ca. 2011; watercolor on paper
by Errol Barron (b. 1941)
4 ¾ × 4 ¾ in.
courtesy of Priscilla and John H. Lawrence

JOHN CLEMMER CENTENNIAL

Architectural Fragment from Belle Grove Plantation
between 1852 and 1857; cypress and paint
by an unknown woodcarver
30 ⅝ × 13 ¾ × 2 ¾ in.
The Historic New Orleans Collection, gift of John and Dorothy Clemmer, 2013.0156.2

Still Life
1940; oil on canvas
by John Clemmer (1921–2014), painter
35 × 24 in.
courtesy of Don Fuson

Interior
1940s; ink and ink wash on paper
by John Clemmer (1921–2014), draftsman
19 ¾ × 24 ¼ in.
courtesy of 3618 Studio, LLC, New Orleans, LA

Batture Dwelling
1941; ink on paper
by John Clemmer (1921–2014), draftsman
9 ¾ × 14 ¾ in.
courtesy of Don Fuson

How Men Their Brothers Maim
1942; oil on canvas
by John Clemmer (1921–2014), painter
35 × 26 in.
courtesy of Edwin and Donna Lupberger

Still Life (Lamp and Radio)
1943; ink on paper
by John Clemmer (1921–2014), draftsman
9 × 6 in.
The Historic New Orleans Collection, gift of Dorothy, Jonathan, and David Clemmer / 3618 Studio, LLC, in memory of John Clemmer, 2016.0041.4

Writing (Marjorie in Floral Shirt)
1943; pencil on paper
by John Clemmer (1921–2014), draftsman
10 × 14 in.
courtesy of David Clemmer, Santa Fe, NM

See Ungeheuer (Sea Monster)
1944; oil on panel
by John Clemmer (1921–2014), painter
24 × 36 in.
courtesy of Jacqueline Bishop and Herbert Halpern

Coup d'Oeil
between 1945 and 1949; oil on canvas
by John Clemmer (1921–2014), painter
18 × 24 in.
courtesy of Don Fuson

Swamp Fire
1947; watercolor and gouache on paper
by John Clemmer (1921–2014), painter
18 × 24 in.
collection of Ogden Museum of Southern Art, gift of Allison Kendrick

Two Nudes in a Landscape
1949; oil on canvas
by John Clemmer (1921–2014), painter
50 × 34 in.
courtesy of Don Fuson

Floral II
1949; oil on canvas
by John Clemmer (1921–2014), painter
35 × 26 in.
courtesy of Mathile and Steven Abramson

Two Figures—Macbeth
1949; oil on canvas
by John Clemmer (1921–2014), painter
59 ¾ × 40 ¾ in.
New Orleans Museum of Art, gift of David J. Clemmer, 97.822

Abstraction
ca. 1949; oil on canvas
by John Clemmer (1921–2014), painter
35 × 22 in.
The Historic New Orleans Collection, 1988.105

Palette formerly belonging to John Clemmer
between 1950 and 1970; laminated wood
16 × 12 × 1 in.
courtesy of Don Fuson

Seated Figure (Dottie)
1951; ink on card stock
by John Clemmer (1921–2014), draftsman
10 ½ × 7 ½ in.
*The Historic New Orleans Collection, gift of Dorothy, Jonathan, and
David Clemmer / 3618 Studio, LLC, in memory of John Clemmer,
2016.0041.23*

Nude with Still Life
1951; oil on canvas
by John Clemmer (1921–2014), painter
36 × 48 in.
courtesy of Don Fuson

Untitled (Self-Portrait)
1951; ink on paper
by John Clemmer (1921–2014), draftsman
36 × 24 ⅛ in.
courtesy of Don Fuson

Parade
1951; ink on paper
by John Clemmer (1921–2014), draftsman
8 ¾ × 10 ⅜ in.
courtesy of Don Fuson

John Clemmer with Mask
1951; photoprint
by a *Times-Picayune* photographer
7 ½ × 5 in.
courtesy of Don Fuson

Blue Vase
1955; oil on canvas
by John Clemmer (1921–2014), painter
42 × 37 in. (framed)
New Orleans Museum of Art, gift of Judith and Robert Stein, 96.239

Mardi Gras Mask
1959; painted buckram
by John Clemmer (1921–2014), artisan
9 ¼ × 7 ¼ × 5 in.
courtesy of Don Fuson

Maze
late 1950s; silkscreen print on deckled paper
by John Clemmer (1921–2014), printmaker
13 × 20 in.
courtesy of 3618 Studio, LLC, New Orleans, LA

Portrait of Wing Macdonald (Florence May Macdonald)
1961–1962; oil on canvas
by John Clemmer (1921–2014), painter
48 × 36 in.
courtesy of Florence Macdonald Boogaerts

Almedia
1962; oil and collage on panel
by John Clemmer (1921–2014), painter
72 × 48 in.
courtesy of David Clemmer, Santa Fe, NM

Collage I—Red, Orange
1962; oil and collage on panel
by John Clemmer (1921–2014), painter
20 × 24 in.
courtesy of David Clemmer, Santa Fe, NM

Siloé
1964; oil on panel
by John Clemmer (1921–2014), painter
47 ⅝ × 42 in.
courtesy of David Clemmer, Santa Fe, NM

Summery—Season II
1964; oil on panel
by John Clemmer (1921–2014), painter
20 × 20 in.
courtesy of David Clemmer, Santa Fe, NM

Portrait of Lin Emery and Shirley Braselman
1967–1968; oil on canvas
by John Clemmer (1921–2014), painter
60 × 50 in.
courtesy of Brooks Emery Braselman

Untitled (French Quarter Scene)
1969; silkscreen on blue paper
by John Clemmer (1921–2014), printmaker
20 × 26 in.
courtesy of 3618 Studio, LLC, New Orleans, LA

Topographia II—Atitlan
1969; oil and acrylic polymer on linen
by John Clemmer (1921–2014), painter
48 × 48 in.
collection of Newcomb Art Museum of Tulane University

Topographia VI—Luna
1969; polymer and oil on canvas
by John Clemmer (1921–2014), painter
48 × 48 in.
courtesy of David Clemmer, Santa Fe, NM

Drawing—Moyen II
1970; ink on deckled Strathmore paper
by John Clemmer (1921–2014), draftsman
10 × 10 in.
courtesy of David Clemmer, Santa Fe, NM

Drawing—Shield
1970; ink on deckled Strathmore paper
by John Clemmer (1921–2014), draftsman
10 × 10 in.
courtesy of David Clemmer, Santa Fe, NM

Topographia IV—Cosmas II
1970; oil on canvas
by John Clemmer (1921–2014), painter
48 × 48 in.
New Orleans Museum of Art, gift of Jonathan C. Clemmer, 97.823

Topographia VIII—Azteca
1970–1971; acrylic polymer and oil on canvas
by John Clemmer (1921–2014), painter
48 × 48 in.
courtesy of 3618 Studio, LLC, New Orleans, LA

Topographia V—Capricorn
1973; oil on canvas
by John Clemmer (1921–2014), painter
60 × 48 in.
courtesy of Jonathan Clemmer and Michael Barnes, Royal Oak, MI

Circles—Homage to JMWT [James Mallord William Turner]
1973; oil on Masonite
by John Clemmer (1921–2014), painter
48 × 48 in.
courtesy of Kimberly and John Ed Bradley

Painting—Sandcasting (Ten-Piece)
1975; oil on canvas with bronze and Portland cement
by John Clemmer (1921–2014), sculptor
30 ¼ × 55 ¾ in.
The Historic New Orleans Collection, 2020.0015.1.6

Areola III
1975; pencil on paper
by John Clemmer (1921–2014), draftsman
14 × 11 in.
courtesy of David Clemmer, Santa Fe, NM

Landscape
1977; watercolor, gouache, and collage on oatmeal paper
by John Clemmer (1921–2014), painter
18 × 24 in.
courtesy of David Clemmer, Santa Fe, NM

Portal II
1978; oil crayon on canvas
by John Clemmer (1921–2014), painter
76 × 44 in.
courtesy of Martha and Rick Barnett

Portal—Itea
1978; oil on canvas
by John Clemmer (1921–2014), painter
30 × 30 in.
*New Orleans Museum of Art, The Muriel Bultman Francis Collection,
86.171*

Floral—Oval
1978; ink on Strathmore paper
by John Clemmer (1921–2014), draftsman
14 × 11 in.
courtesy of Virval Bradley

Self-Portrait
1984; ebony pencil on paper
by John Clemmer (1921–2014), draftsman
38 ½ × 34 ½ in.
courtesy of Kimberly and John Ed Bradley

Sculpture
1986; bronze and nickel silver on Monel
by John Clemmer (1921–2014), sculptor
120 × 30 × 15 in.
courtesy of Martha and Rick Barnett

Il Capannone, Cortona
1987; ink on paper
by John Clemmer (1921–2014), draftsman
9 ¼ × 13 ⅛ in. (sight)
courtesy of 3618 Studio, LLC, New Orleans, LA

Portrait of Richard Charles
1991; oil on canvas
by John Clemmer (1921–2014), painter
36 × 30 in.
The Historic New Orleans Collection, gift of Valerie Charles Beaudette, 2020.0226

San G. II
1993; oil on canvas
by John Clemmer (1921–2014), painter
72 × 36 in.
The Historic New Orleans Collection, gift of Susan Brill and Michael S. Hershfield, 2018.0025

From the Erectheum
1993; mixed media on canvas
by John Clemmer (1921–2014), painter
48 × 56 in.
courtesy of 3618 Studio, LLC, New Orleans, LA

Porta Libera—Todi
1993; colored pencil on Bristol board
by John Clemmer (1921–2014), draftsman
17 × 25 in.
courtesy of Dr. Joseph J. Roniger and Mary Sue Roniger

Trilogy V, San Marco
1994; oil crayon on Strathmore paper
by John Clemmer (1921–2014), painter
30 × 26 in.
courtesy of Martha and Rick Barnett

From the Country House IX
1995; oil on Masonite
by John Clemmer (1921–2014), painter
40 × 48 in.
The Historic New Orleans Collection, gift of Lois Charles, 2019.0434

From the Kitchen
1996; mixed media on canvas
by John Clemmer (1921–2014), painter
48 × 26 in.
courtesy of 3618 Studio, LLC, New Orleans, LA

To the Beach
1997; oil on board
by John Clemmer (1921–2014), painter
15 × 15 in.
The Historic New Orleans Collection, 2014.0464.11

Triunity II
1997; mixed media on canvas
by John Clemmer (1921–2014), painter
70 × 48 in.
courtesy of Kimberly and John Ed Bradley

Self-Portrait
2003; oil on canvas
by John Clemmer (1921–2014), painter
36 × 24 in.
courtesy of 3618 Studio, LLC, New Orleans, LA

Self-Portrait
2003; oil on canvas
by John Clemmer (1921 2014), painter
19 ¾ × 19 ¾ in.
courtesy of 3618 Studio, LLC, New Orleans, LA

Untitled
2004; mixed media on papel de amate
by John Clemmer (1921–2014), painter
15 × 22 ½ in.
courtesy of a private collector

Untitled
2004; mixed media on papel de amate
by John Clemmer (1921–2014), painter
15 × 22 ½ in.
courtesy of a private collector

Belle Grove II
2007; oil on canvas
by John Clemmer (1921–2014), painter
50 × 60 in.
The Historic New Orleans Collection, gift of Susan Brill and Michael S. Hershfield, 2016.0400.1

Floral Circle
2008; oil on canvas
by John Clemmer (1921–2014), painter
48 × 36 in.
courtesy of Kimberly and John Ed Bradley

Untitled
2011; oil on canvas
by John Clemmer (1921–2014), painter
40 × 24 in.
courtesy of 3618 Studio, LLC, New Orleans, LA

CONTRIBUTORS

JUDITH H. BONNER, senior curator and curator of art for The Historic New Orleans Collection, has published widely on southern art and art criticism with a focus on Louisiana. She has curated numerous exhibitions at The Collection and the New Orleans Museum of Art, as well as the Newcomb College Centennial Exhibition held at NOMA. Bonner has taught at Xavier University of Louisiana and the United States Air Force Academy.

Bonner co-edited the *Art and Architecture* volume of *The New Encyclopedia of Southern Culture*. She authored the foreword for Angela Gregory's memoir, *A Dream and a Chisel: Louisiana Sculptor Angela Gregory in Paris, 1925–1928*. Together with her husband, Dr. Thomas Bonner Jr., she wrote biographies for the personalities who are caricatured in *Sherwood Anderson and Other Famous Creoles* (New Orleans: Pelican Press, 2018). Originally published in 1926, the book was a collaborative effort of William Spratling and William Faulkner. For more than twenty years Bonner compiled a bibliography on southern art and architecture for the *Southern Quarterly* published by the University of Southern Mississippi and served on its advisory board. For more than thirty years she has been a contributing editor of the *New Orleans Art Review*.

JOHN ED BRADLEY is the author of eight novels and the memoir *It Never Rains in Tiger Stadium*, which *Sports Illustrated* called "the best sports book of the year" in 2007. His novel for young readers, *The Road to Wherever*, was published by Farrar, Straus and Giroux in 2021. Bradley lives in Mandeville, Louisiana, with his wife, Kimberly, and daughter, Hannah.

DAVID CLEMMER is a writer, photographer, and musician living in Santa Fe. He is a native of New Orleans, Louisiana, where he attended public schools followed by study at Tulane University and the University of New Mexico. He has lived in New Mexico since 1979 and has authored books on the art and artists of the West and Southwest. His critical writing has appeared in numerous local, national, and international publications.

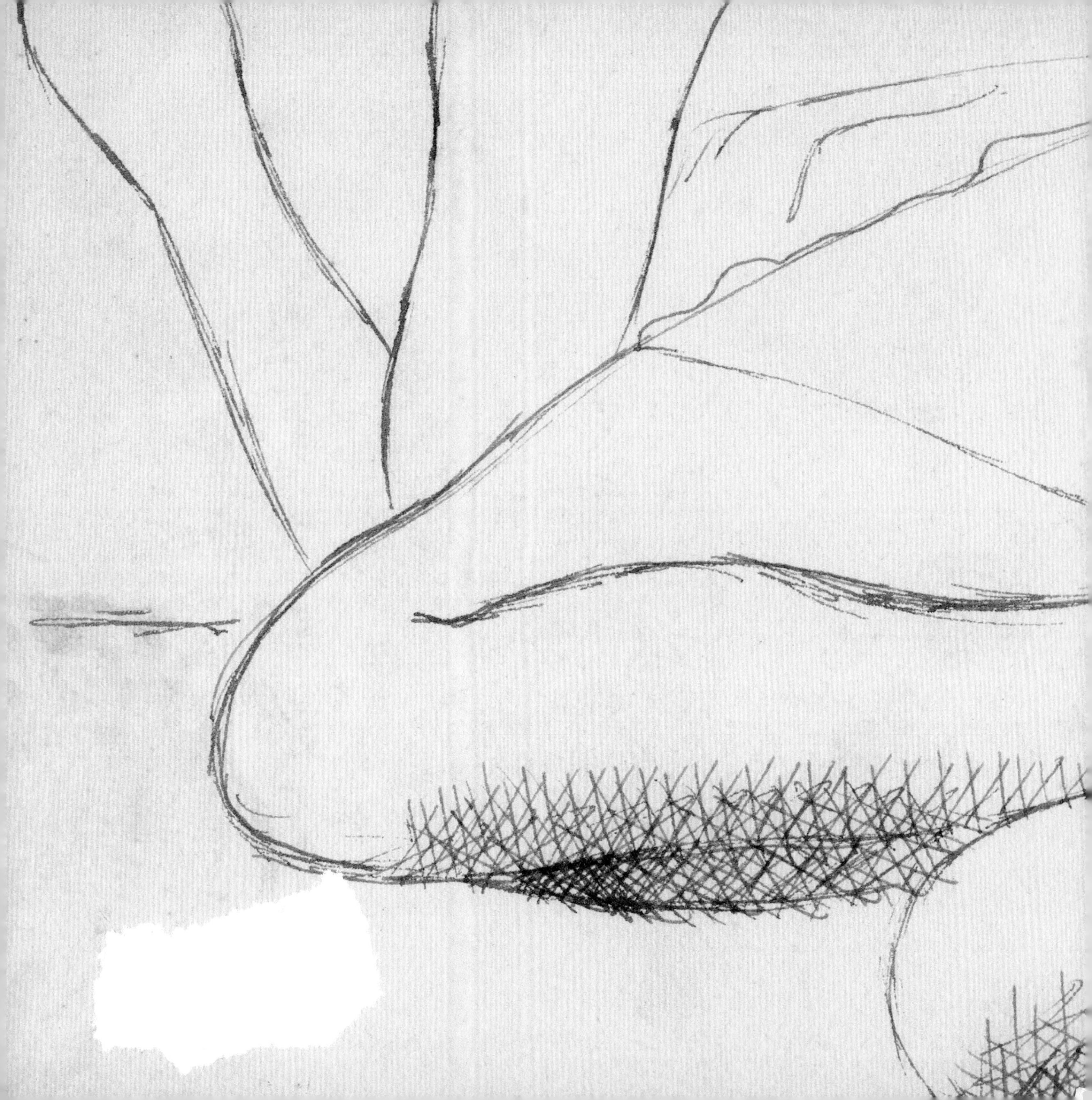